IMAGES
of America

FLORENCE
1870s–1970s

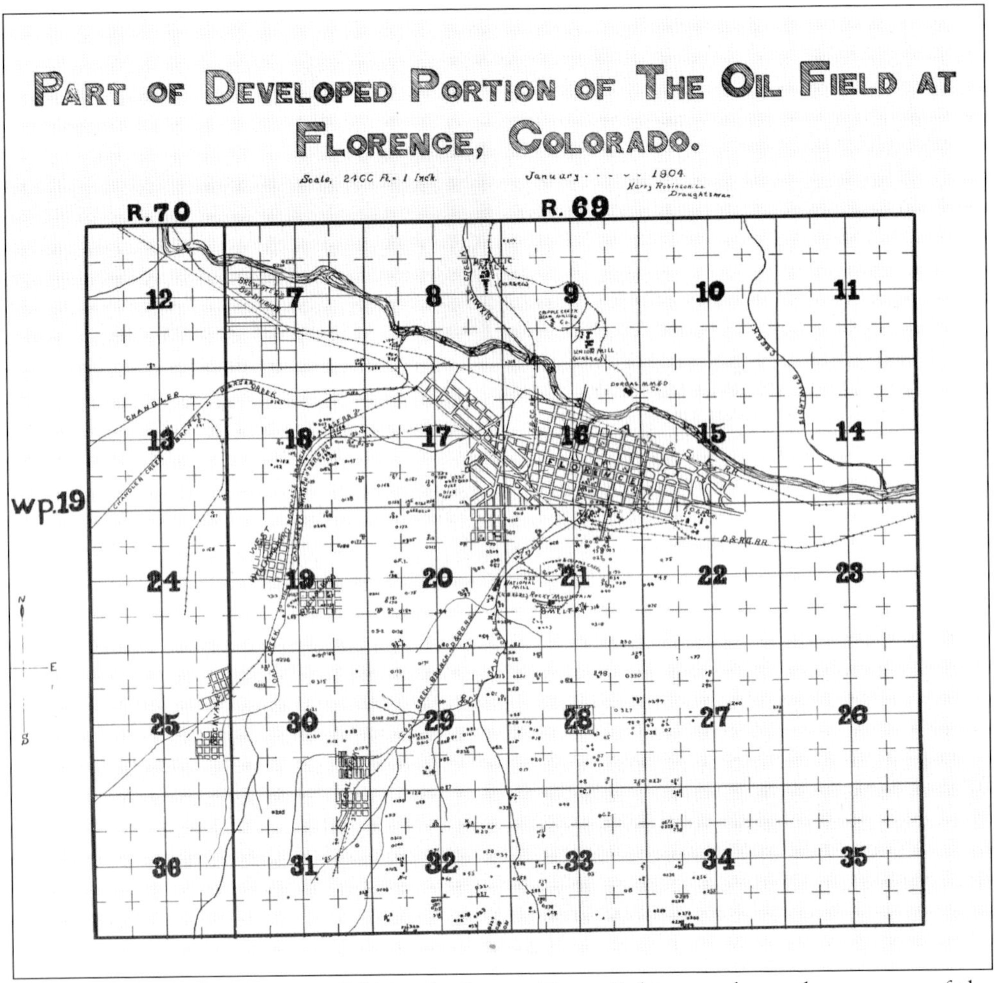

This map, created in January 1904 by draftsman Harry Robinson, shows the expanse of the Florence Oil Field. Commissioned to identify each oil well, the map identifies each operating well by number based on when it was drilled, starting with lower numbers and increasing. It is clearly seen here how the first wells were near the center of present day Florence and expanded southeast out into the oil field. The map also identifies major improvements including the three railroads and various smelters operating in 1904, as well as the smaller outlying communities. (Courtesy Florence Pioneer Museum and Research Center.)

On the Cover: This photograph of the Rainbow Park service station was taken in 1945 with owner Tom Sasser (left) and his son Jack. The Sasser family leased the business from Tom's uncle after moving to Florence from Oklahoma in 1934. Rainbow Park Service, or Tom's Service, was a successful business that sold and delivered fuel, had a service garage, and also sold a few basic food items in the store. In 1946, it was relocated to a new site closer to Florence. When this picture was taken, State Highway 50 ran through Florence and Portland to Pueblo. The service station was on the south side of the present-day junction of Highway 115 and Highway 120. The bridge to Portland can be seen in the background at left. (Courtesy of the Sasser family.)

IMAGES
of America

FLORENCE 1870s–1970s

Dennis M. Lancaster
Foreword by Gayle MacKinnon

ARCADIA
PUBLISHING

ISBN 978-1-4671-0834-8

Published by Arcadia Publishing
Charleston, South Carolina

Printed in the United States of America

Library of Congress Control Number: 2022938576

For all general information, please contact Arcadia Publishing:
Telephone 843-853-2070
Fax 843-853-0044
E-mail sales@arcadiapublishing.com
For customer service and orders:
Toll-Free 1-888-313-2665

Visit us on the Internet at www.arcadiapublishing.com

For Chopper and Toni Price, who show me my past, and for my parents, Carl and Bernice Lancaster, who show me the importance of community.

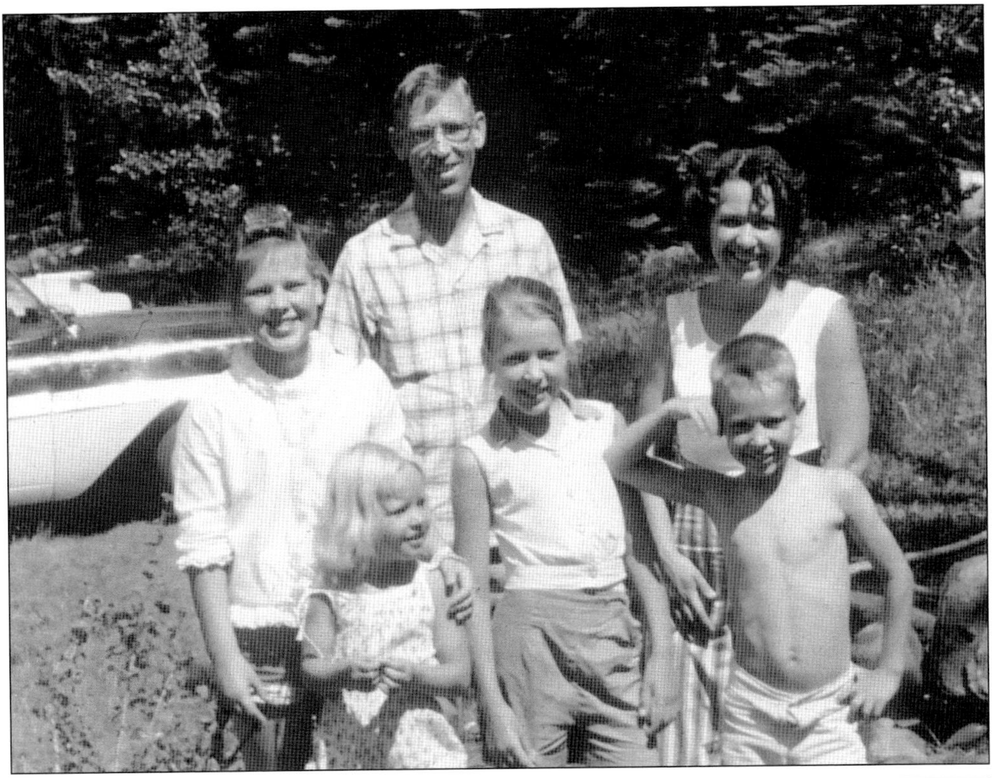

Shortly after returning from his service in World War II, Evan Royal, known throughout his life as "Royal," met and married Betty Jo "B.J." White in 1947. They had four children, Linda Christine, Jo Anna, Mark Evan, and Peggy Darlene. (Courtesy of Royal and B.J. Schmidt.)

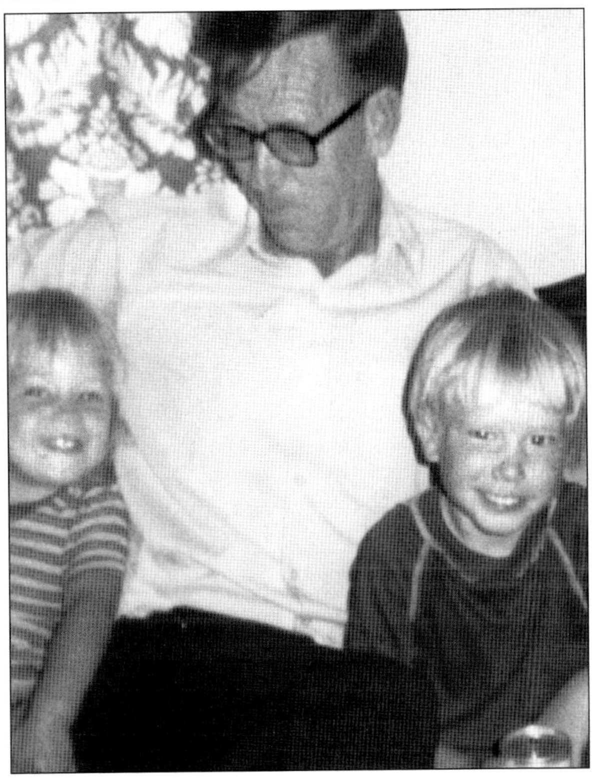

This picture, taken in 1974, shows Royal with two of his grandchildren, daughter Linda's children Melissa and Michael. The Schmidt family, still very active in Florence, can claim over 100 years of attendance in the Florence school system. (Courtesy of Shimla Weare Basile, Dorothy Schmidt Weare collection.)

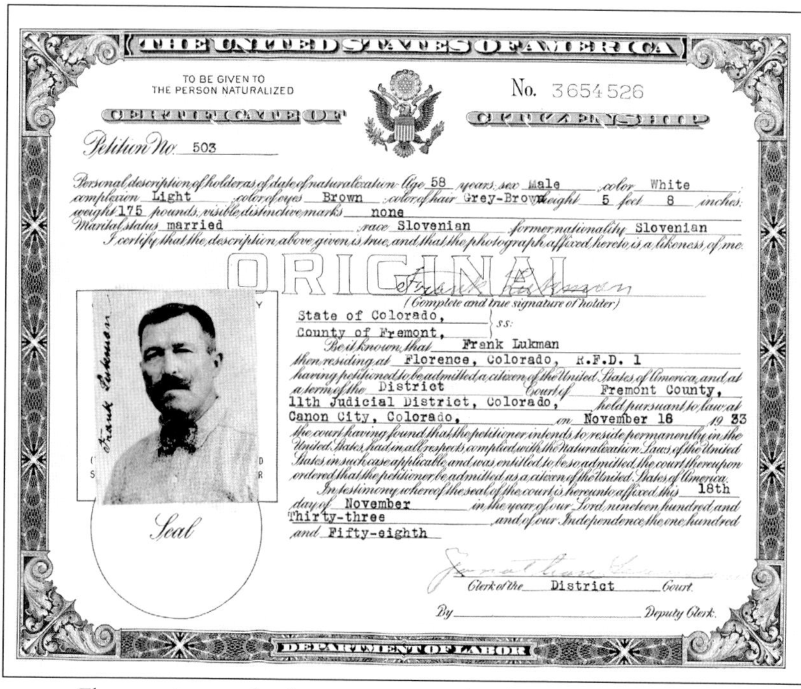

THE UNITED STATES OF AMERICA

TO BE GIVEN TO THE PERSON NATURALIZED

No. 3654526

CERTIFICATE OF CITIZENSHIP

Petition No. 503

Personal description of holder as of date of naturalization: Age 58 years; sex Male; color White; complexion Light; color of eyes Brown; color of hair Grey-Brown; height 5 feet 8 inches; weight 175 pounds; visible distinctive marks none

Marital status married; race Slovenian; former nationality Slovenian

I certify that the description above given is true, and that the photograph affixed hereto is a likeness of me.

ORIGINAL

(Complete and true signature of holder)

State of Colorado, County of Fremont, ss:

Be it known that Frank Lukman then residing at Florence, Colorado, R.F.D. 1 having petitioned to be admitted a citizen of the United States of America, and at a term of the District Court of Fremont County, 11th Judicial District, Colorado, held pursuant to law at Canon City, Colorado, on November 16 1933 the court having found that the petitioner intends to reside permanently in the United States, had in all respects complied with the Naturalization Laws of the United States in such case applicable and was entitled to be so admitted the court thereupon ordered that the petitioner be admitted as a citizen of the United States of America.

In testimony whereof the seal of the court is hereunto affixed this 18th day of November in the year of our Lord nineteen hundred and Thirty-three and of our Independence the one hundred and Fifty-eighth

Seal

Clerk of the District Court.

By ____ Deputy Clerk.

DEPARTMENT OF LABOR

People came to Florence in search of opportunity and a chance to build a new life. Many came from neighboring states, and many from different countries. Frank Lukman arrived in the United States in 1906, and after earning enough money, went back to Europe to marry Agnes, returning to the United States as a married couple. In 1925, Frank and Agnes purchased a farm in Florence with their three children. Frank obtained his valued certificate of citizenship on November 18, 1933, and Agnes received hers on April 24, 1937. (Both, courtesy of Sherrie Stille.)

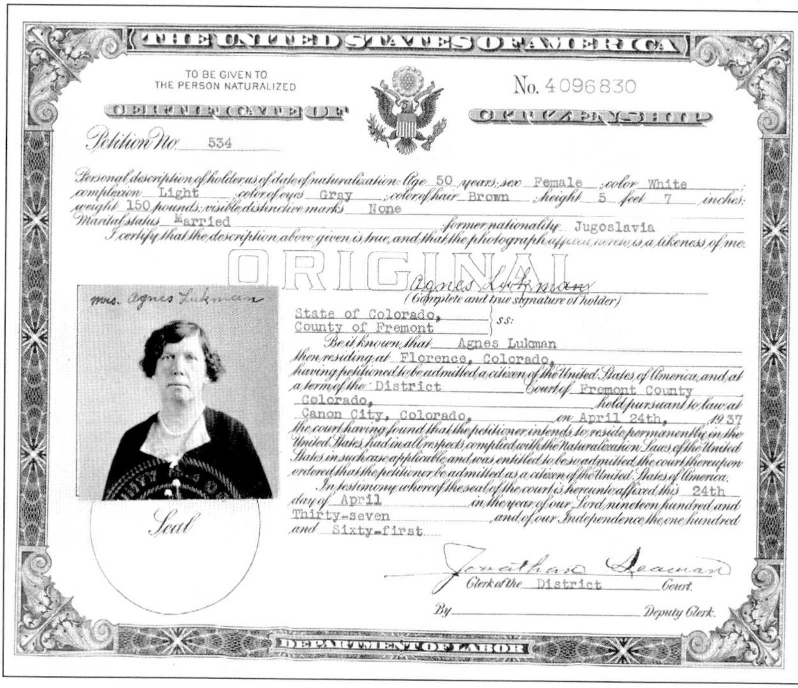

THE UNITED STATES OF AMERICA

TO BE GIVEN TO THE PERSON NATURALIZED

No. 4096830

CERTIFICATE OF CITIZENSHIP

Petition No. 534

Personal description of holder as of date of naturalization: Age 50 years; sex Female; color White; complexion Light; color of eyes Gray; color of hair Brown; height 5 feet 7 inches; weight 150 pounds; visible distinctive marks None

Marital status Married; former nationality Jugoslavia

I certify that the description above given is true, and that the photograph affixed hereto is a likeness of me.

ORIGINAL

Agnes Lukman

(Complete and true signature of holder)

mrs. Agnes Lukman

State of Colorado, County of Fremont, ss:

Be it known that Agnes Lukman then residing at Florence, Colorado, having petitioned to be admitted a citizen of the United States of America, and at a term of the District Court of Fremont County Colorado, held pursuant to law at Canon City, Colorado, on April 24th, 1937 the court having found that the petitioner intends to reside permanently in the United States, had in all respects complied with the Naturalization Laws of the United States in such case applicable, and was entitled to be so admitted, the court thereupon ordered that the petitioner be admitted as a citizen of the United States of America.

In testimony whereof the seal of the court is hereunto affixed this 24th day of April in the year of our Lord nineteen hundred and Thirty-seven and of our Independence the one hundred and Sixty-first

Seal

Jonathan Seaman

Clerk of the District Court.

By ____ Deputy Clerk.

DEPARTMENT OF LABOR

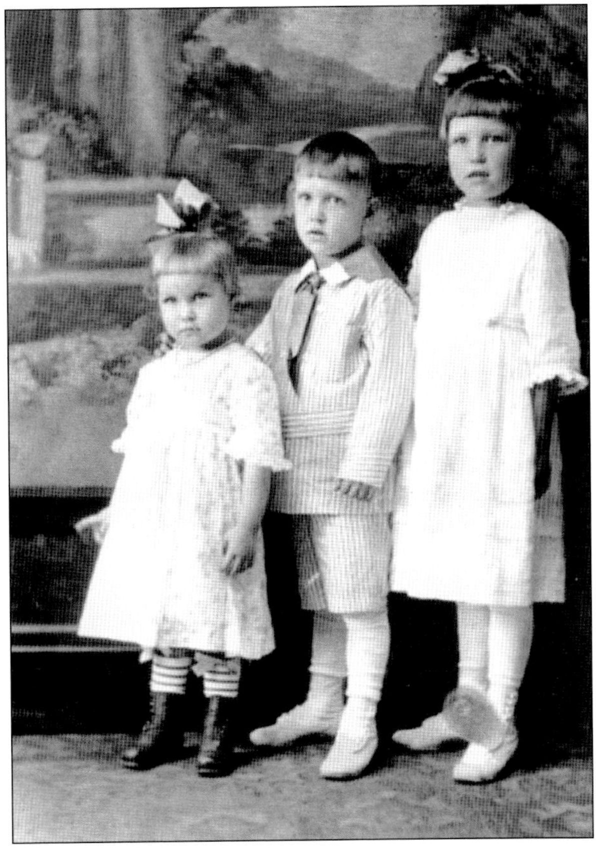

Frank and Agnes Lukman moved with their family to the farm in Rainbow Park in 1925. Here, the three children stand for a photograph in 1919. From left to right are Elizabeth "Irene," Frank Martin Jr., and Amy Mary. (Courtesy of Sherrie Stille.)

This photograph was taken in 1945 next to the Lukman farmhouse in Rainbow Park. From left to right are (first row) Jerry Del Monte, Billy Shriner, George Del Monte, and Sandra Shriner; (second row) Irene Lukman Penny, Doris and Frank Lukman Jr., Amy Del Monte, Frank Lukman Sr., and Agnes Lukman. (Courtesy of Sherrie Stille.)

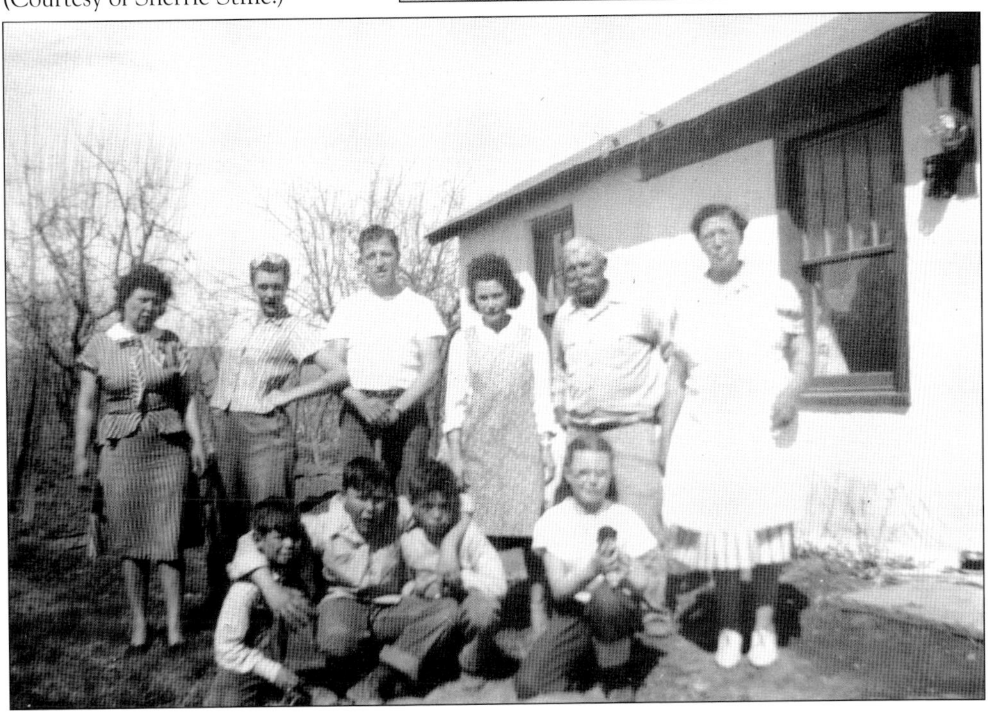

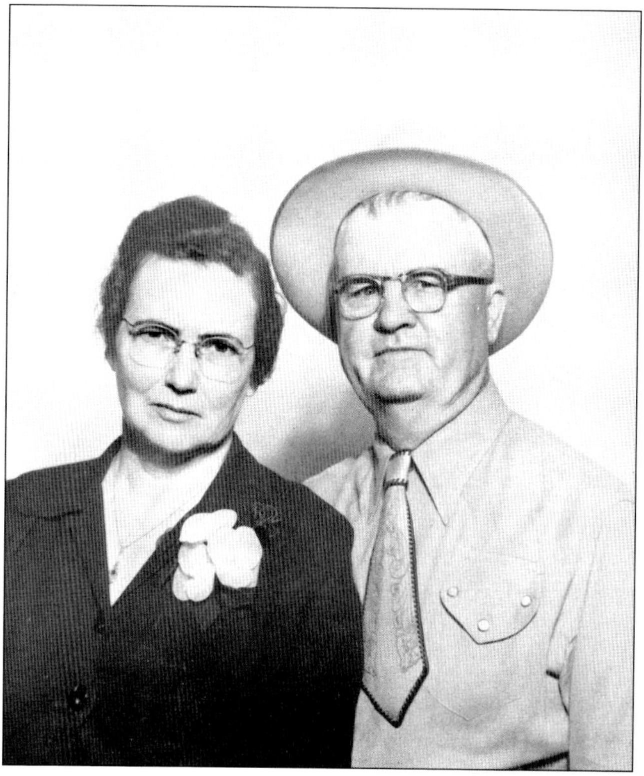

Tom and Sylvia Sasser and their children, Nellie (nine) and Jack (seven), relocated to Florence from Oklahoma in December 1934. During the hard times of the Depression and Dust Bowl, Tom, a shade-tree mechanic, leased a service station here. On January 11, 1935, Rainbow Park Service sold 15 gallons of gas and two quarts of oil. From that first day, the Sasser family developed and grew one of the more prominent businesses in Florence. (Courtesy of the Sasser family.)

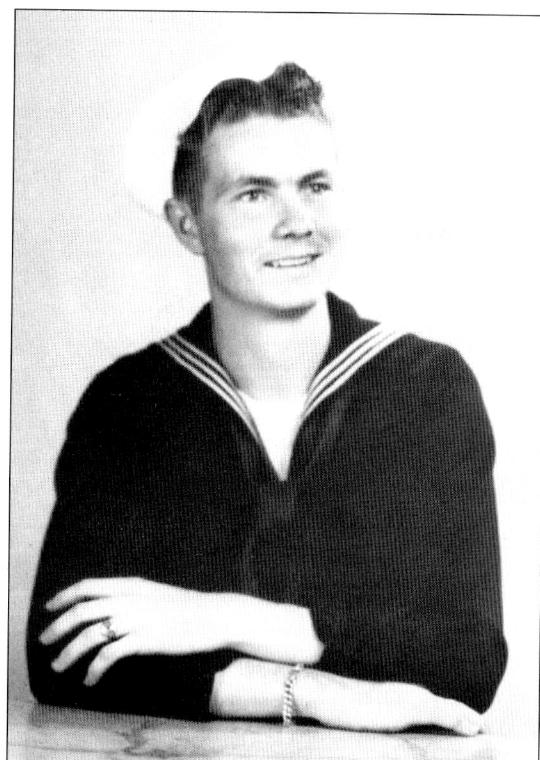

Upon graduating from Florence High School in 1945, Jack Sasser was drafted into the US Navy. After serving on the USS *Rehoboth* in the Pacific toward the end of World War II, he returned to Florence in January 1946 and to the Sasser family business, which had been relocated to the east edge of town. He retired when the service station was sold in 1980. (Courtesy of the Sasser family.)

After returning from the Navy in 1947, Jack met and married Roma Jean Storm from Cañon City, and they had two children, Gary and Marsha. With Lee Nelson, who had joined the Sassers in 1943, Jack took over the Sasser family business in 1959 when Tom Sasser went into semiretirement. (Courtesy of the Sasser family.)

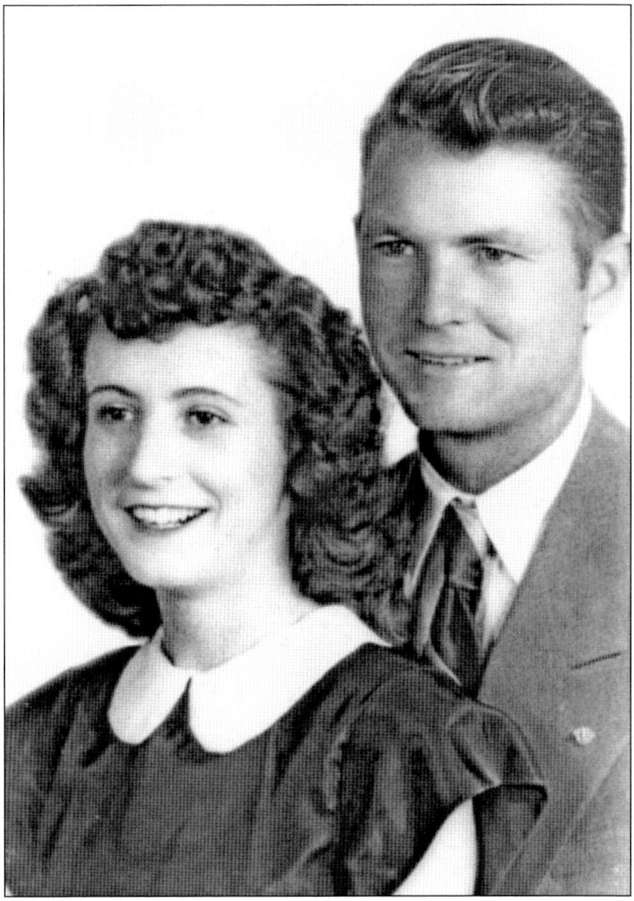

The family behind the successful Sasser and Nelson business poses for this photograph in 1955. From left to right are (first row) children Marsha Sasser, Gary Sasser, Janelle Nelson, and Tom Nelson; (second row) Jack and Roma Jean Sasser, Sylvia and Tom Sasser, and Nellie and Lee Nelson. (Courtesy of the Sasser family.)

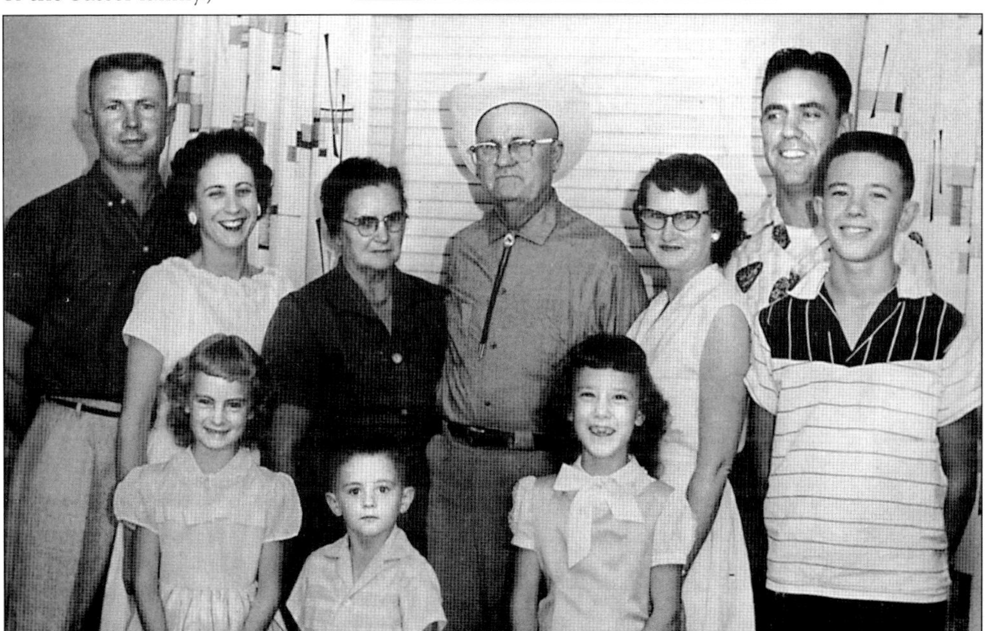

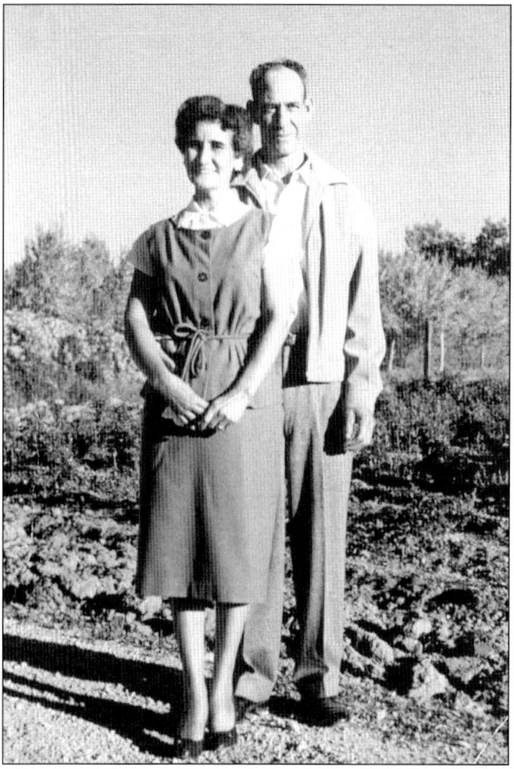

Frank and Alice Villagrana pose shortly after they had settled in Florence and begun their family. Frank came here to work as an inspector in the coal mines in the late 1930s. He was born in Zacatecas, Mexico, in 1909 and came to the United States at the age of 13 to work in the mines with his brother. Frank and Alice were married in 1930 and had four children. (Courtesy of Paul Villagrana.)

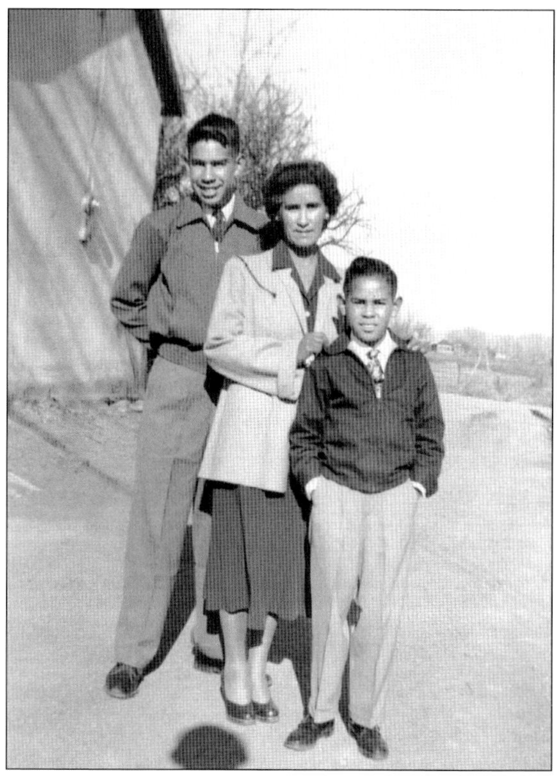

After arriving in Florence, Frank and Alice Villagrana had daughter Bertha and three sons, Reuben, Paul, and Frank. Paul went on to a successful career as a schoolteacher in the Florence school system. Seen here in about 1945 are, from left to right, Paul, Alice, and Frank. (Courtesy of Paul Villagrana.)

Darrell Lindsey was born in Florence in 1935, and after graduating from Florence High School in 1953, joined the military, serving until 1966. He began work at the Florence Post Office in 1966 and was postmaster for 18 years before retiring in 2001. Throughout his entire life, Lindsey was tremendously involved in the community of Florence. Known as the "voice of the Huskies," he announced football and basketball games for over 40 years and worked tirelessly on the creation of the Pioneer Museum. (Courtesy of Nancy Lindsey.)

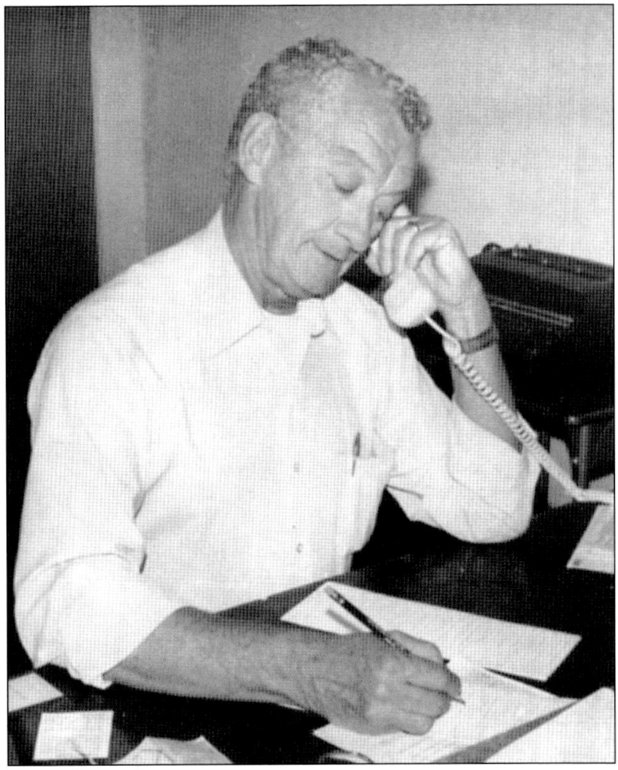

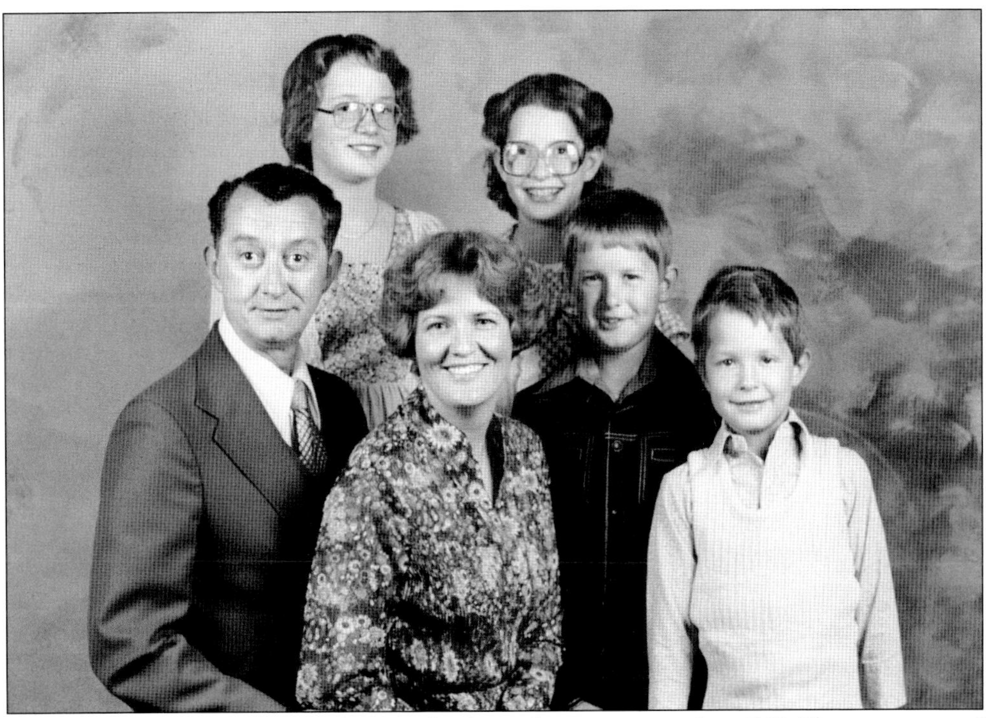

Darrell Lindsey and Nancy Singleterry, also from Florence, married in 1965. They are pictured herewith their four children (from top), Jennifer, Elaine, Jeff, and Steve. (Courtesy of Nancy Lindsey.)

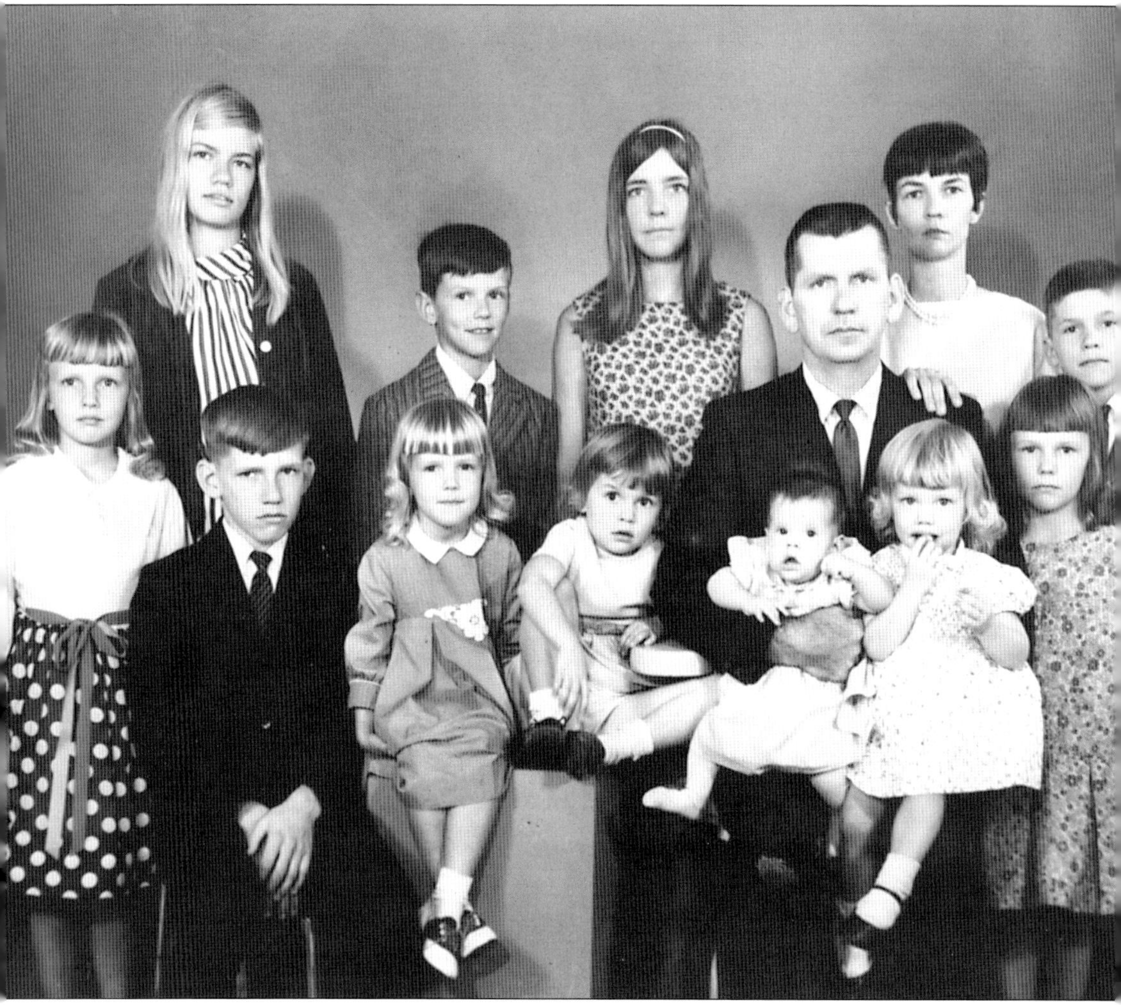

John Fox brought his family to Florence in 1963 after purchasing the Florence Pharmacy, changing the name to Fox Drug. The Fox family, sitting for this photograph in 1967, are, from left to right, (first row) Jane (Gifford), Steve, Kit (Lamborn), Gennie (Barrett), Julie (Privette) and Barb on John's lap, and Joanna (Wilson); (second row) Peg (Piltingsrude), Joe, Joyce (Conners), John, Carol, and Dan. The Fox family commitment to the development of Florence is recognized in numerous aspects, including being a driving force behind the Florence Swimming Pool and the growth of the former St. Joseph Hospital and as a catalyst for the current Florence Archives organization. Peg and Kit were the instigators behind converting downtown to the current retail shopping district, and Steve took over his father's business as a pharmacist until selling Fox Drug in 2017. (Courtesy of Steve Fox.)

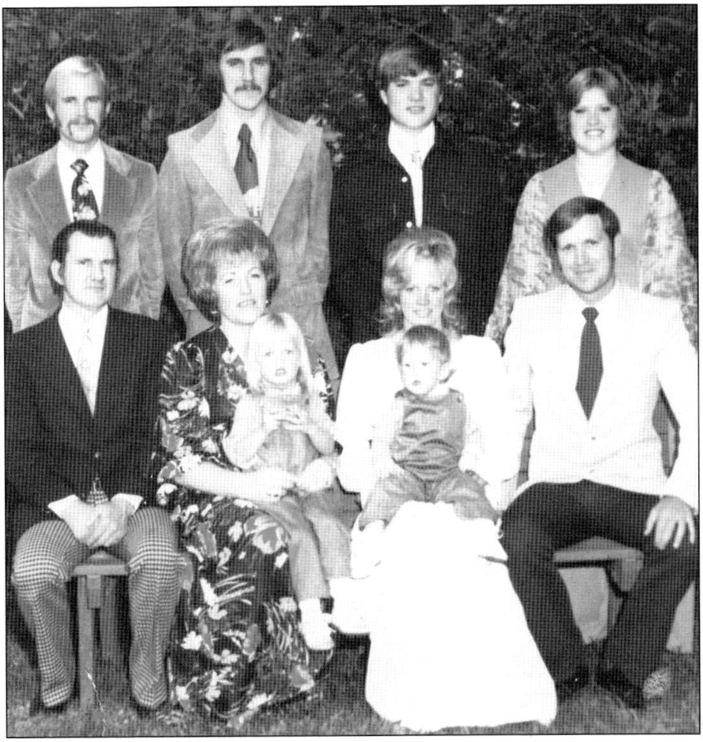

The Carl Lancaster family relocated to Florence in 1961 as Carl began work at Florence Hardware. In 1973, the family opened Lancaster's Home Maintenance, a successful downtown business sold in 1996. The entire family was involved in community endeavors. Three generations gather for this picture. From left to right are (first row) Carl, Bernice holding granddaughter Kristi, Jim's wife Ellen (Nichols) holding second daughter Katie, and Jim; (second row) George, Tom, Dennis, and Lori Ann. (Courtesy of the Lancaster family.)

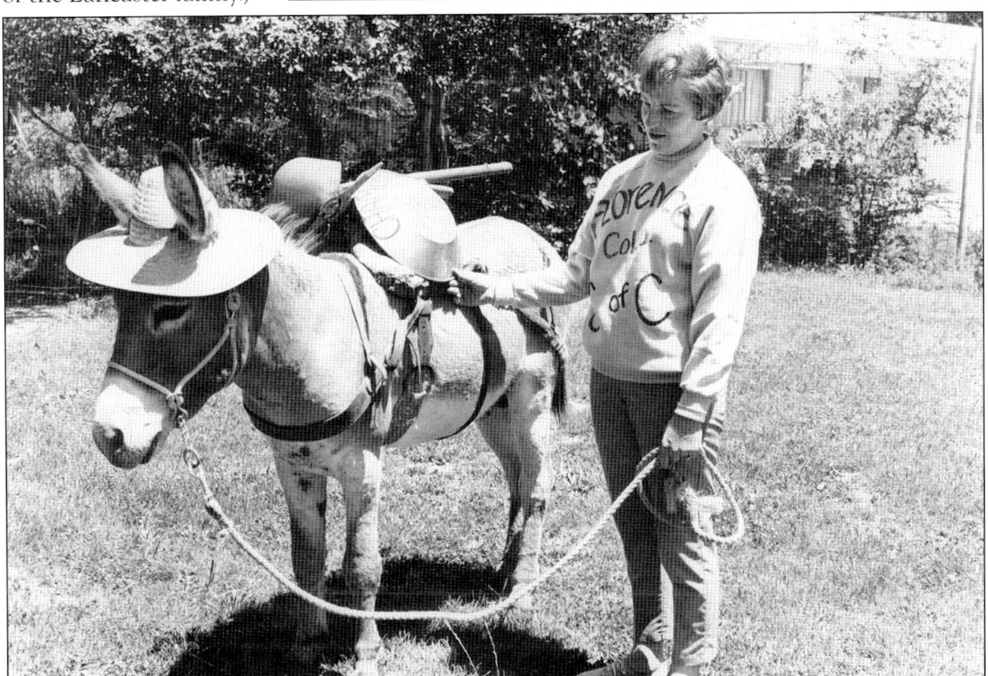

The Florence Chamber of Commerce sponsored Bernice Lancaster in the 1969 World Championship Burro Race from Fairplay to Leadville. Carl and Bernice Lancaster participated in numerous community organizations throughout the years, including the chamber of commerce and Pioneer Day Association, and often helped out at the Pioneer Museum. (Courtesy of the Lancaster family.)

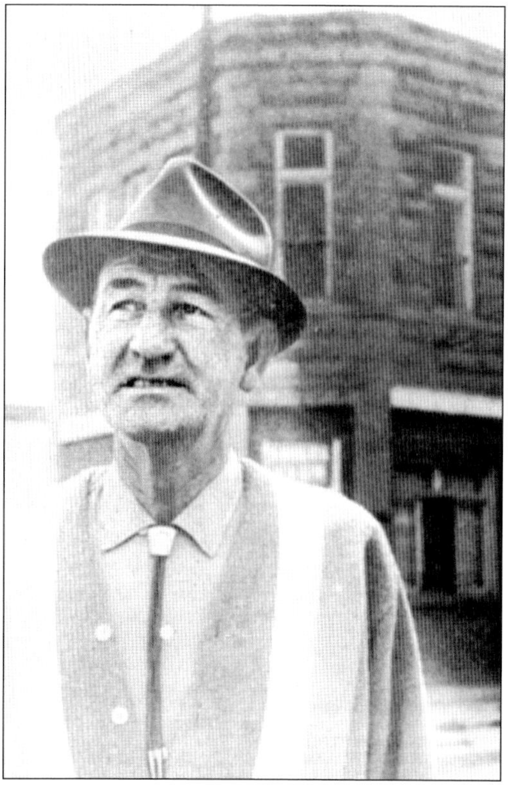

Charles Edwin Price, known to everyone as "Chopper," provided the vision of a museum for the community. In 1963, the Florence Pioneer Day Association tasked him with purchasing a building to house a museum. In 1964, with fundraising spearheaded by Chopper, the Braden-Griffiths Building, constructed in 1894, was purchased for $1,500. It has been the home of the Florence Pioneer Museum and Research Center ever since.

Charles Cristelli (left) and Chopper Price proudly display an original ballot box donated to the museum by the Town of Coal Creek. Cristelli was one of the many dedicated volunteers who have committed countless hours to ensure the success of the museum.

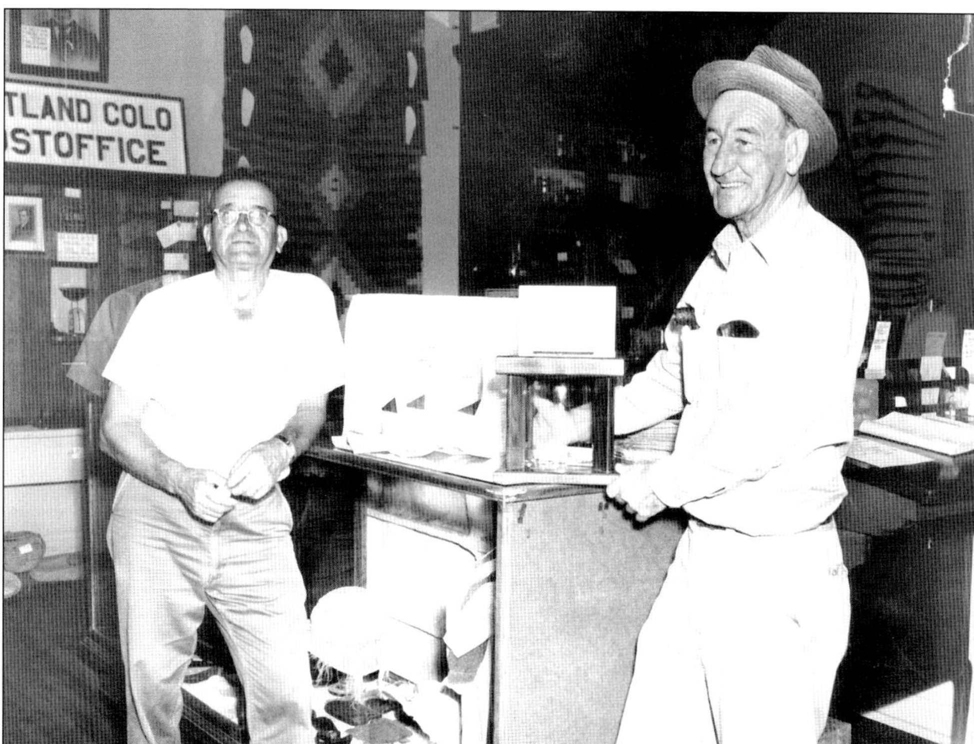

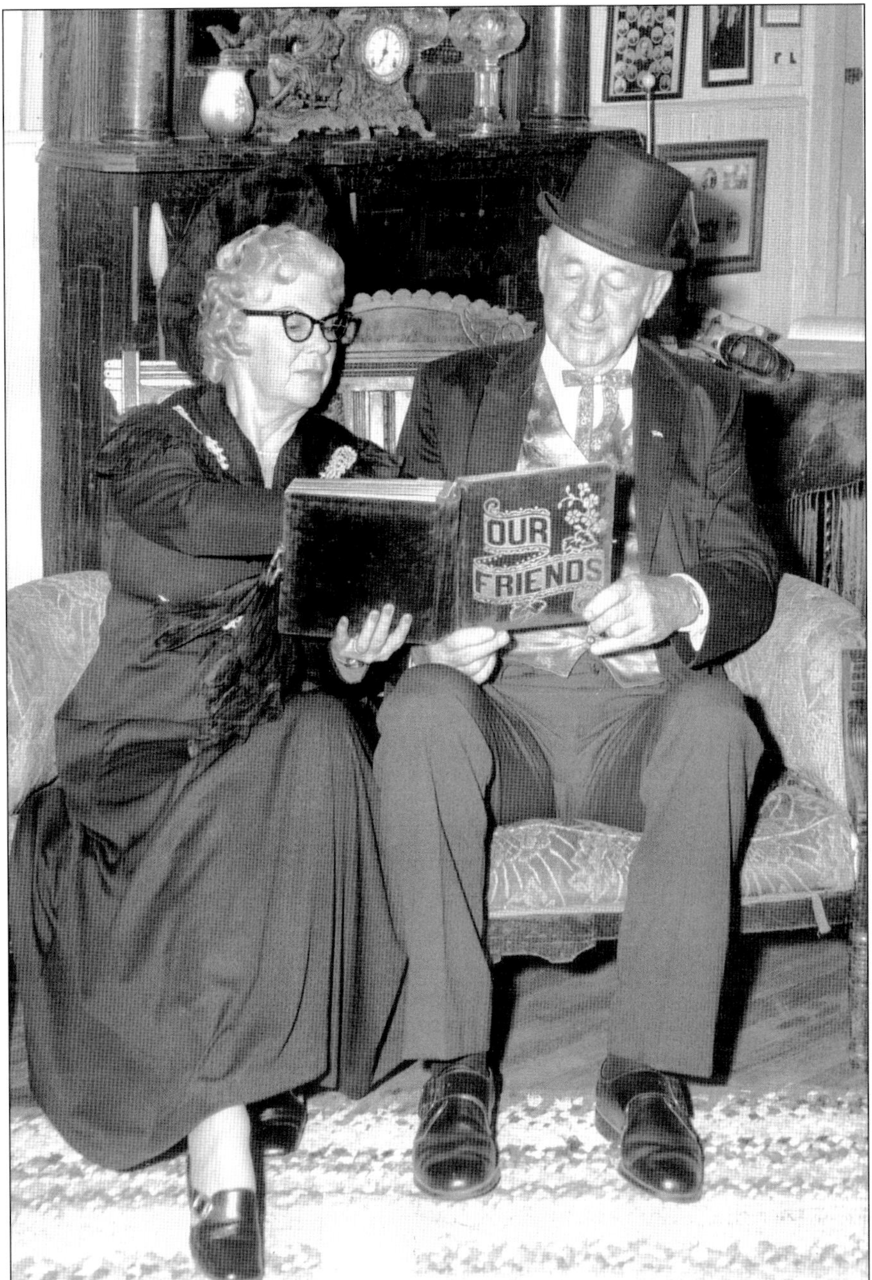

Chopper and Velma "Toni" Price were longtime residents of Florence. Chopper was born in Coal Creek in 1911, graduated from Florence High School in 1929, and made a career as a master electrician. Toni was born in Kansas, and after becoming a schoolteacher, moved with her parents to Florence. Chopper and Toni married in 1937. They made their home in Florence, and both became intensely involved with the community. With their interest in collecting historic information, antiques, and relics, they were naturally drawn to Florence's celebration of its pioneers. They were eventually charged with further developing the concept of a local museum to preserve the story of Florence. They were the founders of the Florence Pioneer Museum.

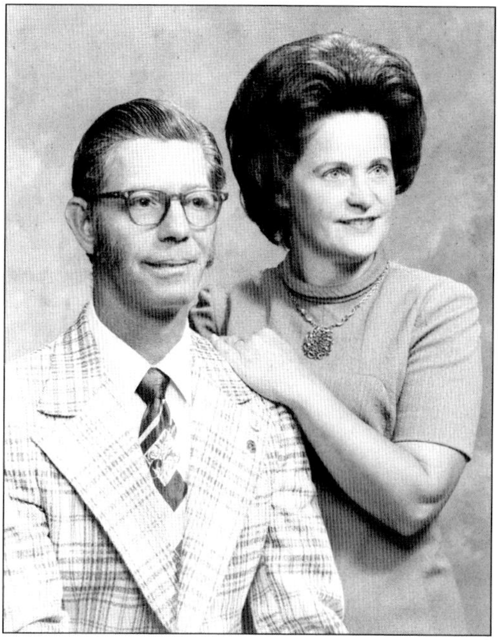

Roy Palmer Jr. and Gwynn Woods married in 1949 and had three children. Coming from a pioneering family in the telephone industry, Roy accepted a position with Mountain States Telephone and transferred his family to Florence in 1961. He became active in the community, serving on the fire department, city council, school board, and numerous other organizations. (Courtesy of Gayle Palmer Mackinnon.)

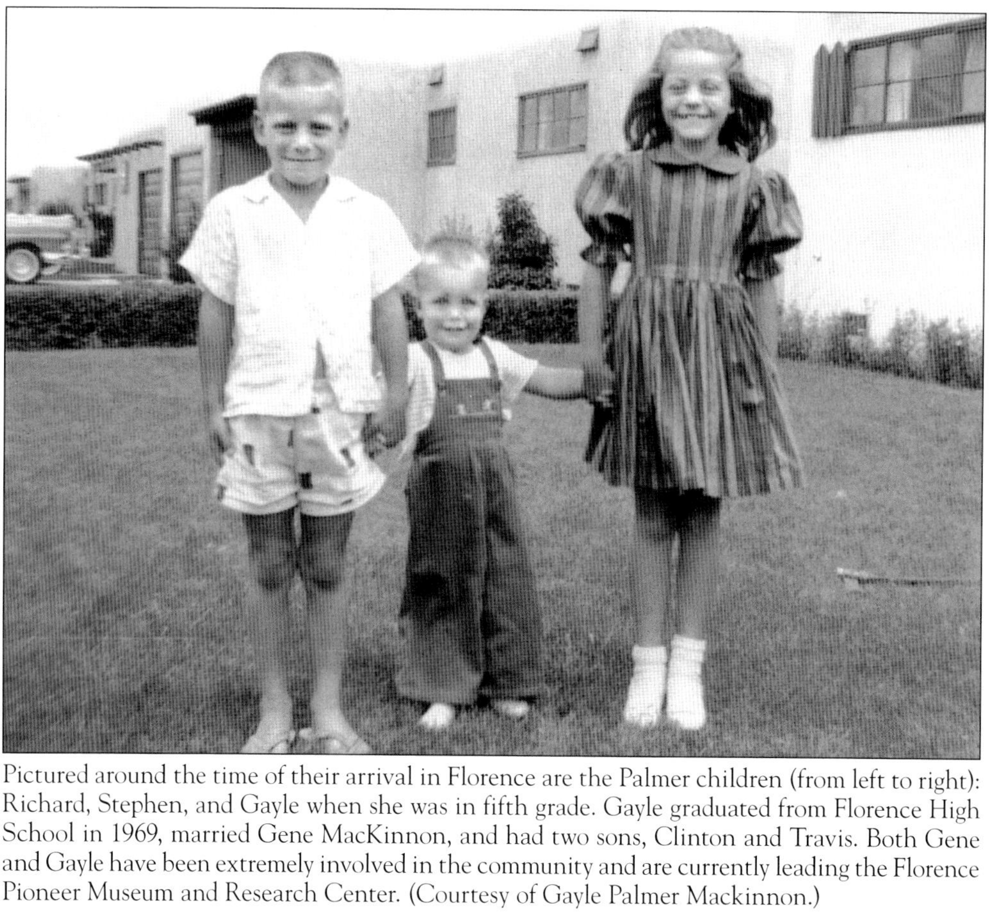

Pictured around the time of their arrival in Florence are the Palmer children (from left to right): Richard, Stephen, and Gayle when she was in fifth grade. Gayle graduated from Florence High School in 1969, married Gene MacKinnon, and had two sons, Clinton and Travis. Both Gene and Gayle have been extremely involved in the community and are currently leading the Florence Pioneer Museum and Research Center. (Courtesy of Gayle Palmer Mackinnon.)

Three

Natural Resources

For centuries, natural resources attracted humans to the area surrounding Florence. The abundance of wild game for food and the moderate climate drew many different Native American tribes, although the area has been inhabited mostly by the Ute, who claim their creation in the area. The numerous local hot springs and mineral oil springs were used by these groups. Europeans came to the area to trade with the Native Americans, who desired the newly introduced materials of the non-natives in exchange for animal pelts and the foods so readily available here.

Gold discoveries near Denver led to the growth of a population that needed a steady food supply. The traders of the Florence area saw the value in the rich soils and ample waters of the Arkansas River for agriculture, and using these resources, were able to meet that demand.

With the many raw material discoveries in the area, farmers and stockmen soon turned to these resource deposits to supplement their income. Outcroppings rich with coal, large pools of oil, vast gypsum and limestone deposits, and precious metal discoveries to the north led to a dependance on Florence to supply the necessary materials and manpower for extracting, refining, and delivering these discoveries.

Florence's base for growth became the natural resources of the area. It grew and prospered, and because of the value of these resources, it often did not experience the recessions and downturns of the national economy. Though Florence was established on natural resources, the community was built on the backs of the individuals who were needed to acquire them: the farmers, ranchers, and stockmen; the coal miners, gold miners, and oilmen; the brick foundry workers, cement plant employees, and homebuilders; the businessmen, railroad workers, and truck drivers; and the visionaries, tycoons, and dreamers.

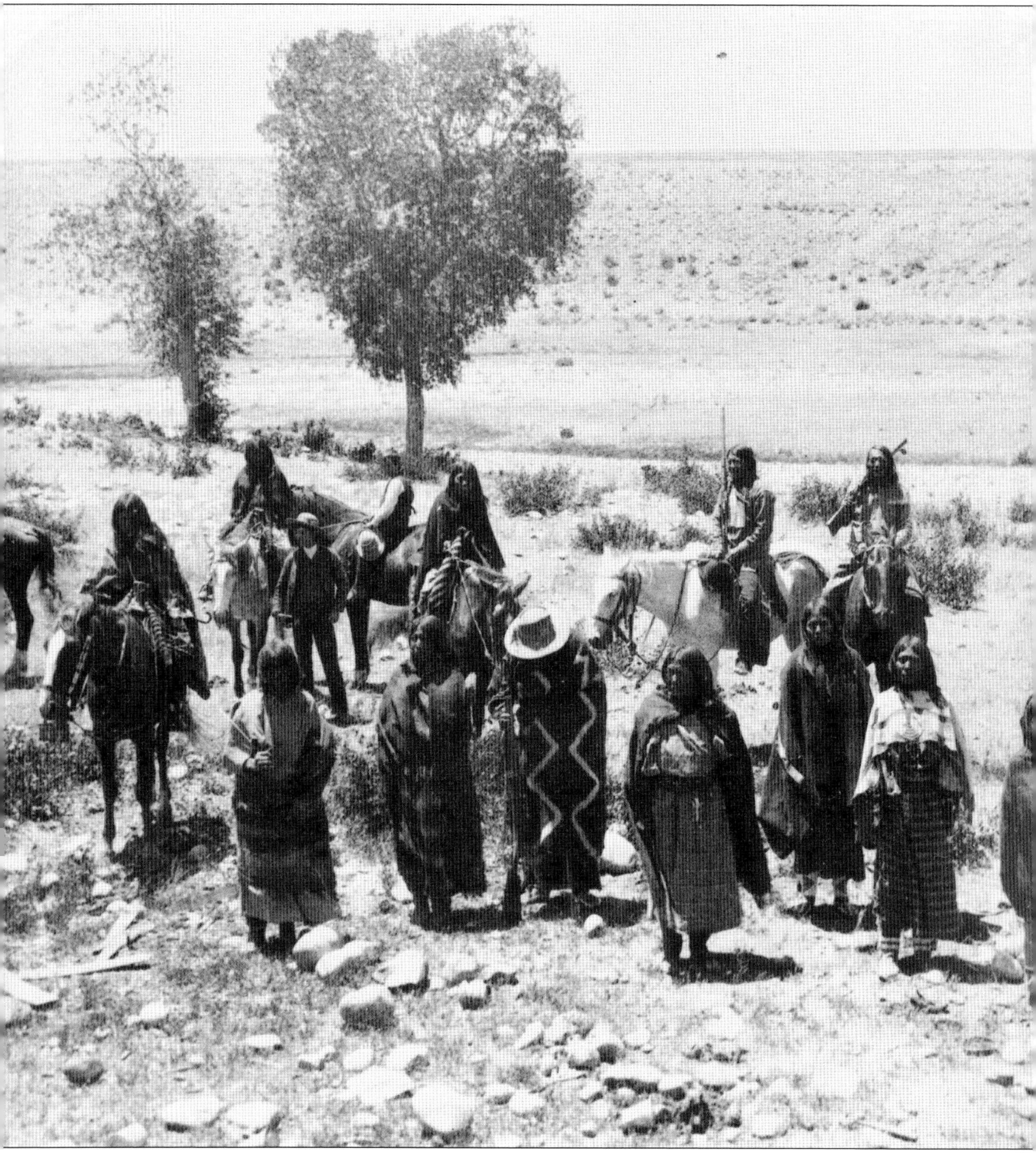

Of the many Native American tribes who have called this area home, the Ute in their stories claim their creation in the area surrounding Pikes Peak. Historic records clearly demonstrate the dominance of the tribe well into the time when Europeans were settling along the Arkansas River. Though now on small reservations in southwestern Colorado, the Ute tribe and its many affiliations roamed broad tracts of land throughout Colorado. The Fremont County area around Florence was a favorite because of the abundance of food, moderate climate, and many hot springs, mineral oil springs, and other natural resources that were readily accessible. Although this is a more recent image, demonstrated by the Western-style hats some are wearing, this is a typical Ute family moving through the area, most likely on an excursion to stock up on food and mineral oil for medicinal purposes. (Courtesy of Library of Congress, LC-USZ62-110874.)

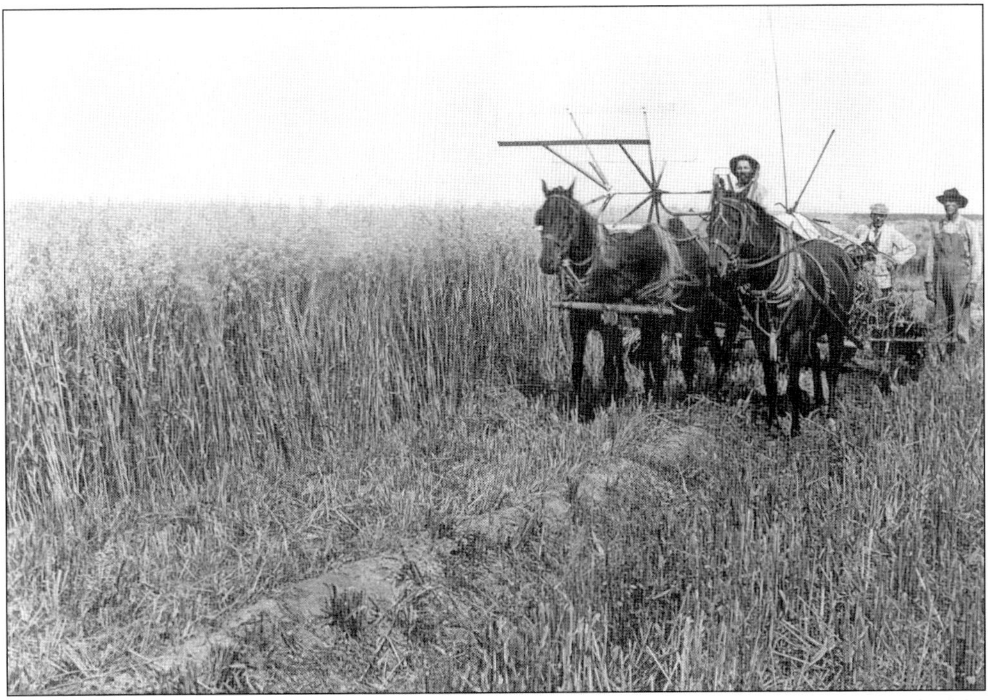

The fertile soils and the abundant waters of the Arkansas River made the Florence area ideal for meeting the increased demand for food in Colorado, including produce and livestock. By 1887, all regular water rights of the Arkansas River were appropriated. Here, workers harvest a field of sorghum, a popular crop at the time.

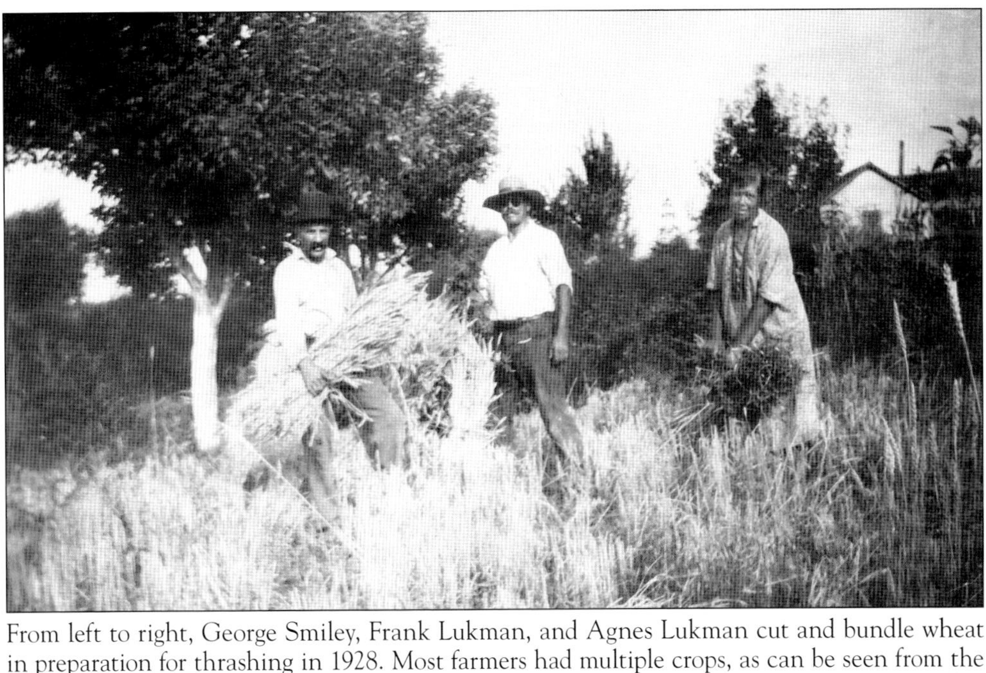

From left to right, George Smiley, Frank Lukman, and Agnes Lukman cut and bundle wheat in preparation for thrashing in 1928. Most farmers had multiple crops, as can be seen from the fruit tree in the background, making for a very busy harvest season. (Courtesy of Sherrie Stille.)

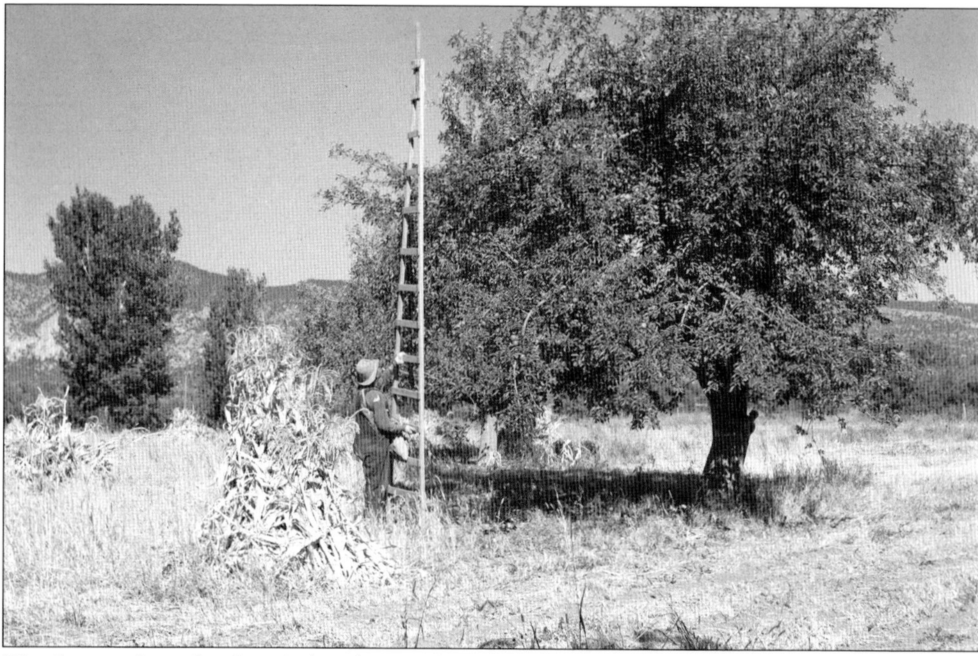

The first apple orchard in Colorado was planted by Jesse Frazer on the west side of present-day Florence. His plot was acquired in 1863 through the Homestead Act. By 1867, Frazer had over 2,000 apple trees on his orchard. Florence and the surrounding area became known for successful apple production. In 1888, Fremont County shipped out over 700,000 pounds of fruit, primarily apples. That same year, the entire state produced 60,000 bushels of apples, of which 40,000 bushels were produced in Fremont County. These photographs demonstrate the apple harvest process in Fremont County in the late 1930s. (Both, courtesy of Library of Congress; above, LC-DIG-fsa-836539; below, LC-DIG-fsa-8636537.)

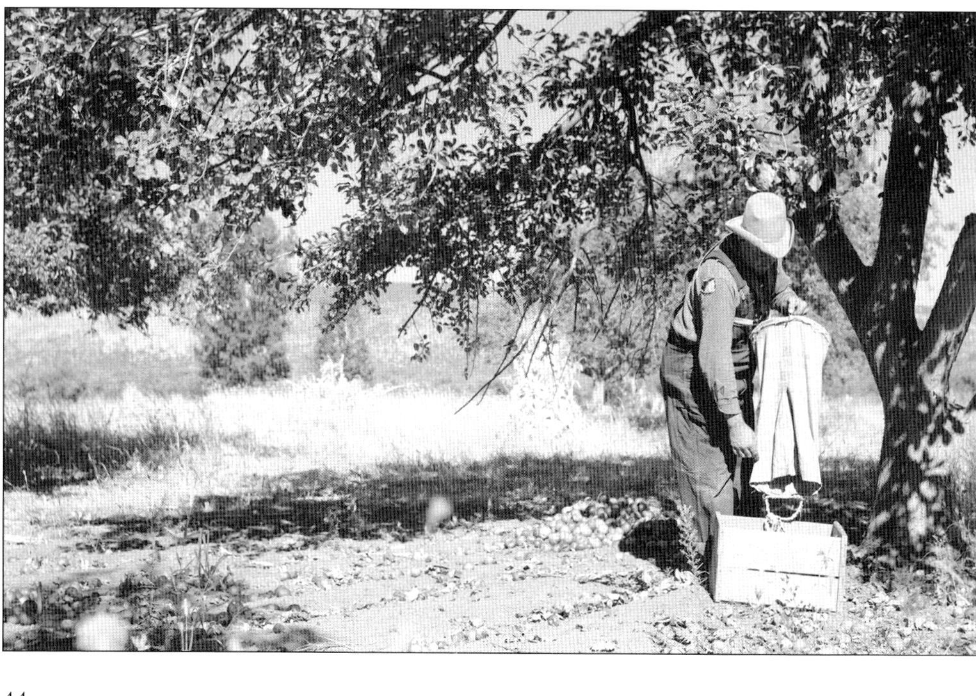

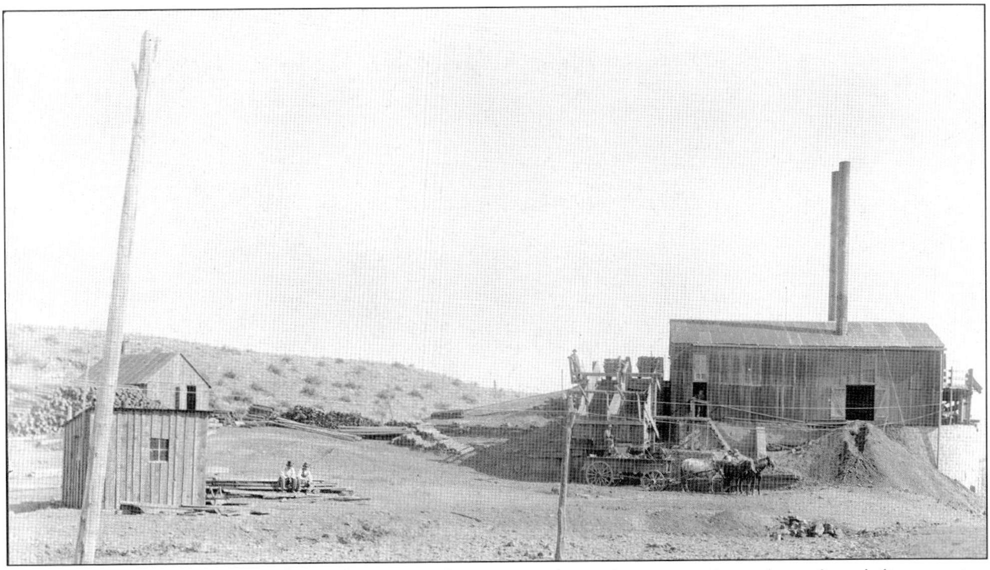

Florence began with agriculture, but soon, farmers and ranchers saw the value of coal discoveries in the surrounding area. Pioneer agriculturist Jesse Frazer himself supplemented his farming income by delivering coal for heating homes and to blacksmiths for their forges. Many families started their own mining operations, as shown here with an area family loading a horse-drawn wagon with coal extracted from their mine.

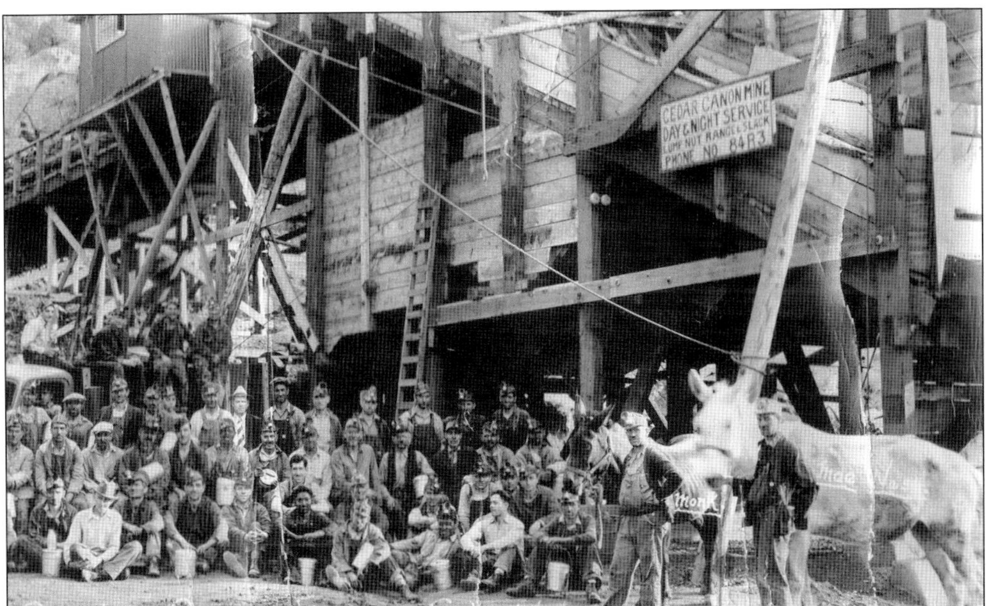

Coal became a driving force behind Florence's growth and development. The town transformed into a hub for its extraction and delivery, supplying manpower, equipment, transportation, and supplies to the over 50-square-mile area, maintaining over 180 individual coal mines, the last closing in 2001. This photograph of the Cedar Cañon Mine, one of the larger mines, was taken in 1935.

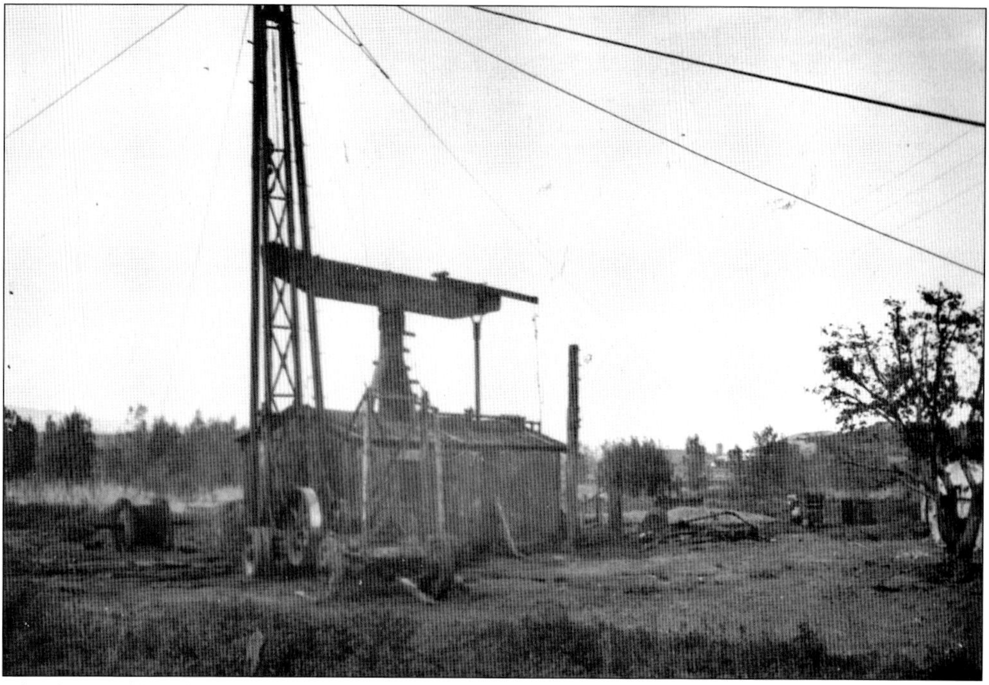

The first viable oil-producing well was drilled on Edwin Lobach's property in Florence in 1876 by Isaac Canfield. The well led to the discovery of the Florence Oil Field, which by 1992 produced 824,000 barrels of oil. Florence was soon dotted with 1,300 oil wells such as the one pictured here.

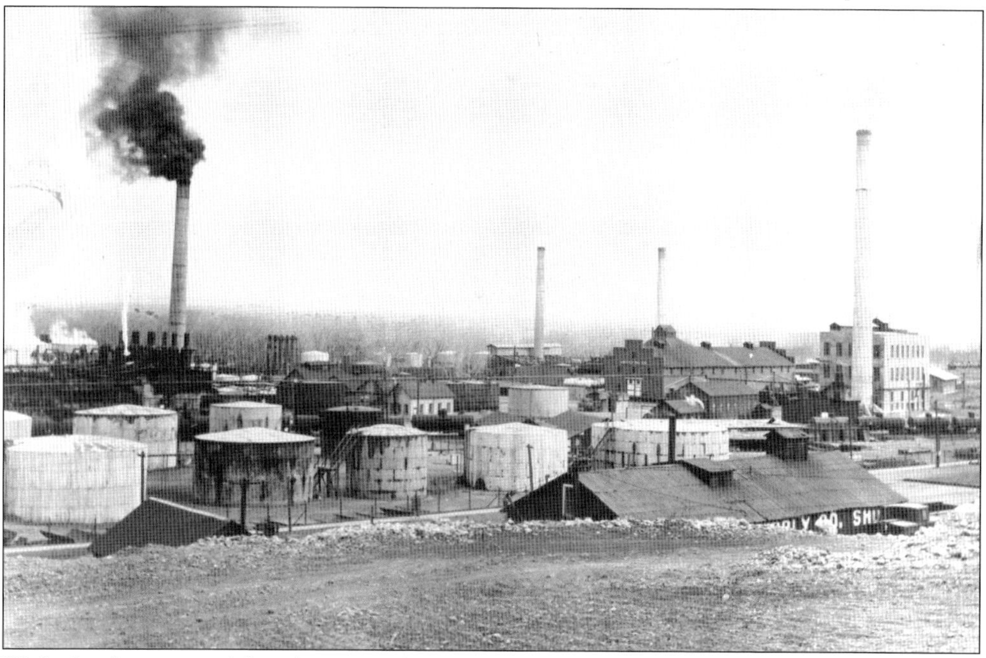

With the discovery of the Florence Oil Field, oil extraction, refining, and transportation were soon added to the Florence economy. In the beginning of the 20th century, Florence claimed 1,300 oil wells, 26 oil companies, and 5 oil refineries. This image of the Continental Oil Refinery shows the massive size of the stack and building on the right, still standing today.

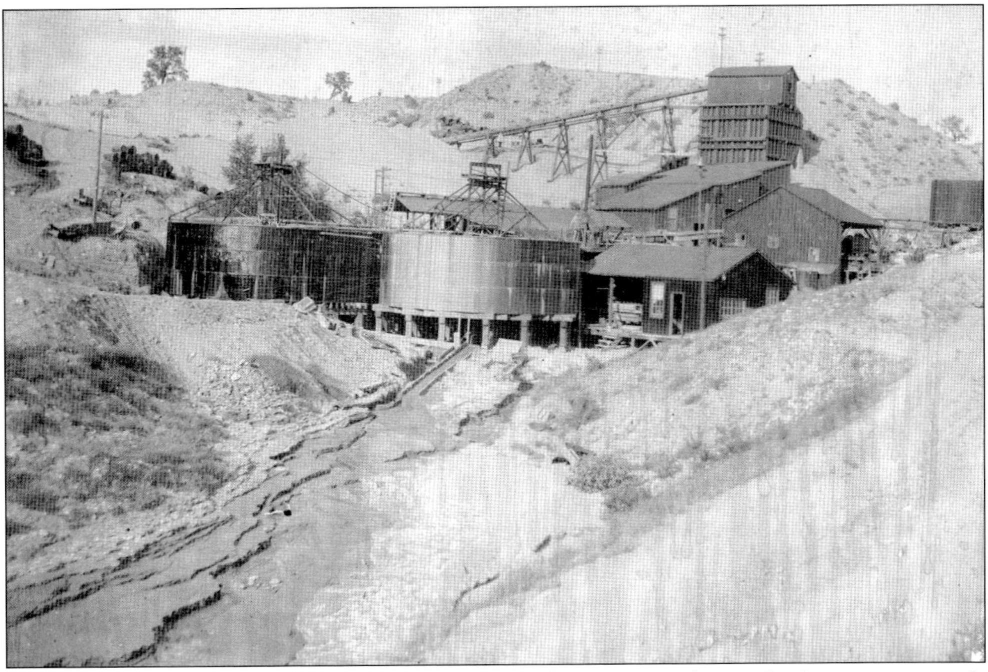

Community leaders also took advantage of the natural resources to the north, the precious metals found in the Cripple Creek goldfield. A group of Florence businessmen drove the construction of the Florence & Cripple Creek Free Road and soon spearheaded the Florence & Cripple Creek Railroad along the same route. Twenty-two smelting and reduction mills operated in Florence between 1887 and 1912, including the Union Mill (above) north of town and the El Paso Reduction Works mill (below) on the south side of town. In addition to refining ore, Florence again succeeded as a transportation hub supplying material and manpower to the Cripple Creek area.

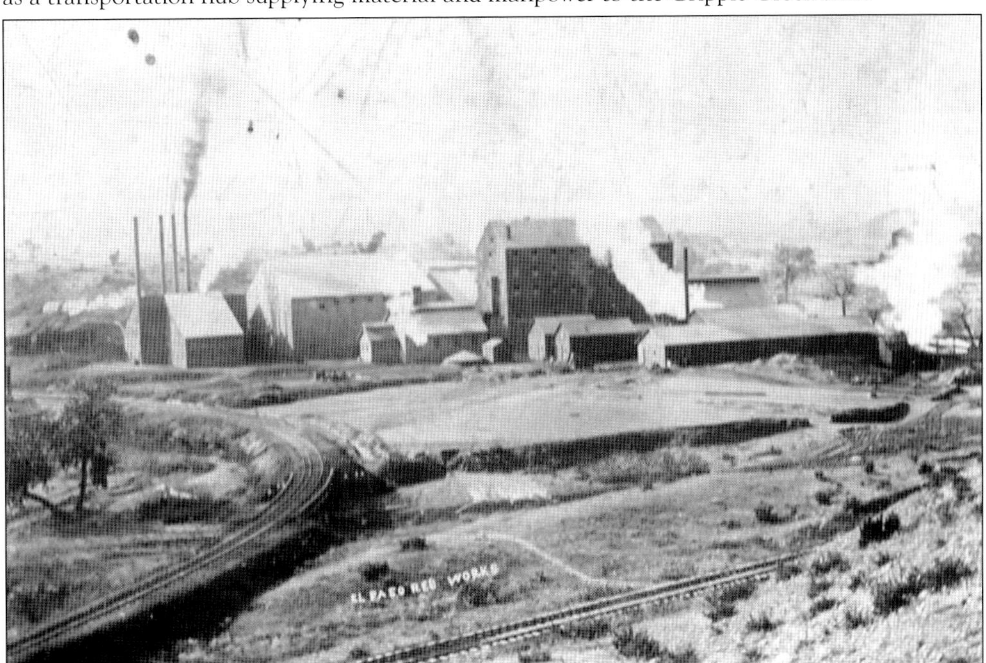

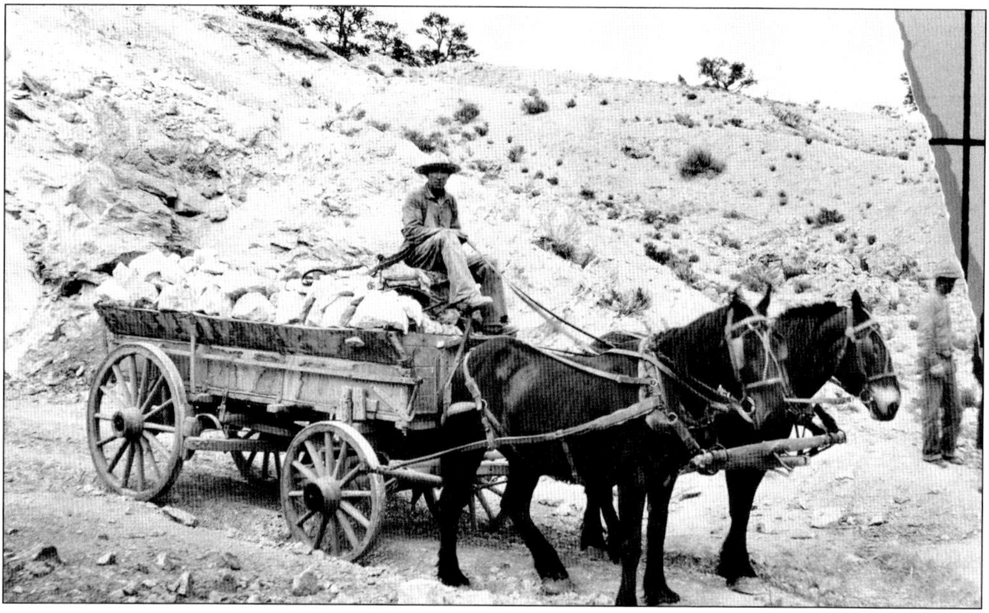

Limestone discoveries along the banks of the Arkansas River east of Florence soon developed into the booming production of cement, an important building material. This eventually led to the establishment of three no longer existing communities, Portland, Concrete, and Cement, for housing employees. Although no longer supporting any residential neighborhoods, cement production in the area continues to be strong today.

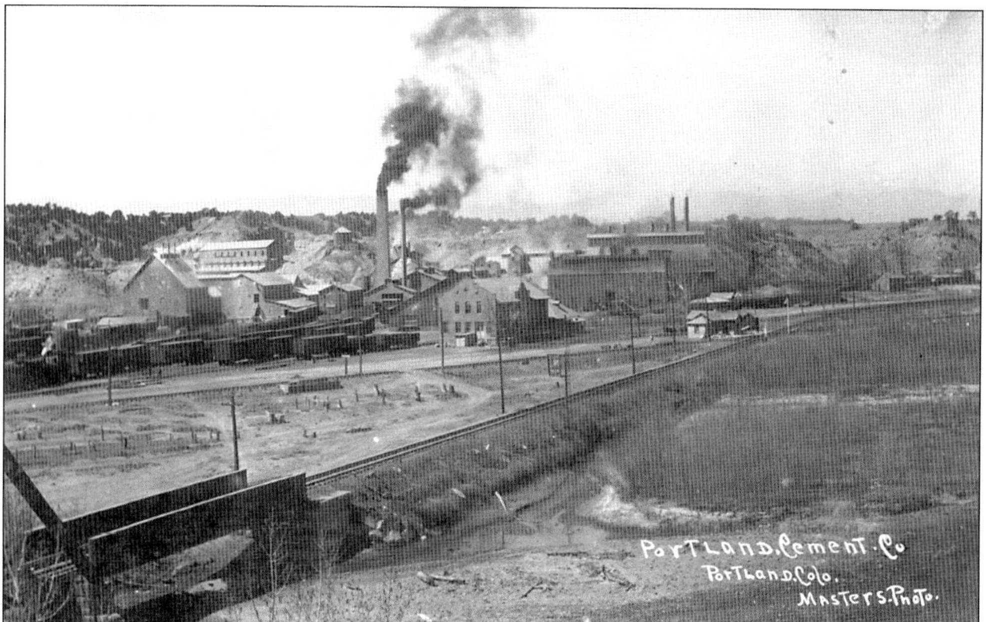

Cement has been produced in eastern Fremont County continuously since prior to 1900. Though the buildings have taken many different shapes and sizes, cement production has always been an important force in the area economy. This photograph, taken in the mid-1920s, shows a factory at that time. The road and railroad at center remain in use today. At one time, this was the only connection between Florence and Pueblo.

Four

Transportation

One of the key elements to the establishment and growth of Florence was the advance in transportation. Settlement began in the horse-and-buggy era, when entire families crossed the plains in horse-drawn wagons to find the fertile soils needed to grow their crops on the banks of the Arkansas River. Freight wagons were used to transport supplies and goods to and from the area, and soon the paths became roads. Wagons and carts were used to move people, materials, supplies, and crops within the growing area.

In 1869, the transcontinental railroad connected the East and West Coasts, and railroads were soon expanding into rural areas, making transportation easier and quicker. With his interest in railroad building, William Jackson Palmer needed the coalfields of the Florence region to fuel his trains and manufacture his steel. Competition between Palmer's Denver & Rio Grande Railroad (D&RG) and the Atchison, Topeka & Santa Fe Railway (ATSF) led to the accelerated growth of rail transportation to rural Florence.

In 1872, J.A. McCandless platted the town of Florence, encompassing what was becoming known as the farming community of Frazerville. In 1873, immediately adjacent to the east boundary of Florence, Palmer spearheaded the platting of the town of Labran as his railroad's last stop before heading south up Oak Creek into the coalfields.

Mine owners and miners of the Cripple Creek District relied on Florence to bring in necessary supplies and to haul out and process the products of their labor. The Florence & Cripple Creek Free Road, soon to become the Florence & Cripple Creek Railroad (F&CC), served that purpose. With all the resources found in the area, Florence became a crucial and popular waypoint for rail transportation, easily supporting the D&RG, the ATSF, and the F&CC.

The oilfield that surrounded Florence was becoming essential for supplying the oil needed for heating and lighting. The demand for oil and gasoline products grew exponentially with the arrival of the automobile. Florence stepped up to supply that demand with crude oil from the over 1,300 wells in the region, five large refineries within its boundaries, and the ability to transport those products throughout the entire nation.

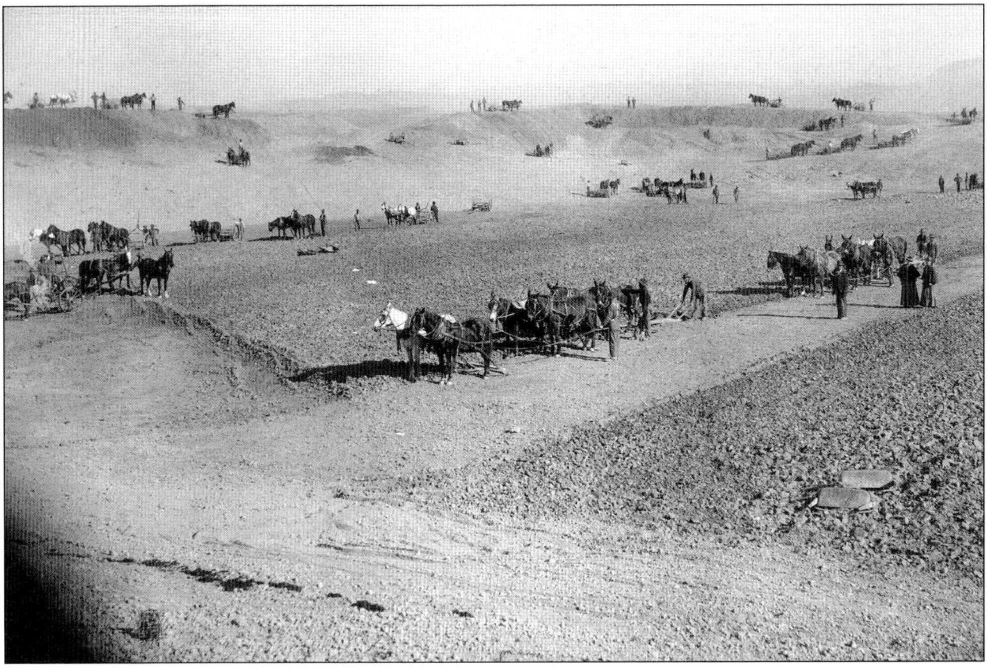

When Florence was established, the horse was the main mode of transportation and also the method used to get work done. In this photograph, teams of horses and men work to complete water reservoirs south of the city. These reservoirs held and supplied water for Florence for years to come.

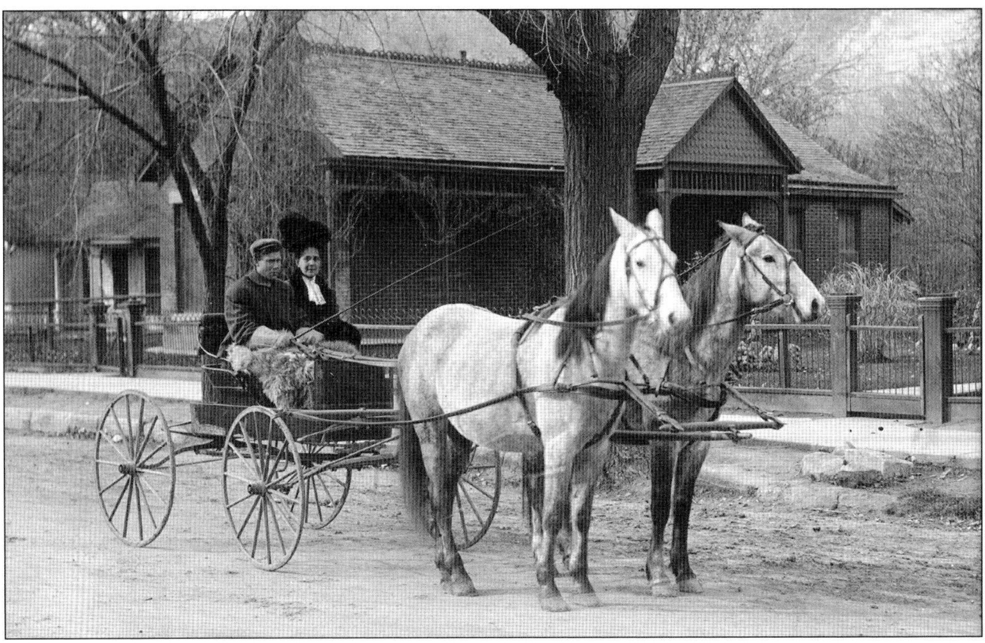

The horse and buggy was the main mode of transportation when Florence got its start. Concrete sidewalks were not added to the residential areas until 1910, and streets remained dirt until the 1920s. This photograph shows a typical couple out for a ride during that era.

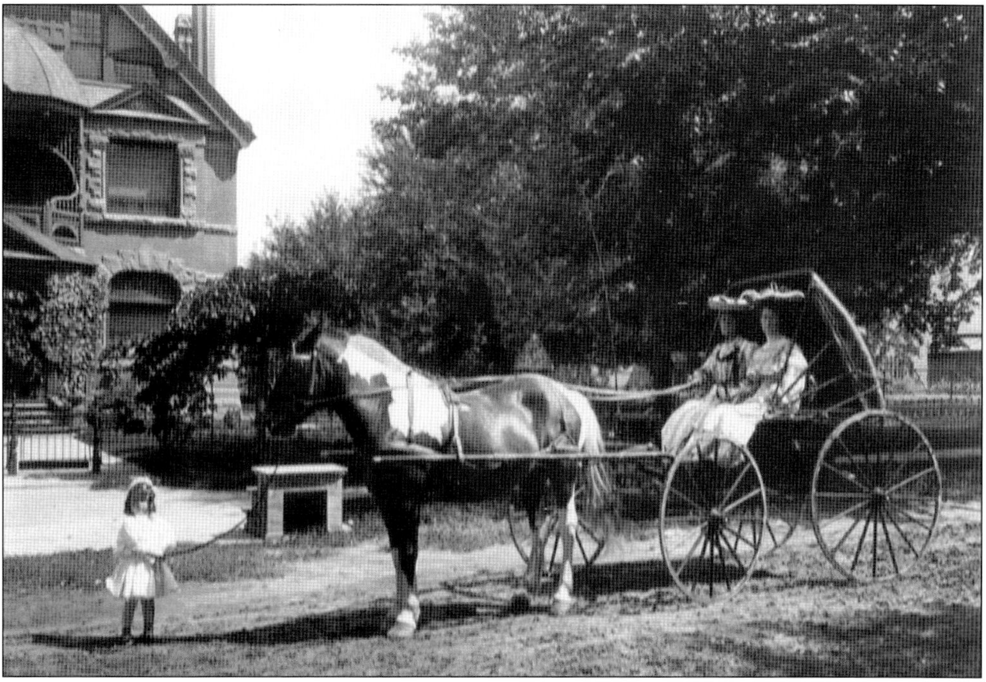

Sitting in the buggy in 1905 are Katherine McCandless (left), wife of Florence's founder, J.A. McCandless, and her daughter Ida Carlin. The young girl holding the reins is three-year-old Thelma Carlin, Ida Carlin's daughter. This is in front of the McCandless home in the 100 block of North Pikes Peak Avenue looking east from the site of the current Florence Post Office.

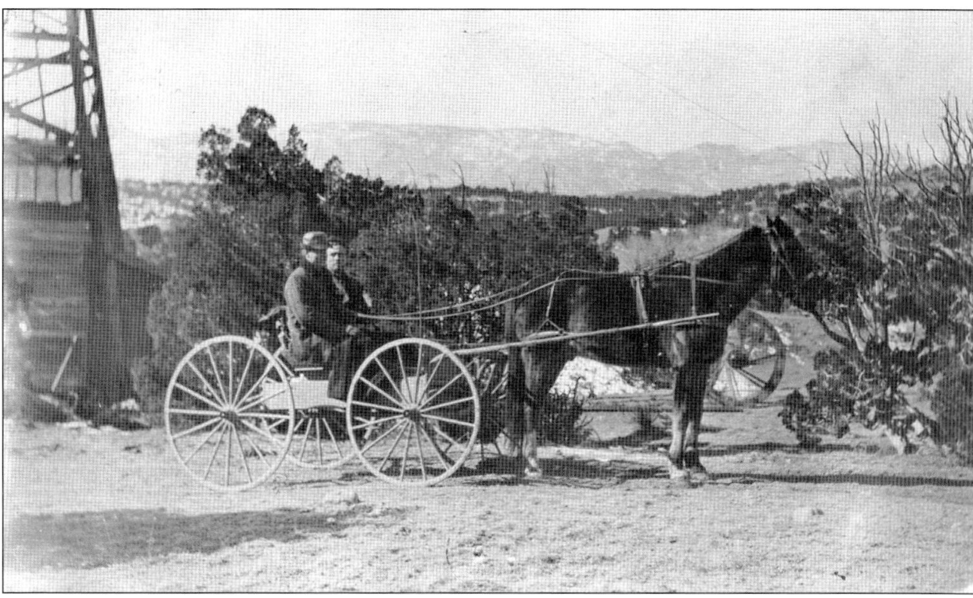

Speculators involved in the early oil industry came to Florence from all over the world. The John family emigrated from Wales to try their luck in the oil business with the Radium Oil Company. Here, two John brothers in their single-horse buggy are presumably out for a daily inspection of one of the 1,300 wells that would eventually pump oil from the Florence Oil Field.

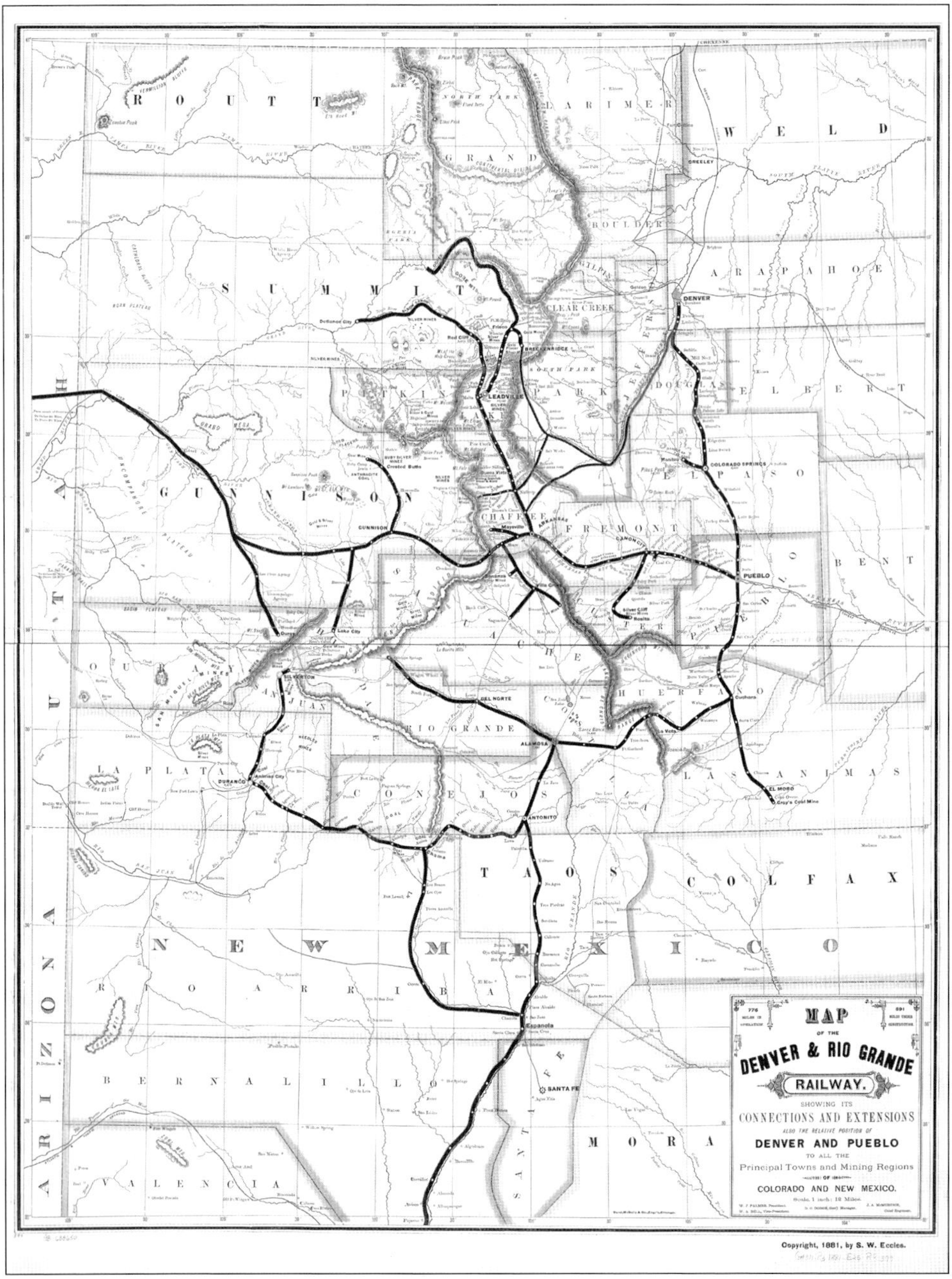

This 1881 D&RG map of connections and extensions shows the importance of the railroad to the settling of the West. Railroads made access to rural areas much easier and faster and supported the marketing and delivery of the natural resources found in remote areas such as Florence. At the time this map was drafted, William Jackson Palmer had 776 miles of railroad in operation and 691 miles under construction, demonstrating the significance of his railroad not only to Florence but also to the surrounding states. At the time, the ATSF and the F&CC were also adding rails and contributing to the growth and development of Florence. The train became the primary mode of transportation for both passengers and freight. (Courtesy of Library of Congress, Geography and Map Division, G4311.P3 1881. E25 RR399.)

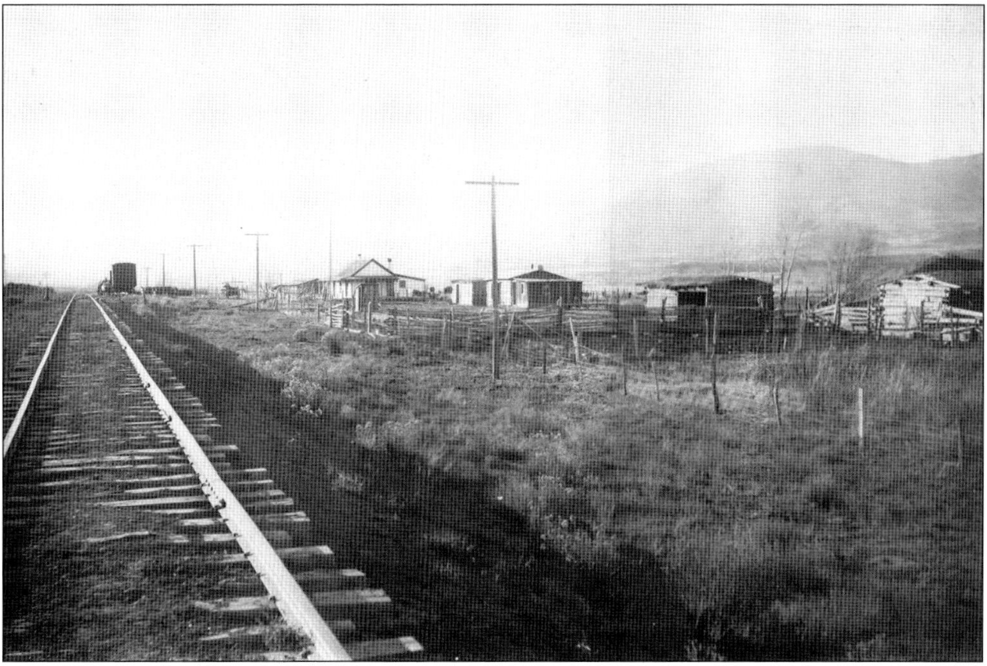

The D&RG came to the area in 1872, following the Arkansas River from the east. Railroads needed coal to fuel their steam engines and to fire their furnaces for making rails. The coalfields southeast of Florence contained a coal that burned hotter for better efficiency, and it was in high demand.

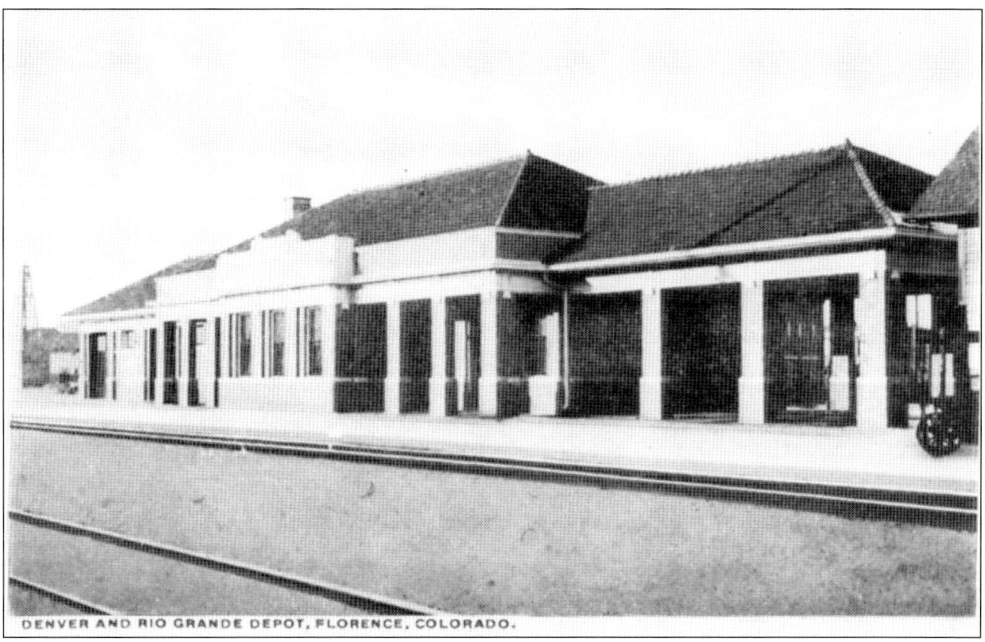

This is the second building to house the Denver & Rio Grande Railroad in Florence. Built in 1917 to replace the first D&RG station, which was slightly to the east, this depot was used by the railroad from the day of its completion until 1968, when, because of the decline in passengers, the railroad donated the building to the City of Florence.

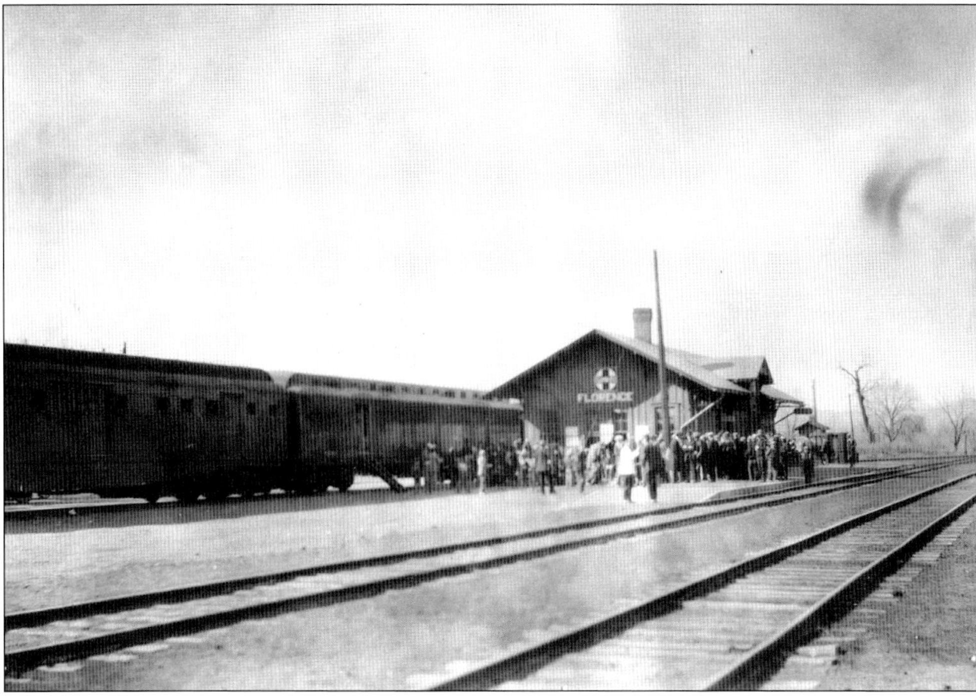

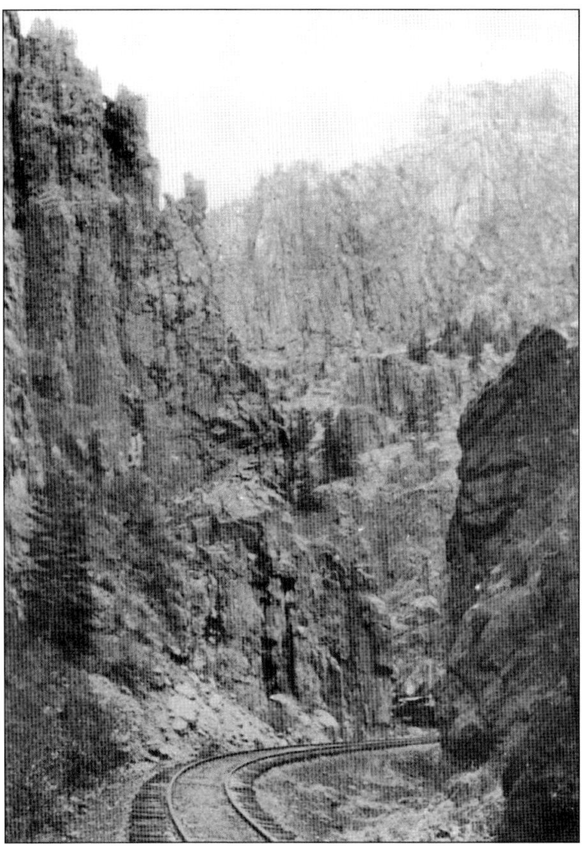

By 1873, the ATSF had arrived in Florence seeking the coalfields as well as expanding its freight and passenger traffic to the growing area. The railroad serviced Florence until 1947. This photograph, taken in 1903, shows the station on the north side of Florence near present-day McCandless and Eighth Streets.

The F&CC carried passengers and freight, including coal for heating and bricks for construction, from Florence to the Cripple Creek goldfields. Return trips carried the precious metal ore for processing in Florence or other destinations. The F&CC operated from 1894 to 1915. This photograph of Eight Mile Canyon, now Phantom Canyon, shows the steep canyon walls and ravines of the route, originally built as the Florence Free Road and closed to train use by a July 1912 flood.

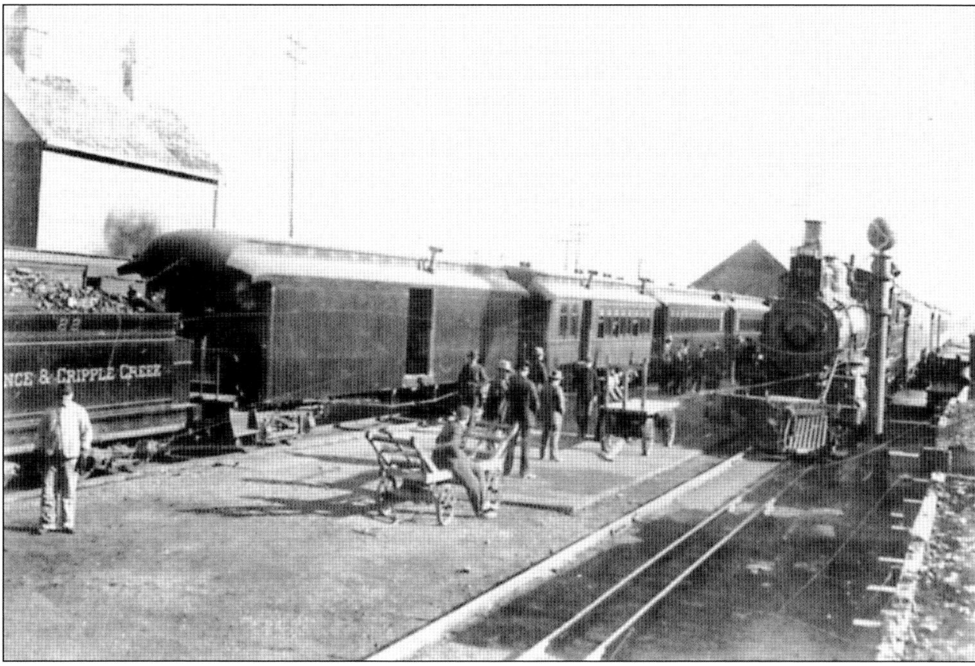

The three-track rails seen in the foreground became common in areas that served both standard-gauge trains with rails four feet, eight inches wide and narrow-gauge trains with rails two feet, six inches wide. The three railway companies of Florence, the D&RG, the ATSF, and the F&CC, shared many areas of track, the Florence & Cripple Creek being the only narrow-gauge road. Here, an F&CC passenger train prepares for departure.

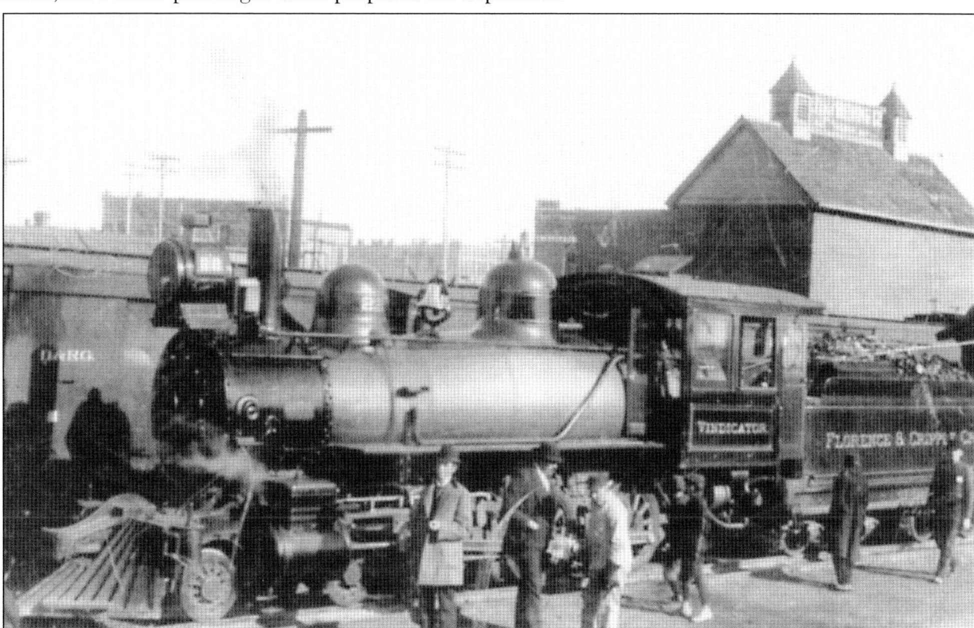

Over the course of its 21-year lifespan, the F&CC owned and operated 19 steam locomotives. Here, No. 22, named *Vindicator*, was one of three built and delivered by Schenectady Locomotive Works to Florence in 1900. The *Vindicator* was used for passenger transportation.

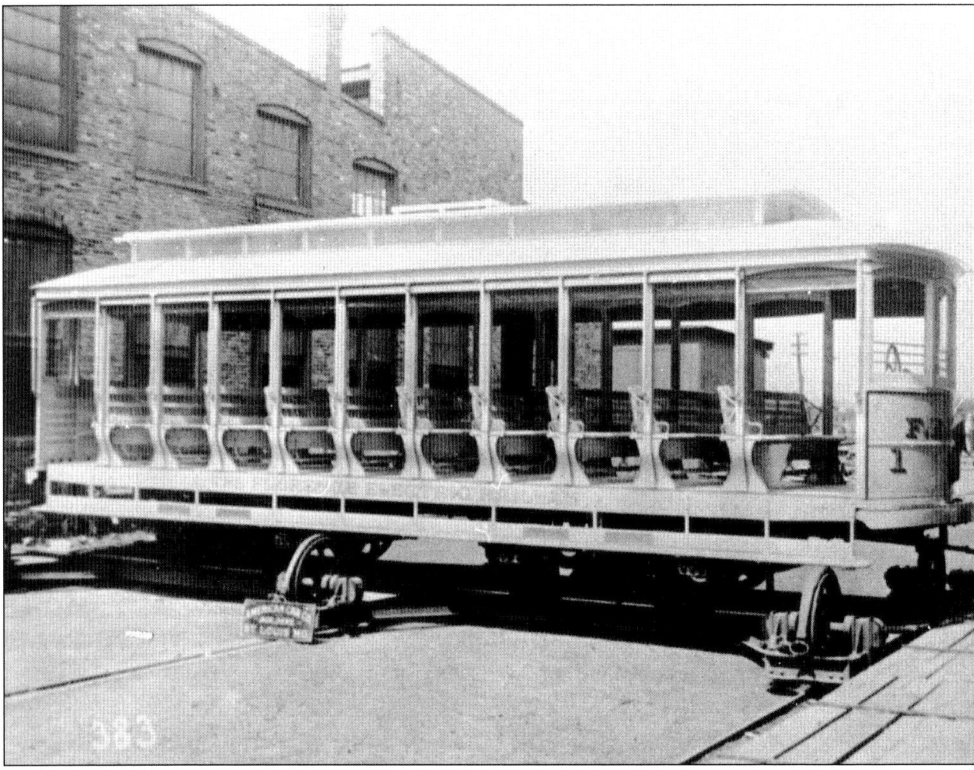

In 1900, Thomas Robinson and other businessmen of Florence incorporated the Florence Electric Railway. The plan was to establish an electric streetcar system for the growing community. Although receiving significant local investment, after nearly 10 years, the project was scrapped as unfeasible. The project had started mapping the streetcar route and had ordered the streetcars from the American Car Company in St. Louis, shown here being constructed.

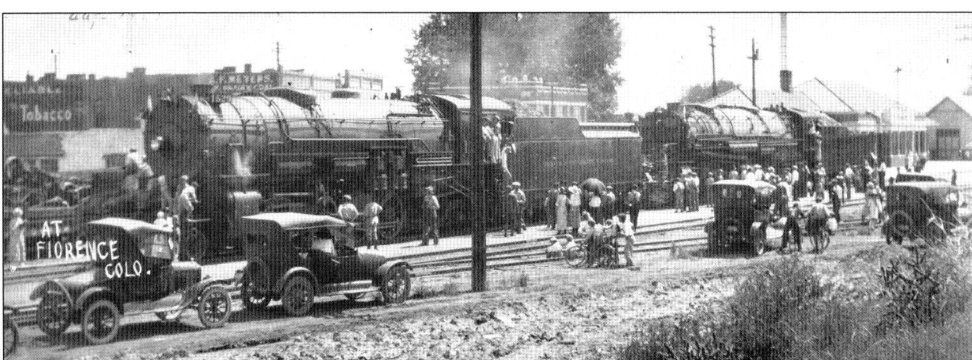

The D&RG grew and expanded throughout the West, adding routes and trains to service the rapidly expanding population. In this photograph, at the height of operations, the railroad takes two of its newest additions on tour. In August 1923, engines 1529 and 3509 stop for a couple of hours in Florence to allow citizens the opportunity to view the two massive locomotives, the largest freight and passenger engines ever built.

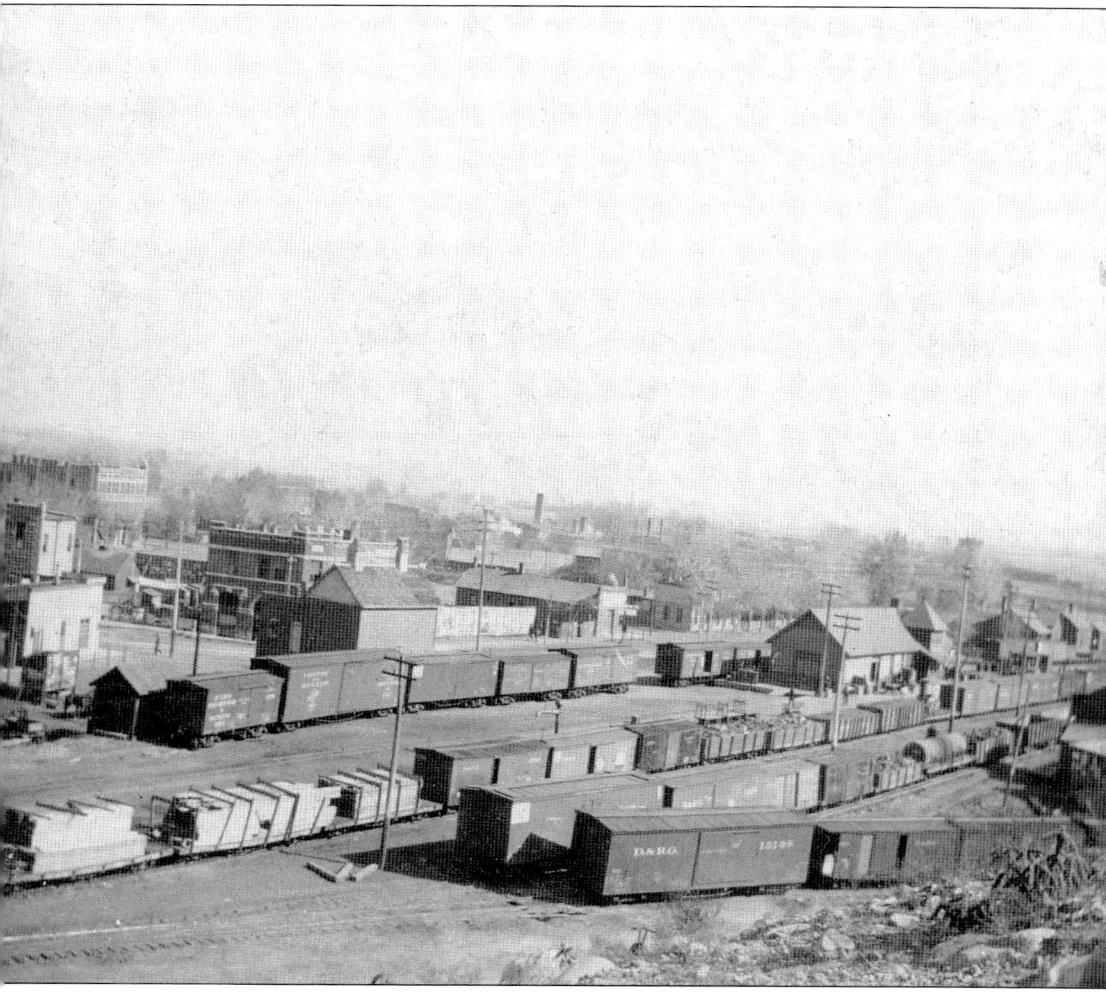

Railroad transportation played a major role in the establishment and growth of Florence. At the turn of the 20th century, at the peak of its development, three rail lines served the area: the D&RG, the ATSF, and the F&C. This photograph of the area just south of downtown that served as the central switching area for all three railroads demonstrates the vigorous rail activity of the time. From initially seeking the coalfields southeast of Florence for fuel to becoming the method for supplying men and materials and delivering the natural resources found in the area to the rest of the world, the rail transportation system became the lifeblood of Florence.

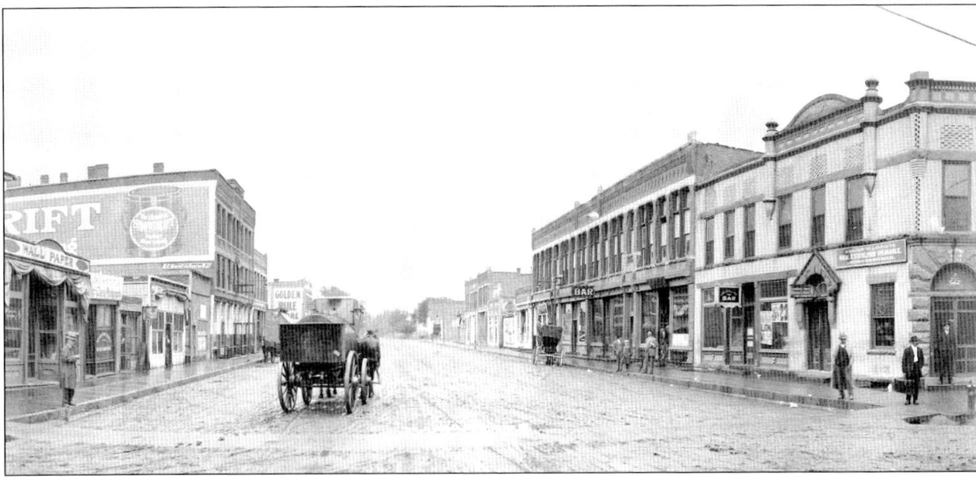

These photographs were taken in 1915, just as the automobile era was arriving in Florence. The first automobile in Florence was a steam-powered Locomobile, delivered in 1900 for William M. Rogers. Like everywhere, cars slowly took over horses as the preferred mode of transportation, and communities had to deal with the changes. The photograph above shows Main Street looking east from Pikes Peak Avenue. Sidewalks were constructed in 1911, but there was really no consideration for the streets themselves. The photograph below is from the same position looking southeast, with South Pikes Peak Avenue on the left and West Main Street on the right.

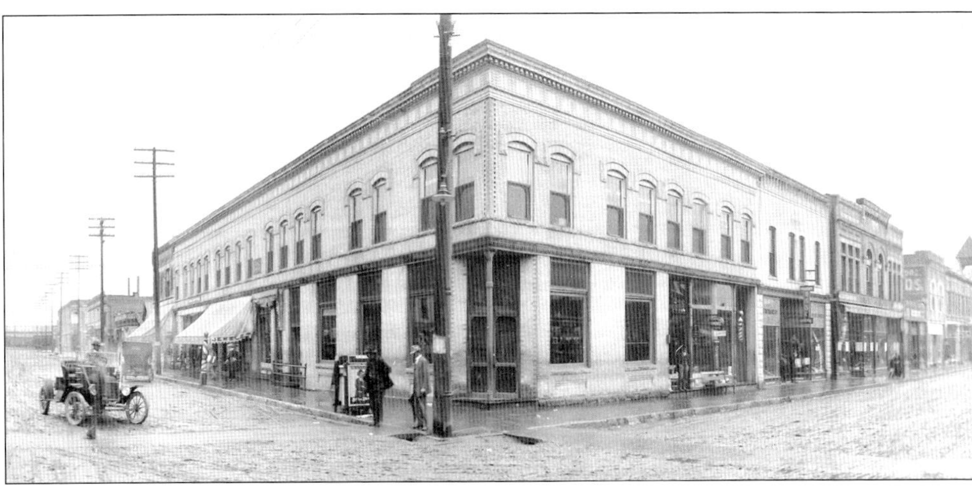

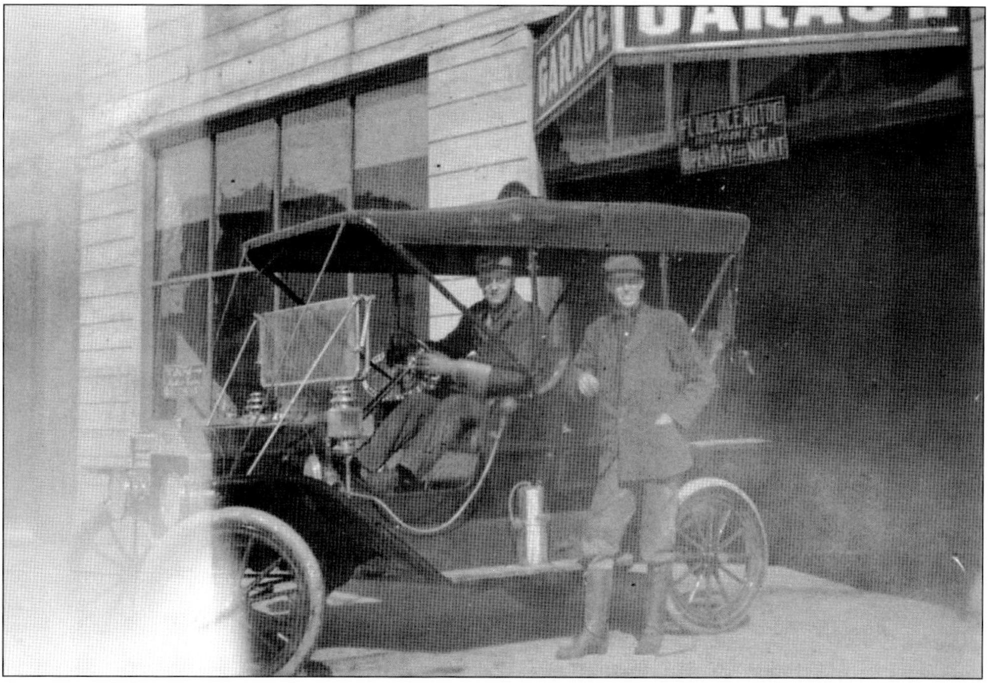

As automobiles grew in popularity, Florence saw the introduction of dealerships and service shops. This photograph of the Florence Auto Company at 111 West Front Street was taken in 1920. Florence Auto was owned by Henry Fox, who is sitting in the driver's seat. It was one of the first businesses in Florence specifically related to the automobile.

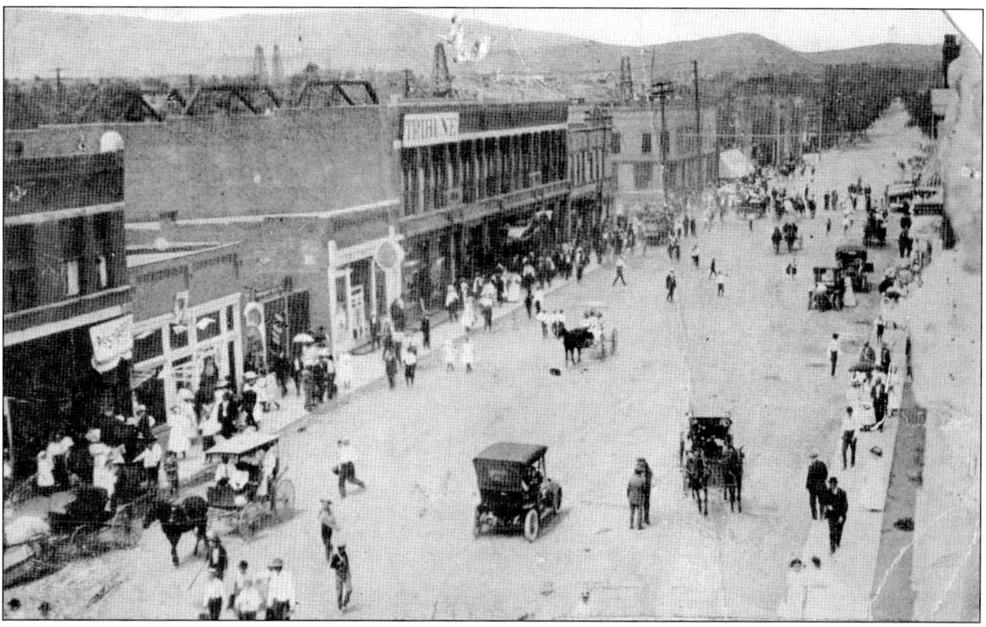

The transition from horses to automobiles was rapid and exciting for Florence. Looking west along Main Street, horse-drawn wagons, automobiles, and pedestrians gather for a Fourth of July celebration. The number of oil wells in the background would continue to grow along with the popularity of the automobile.

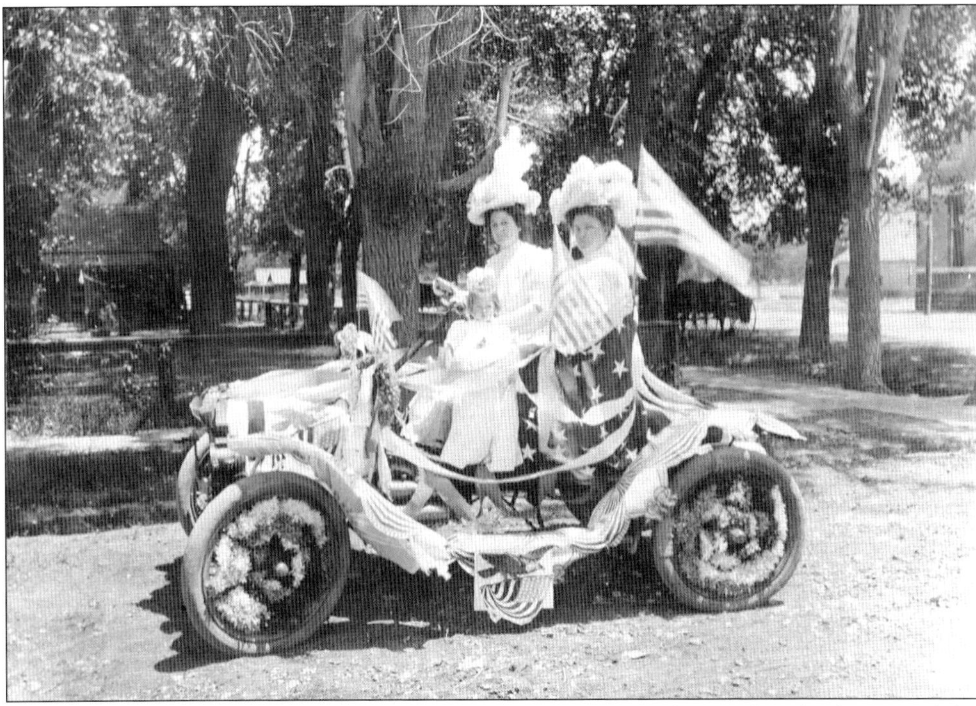

This 1906 photograph, entitled "McCandless Women," illustrates the novelty of early automobiles. Decorated here for a Fourth of July parade, the automobile was soon to become a way of life and major contributor to transportation and economic growth in Florence.

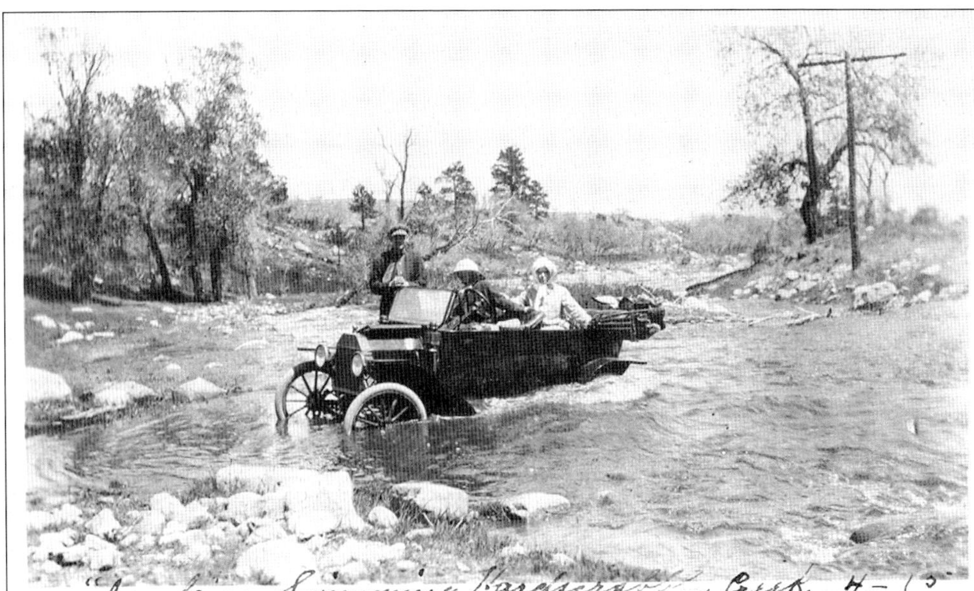

Citizens of Florence quickly learned the usefulness of the automobile. Personal vehicles made transportation easier but also required improvements to roads that were once only maintained for horse traffic. This photograph of Hardscrabble Creek during the spring runoff of April 1915 shows the new necessity of bridges in the Florence area.

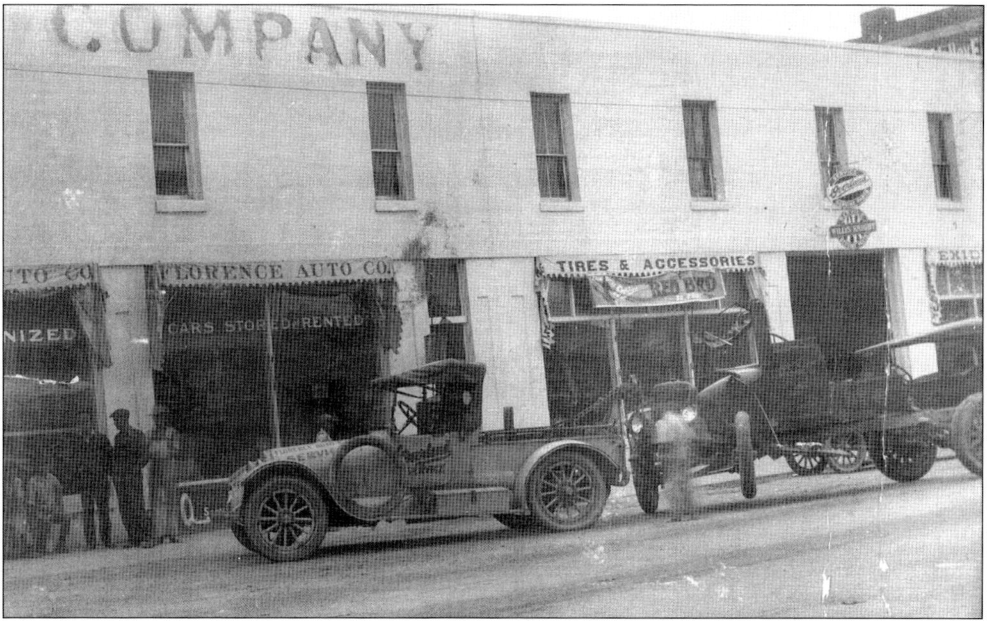

In 1912, Henry Fox acquired the Ford Auto Agency on East Main Street and renamed it Florence Auto Company. As his business grew between 1917 and 1926, he constructed two new buildings, 115 and 123 East Main Street. In 1949, Luke's Motor Company opened in the west building, while Florence Auto continued operations in the east building. With the prosperous automobile industry, Luke's Motor Company purchased the Ford dealership in 1951 and remodeled the front of the building in 1963.

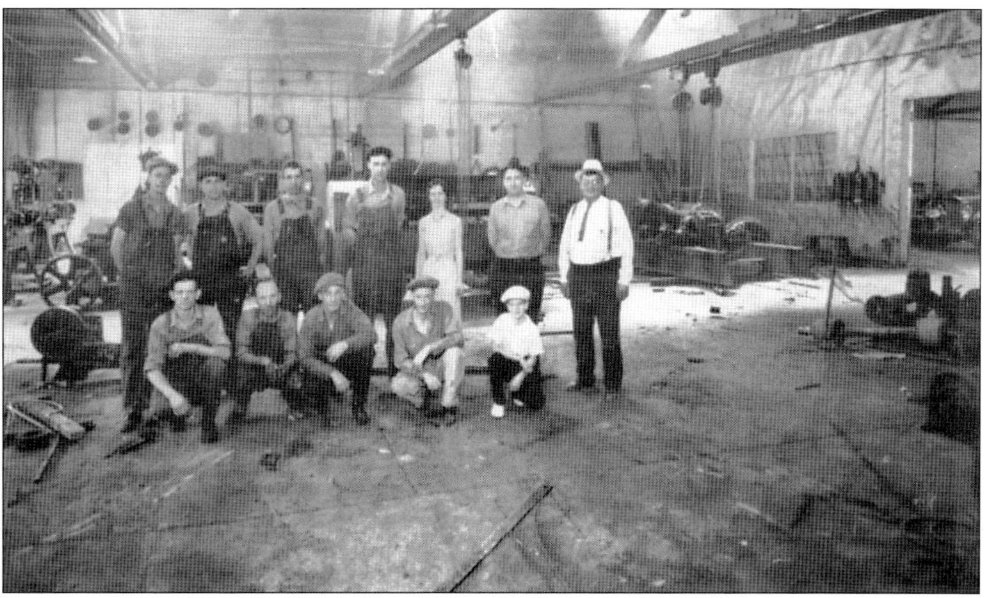

Ford Motor Company required a machine shop within each franchise. The building Henry Fox constructed at 123 East Main Street housed Fox Machine Shop for that purpose. In this photograph, he is on the far right, his brother Nicholas Fox stands next to him, and grandson Henry Fox is kneeling in front at far right. Young Henry Fox continued to own and operate Fox Machine Shop, relocating it to Front Street and selling it to the Carochi brothers (page 27) in 1987.

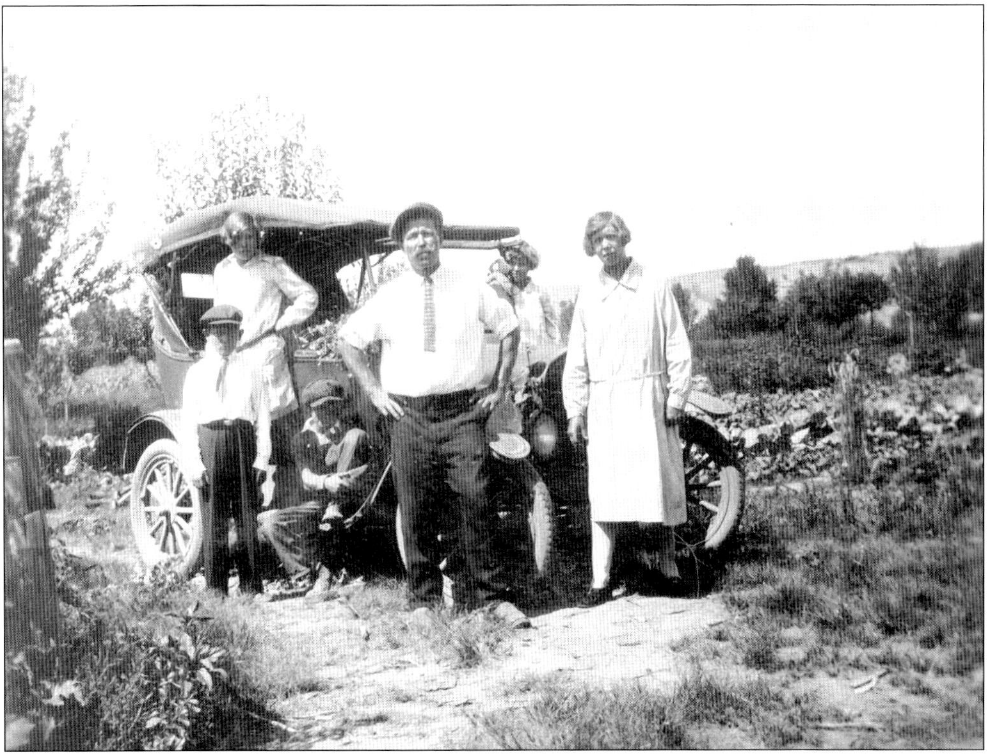

The automobile made life in general a bit easier. It also created what became known as the Sunday afternoon drive. Many families enjoyed a drive in the country after church with a picnic lunch packed. Here, in 1928, the Frank Lukman family stops for a photograph on a Sunday afternoon. (Courtesy of Sherrie Stille.)

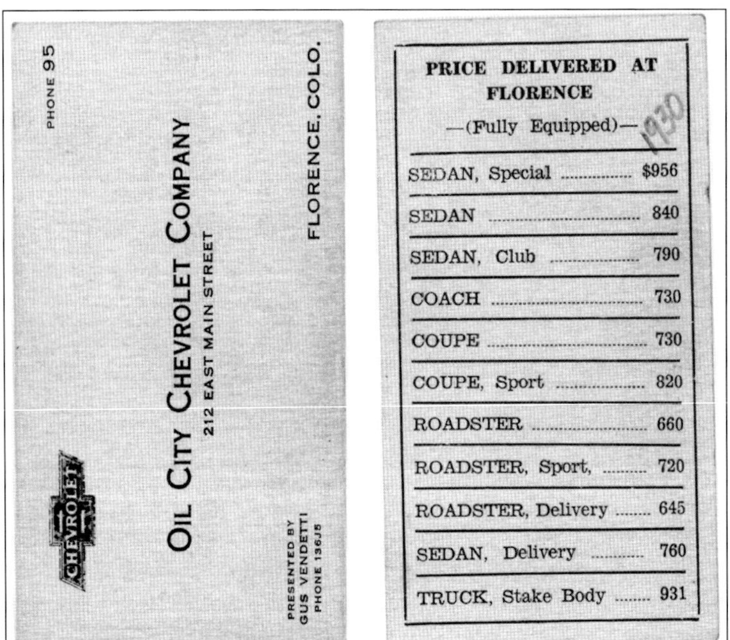

PHONE 95

CHEVROLET

OIL CITY CHEVROLET COMPANY
212 EAST MAIN STREET

FLORENCE, COLO.

PRESENTED BY
GUS VENDETTI
PHONE 136J5

PRICE DELIVERED AT FLORENCE
—(Fully Equipped)—

1930

SEDAN, Special	$956
SEDAN	840
SEDAN, Club	790
COACH	730
COUPE	730
COUPE, Sport	820
ROADSTER	660
ROADSTER, Sport,	720
ROADSTER, Delivery	645
SEDAN, Delivery	760
TRUCK, Stake Body	931

This business card of Gus Vendetti Sr. shows the cost of automobiles sold at the Oil City Chevrolet Company in 1930. The car dealership, located at 212 East Main Street at that time, eventually became Vendetti Chevrolet. The price for a Special Sedan adjusted for inflation would be about $16,000 today. (Courtesy of Gus and Barbara Vendetti.)

As the automobile industry grew, so did the need for fuel and service stations. The Sasser family came to Florence in 1934 to operate Rainbow Park Service. Here, Tom Sasser pumps gasoline into the visible cylinder of one the original gravity-fed gas pumps. (Courtesy of the Sasser family.)

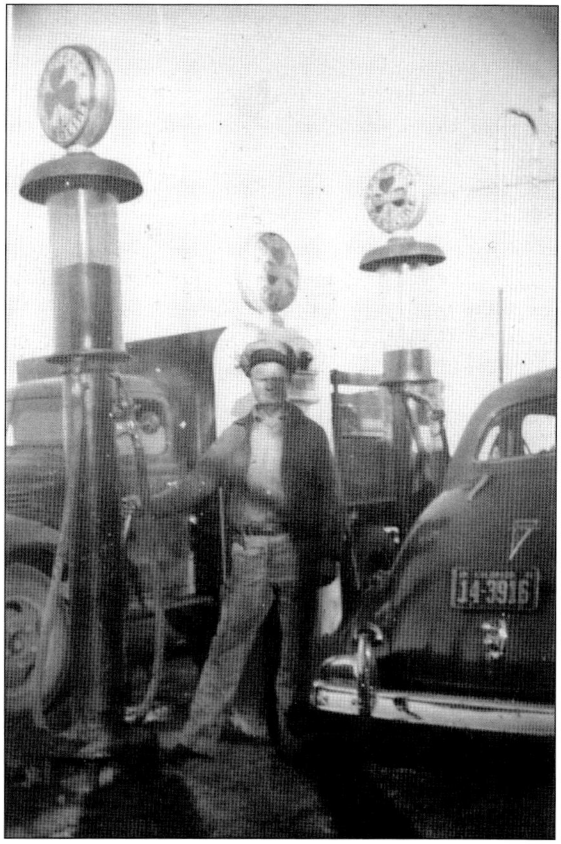

Just as automobiles replaced trains for passenger transportation, trucks soon replaced horse-drawn freight wagons for local transport of materials. Ralph Carestia, of the Carestia coal mining family, owned and operated the successful Carestia Trucking Company in Florence until the 1990s. This photograph shows three of his trucks loaded with coal fueling at Rainbow Park Service. (Courtesy of the Sasser family.)

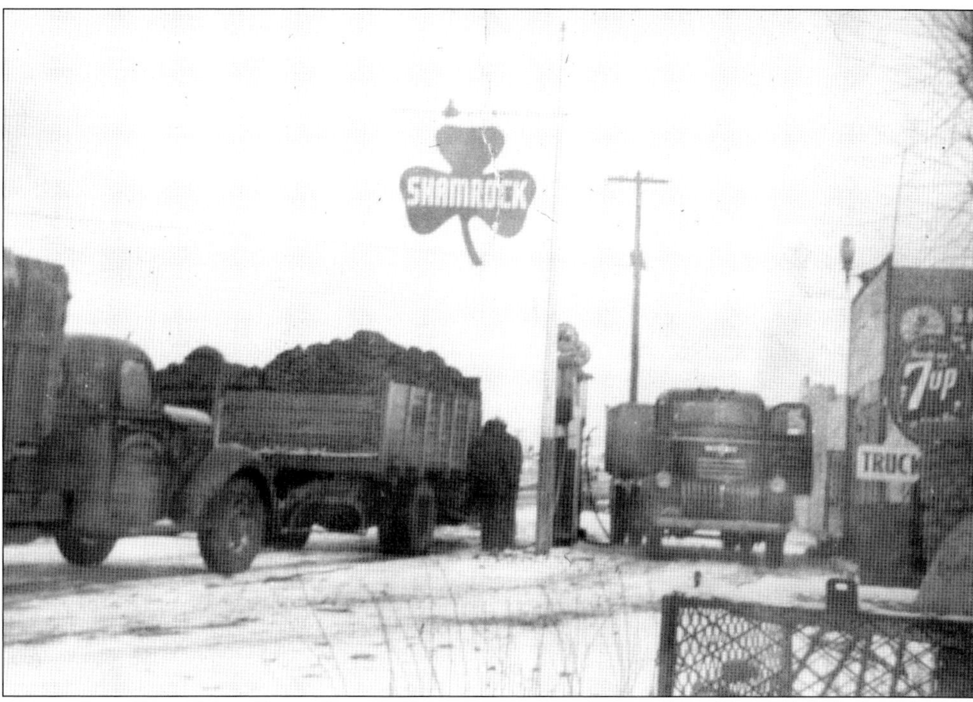

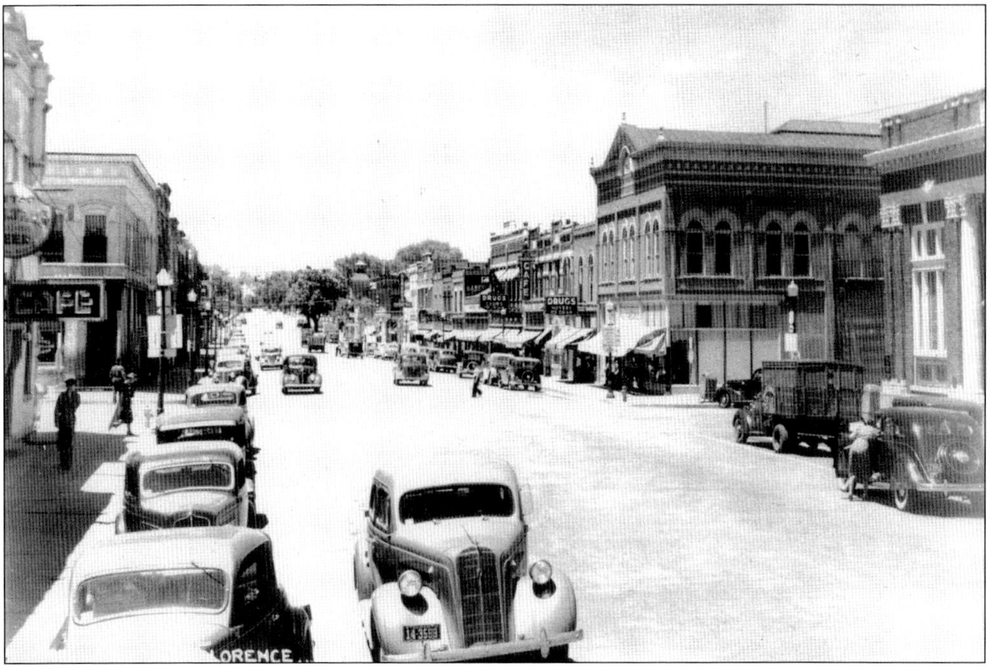

The popularity of the automobile drastically changed the look of downtown Florence by the end of the 1930s. Many streets were paved in the late 1920s. This photograph shows the intersection of Main Street and Pikes Peak Avenue, with parallel parking along the length of Main Street.

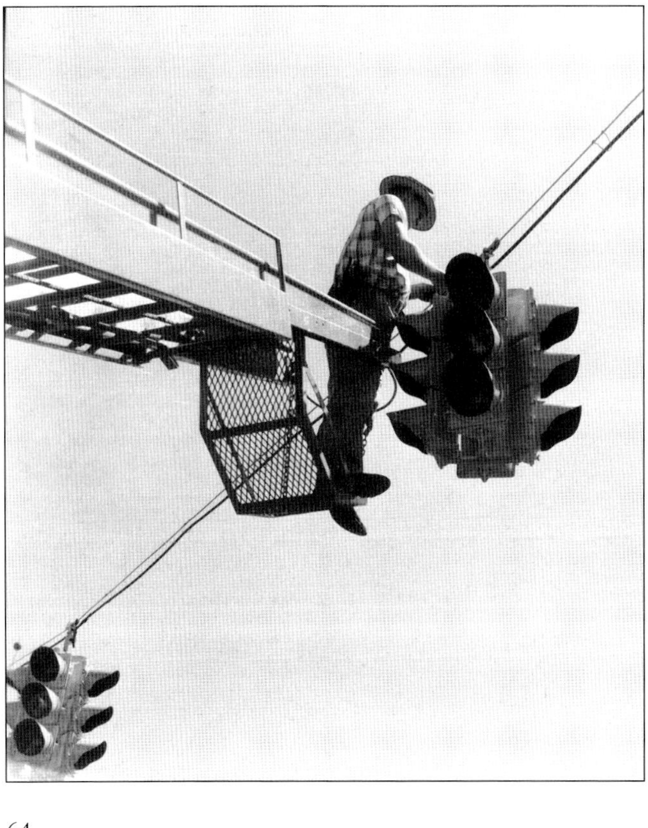
The popularity of the automobile continued to grow as more and more vehicles were purchased and used on the streets of Florence. Eventually, a traffic signal was required at the busy intersection of Main Street and Pikes Peak Avenue. This photograph, taken by city manager Frank Carochi, shows a Colorado Highway Department employee hanging the first—and for a long time only—stoplight in Florence. (Courtesy of the Carochi family.)

Five

Business

The success of a community is often measured by the businesses it supports. The success of a business is often measured by the impact it makes on a community. These are both obvious in the history of Florence. It may have been the natural resources of the area that attracted the first settlers, but it was the dedicated businessmen and businesswomen who ensured the prosperity of Florence. They saw a need in a community and took it upon themselves to fulfill that need.

The entrepreneurial spirit has always been alive and well in Florence. It is in that spirit that the bottom line of a successful business is calculated, not by how much it received but rather how much it received and then put back into the community. The businesspeople in Florence have consistently demonstrated that concept. When looking at volunteer organizations, city government, school administration, volunteer fire departments, and others, a high percentage have volunteered their time to sit on boards of directors, to help with events, and otherwise assist the community. These same businesses are the first resources sought when in need, be it for t-shirts for the Little League baseball team or to clean up mud after a flood.

So the success of a community is often determined by the businesses within that community. Throughout the history of Florence, the businessmen, the businesswomen, and the business families have demonstrated their desire to be involved in the development and the future of Florence and its citizens. They have demonstrated the desire to make an impact on Florence.

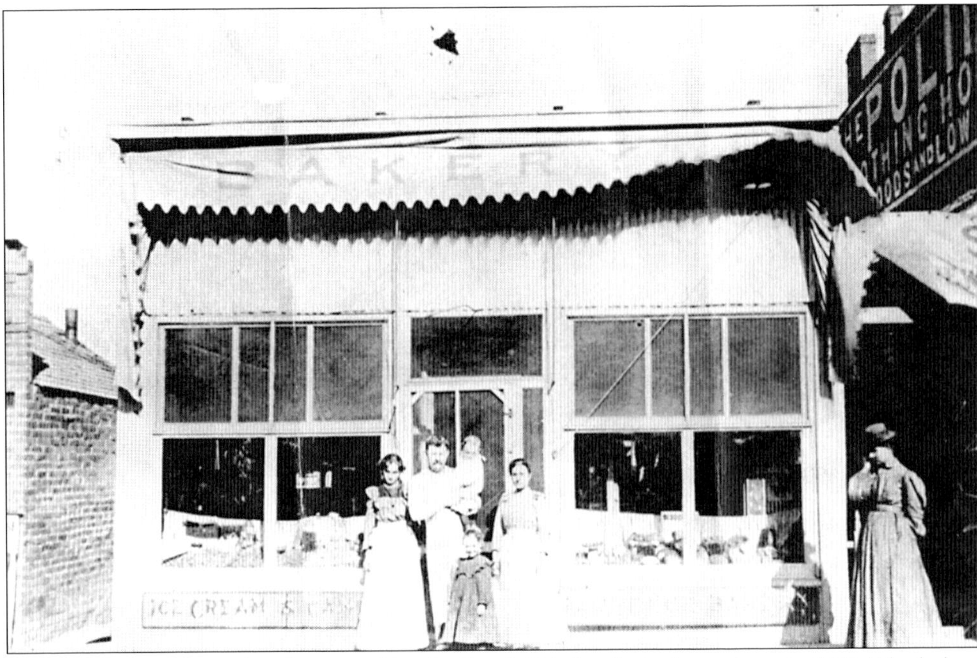
Florence Bakery, owned and operated by the Frank Ebb family, is shown here in 1902. The bakery sat at the northeast corner of Pikes Peak Avenue and Main Street. The small wooden structure was one of the original buildings soon replaced by newer brick construction.

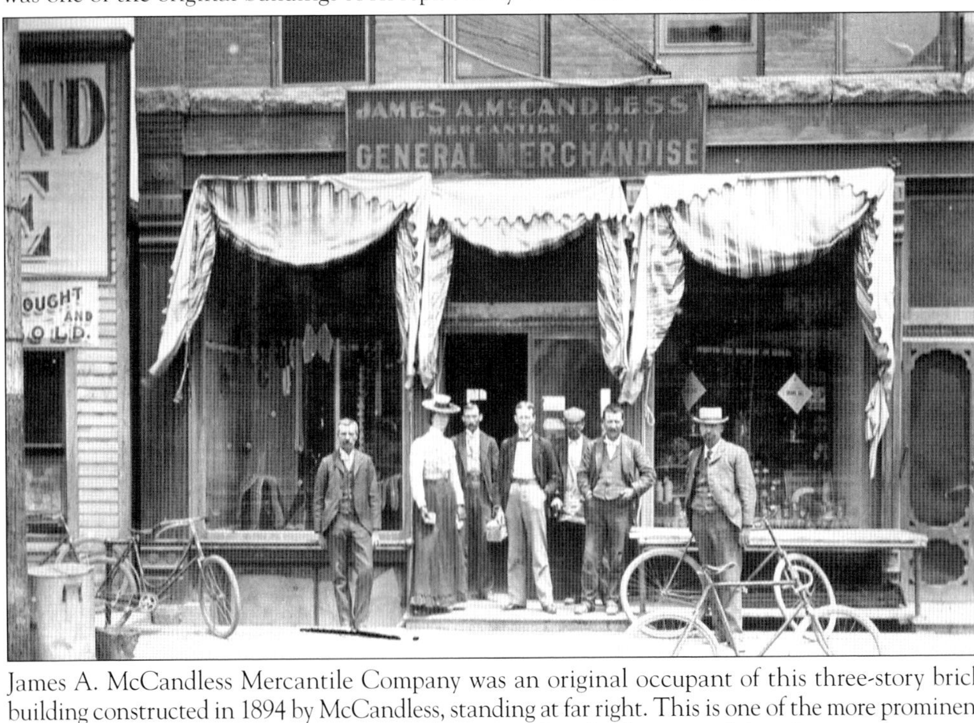

James A. McCandless Mercantile Company was an original occupant of this three-story brick building constructed in 1894 by McCandless, standing at far right. This is one of the more prominent brick buildings remaining in downtown Florence today. At the time of this photograph, general retail sales occupied the ground floor, with hotel rooms, office space, and a public meeting hall on the second and third floors.

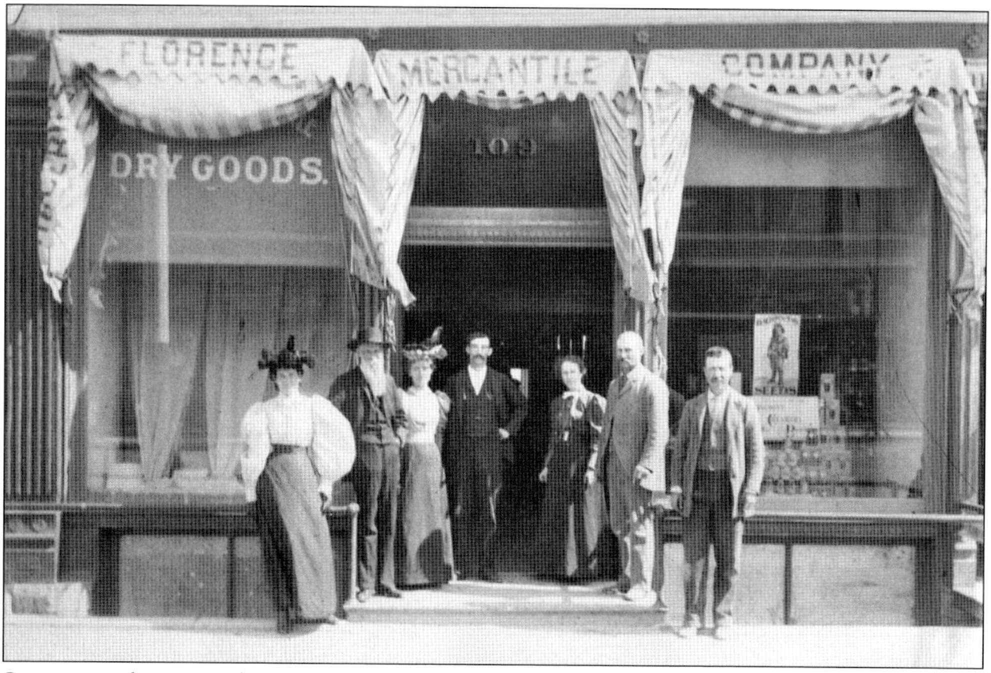

Sometime after 1900, the Hadley family purchased the James A. McCandless mercantile store and operated a dry goods and grocery store here called the Florence Mercantile Company. They offered wholesale and retail merchandise including clothing, carpet, curtains, suitcases, and groceries up until 1921, when the business space was purchased by the Butler Sauer Furniture Company.

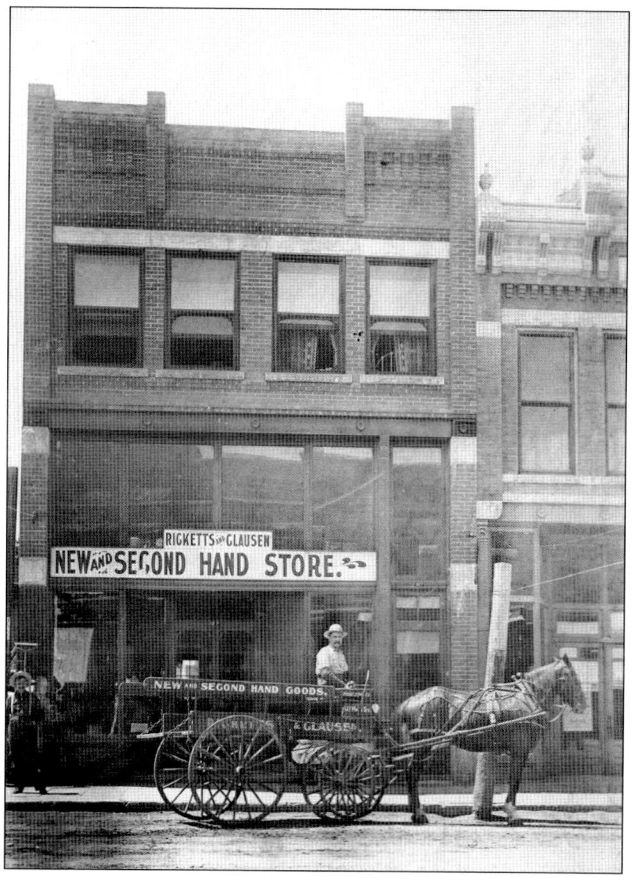

William G. Ricketts settled in the Florence area around 1890. He became a prominent businessman selling new and second-hand carpets, furniture, and other household goods. He had his business building constructed in two sections, the west side first in 1899 and then the matching east side in 1915. After Ricketts died in 1928, his widow, Nettie, continued to live upstairs and run the business downstairs until her passing in 1953.

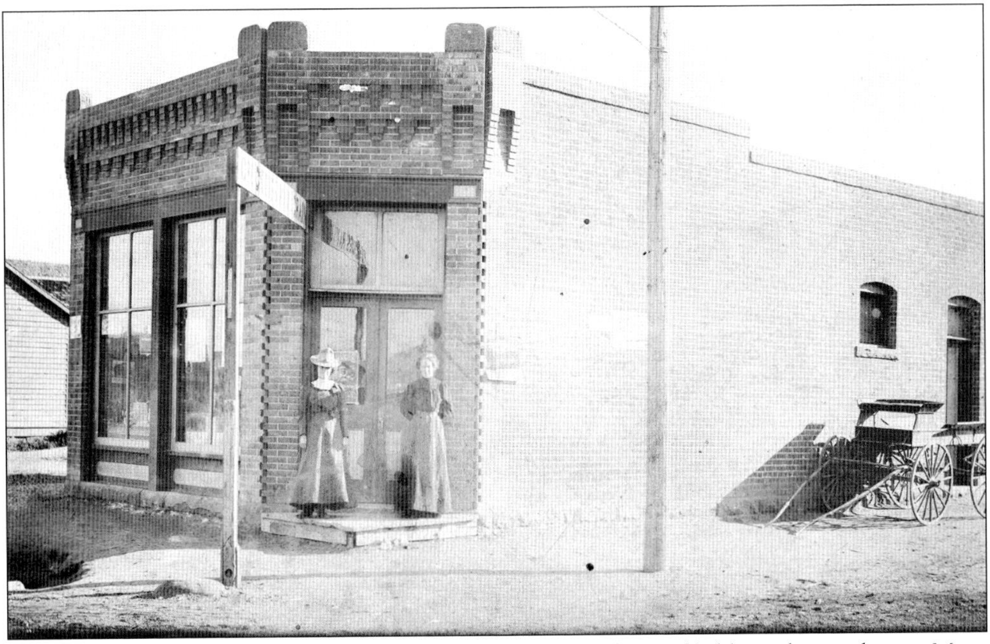

As Florence continued to grow as the hub for supplies for the coalfields to the southwest, Main Street grew as well. The Van Lew family operated their grocery store and livestock supply at the southeast corner of West Main Street and Frazier Avenue. It had a livery stable in the rear.

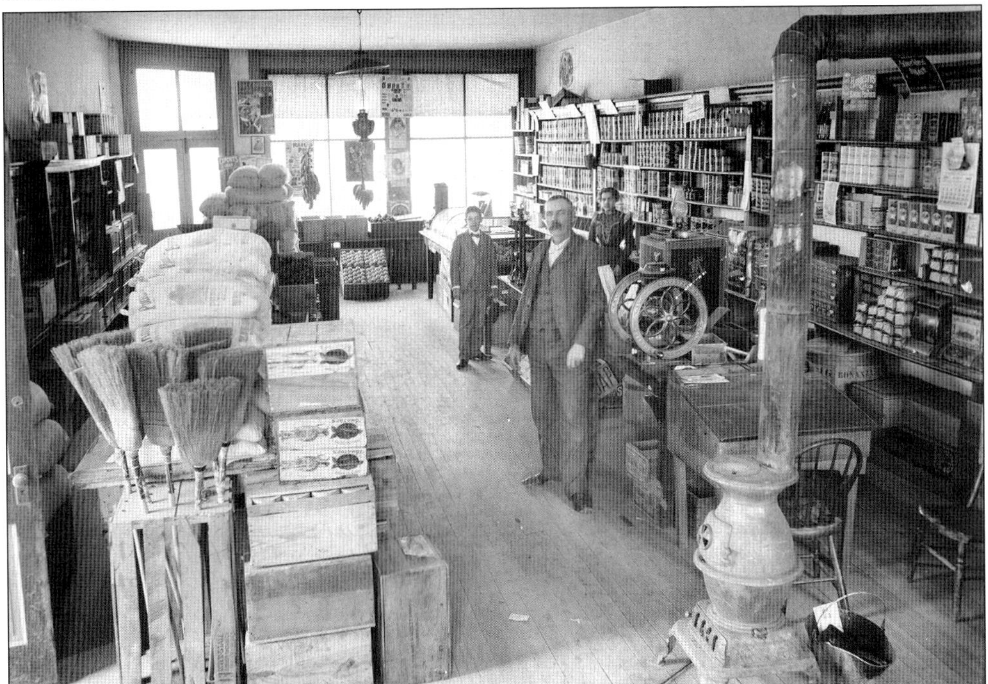

The interior of the Van Lew business shows the well-stocked shelves of the grocery store around 1908. The store became a popular stop for citizens on the west end of Florence and those heading out to the coal camps. Notice the coffee grinder and potbellied stove in the foreground, two very important and popular pieces in any store of that time.

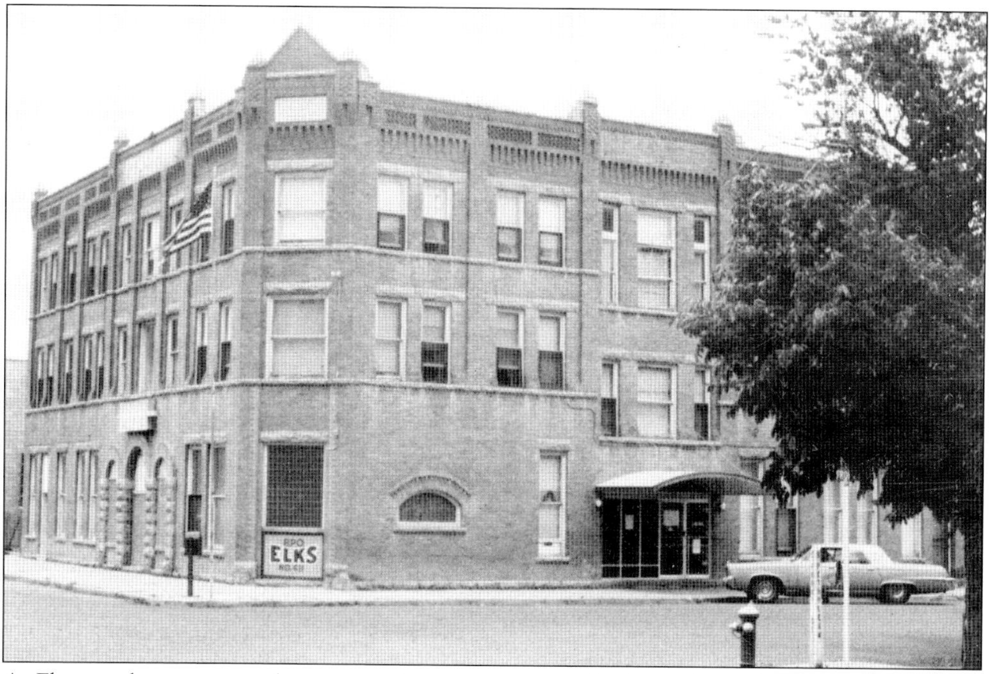

As Florence became a supply center and transportation hub, demand grew for temporary lodging. H.L. Rice responded with the purchase of lots at the corner of East Front Street and South Petroleum Avenue, where he built the Fremont Hotel in 1897. The hotel closed in 1912, and in 1915, the Fremont Benevolent and Protective Order of the Elks No. 611, chartered in 1901, purchased the building and moved in. The Elks have occupied the space since.

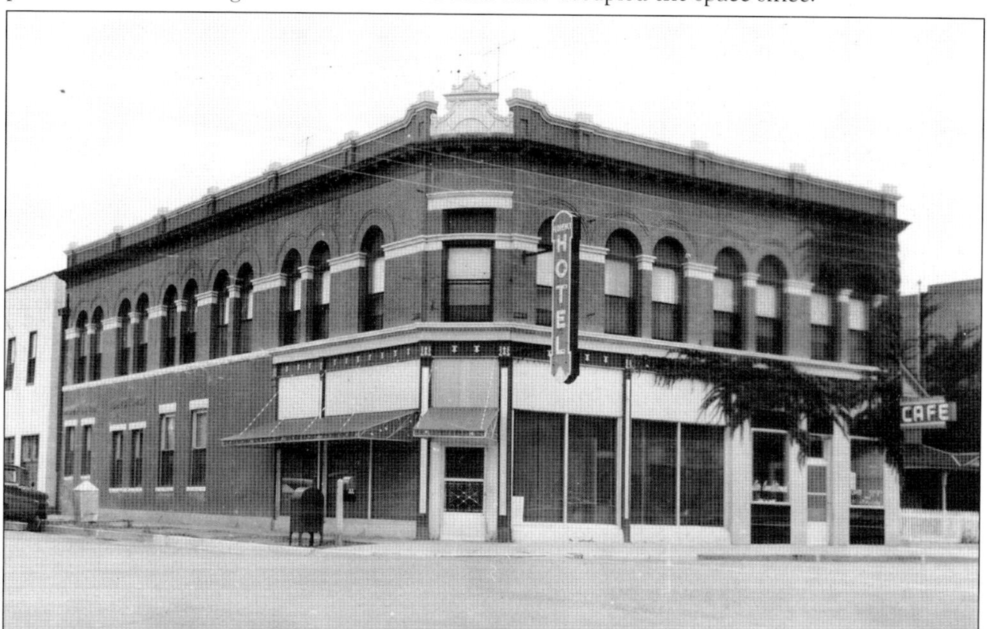

The Florence Hotel at 201 West Main Street was popular during the 1910s and 1920s, marked by its fine design and architecture. When construction was completed in 1906, the building housed the Lenox Hotel, but it became the Florence Hotel by 1924.

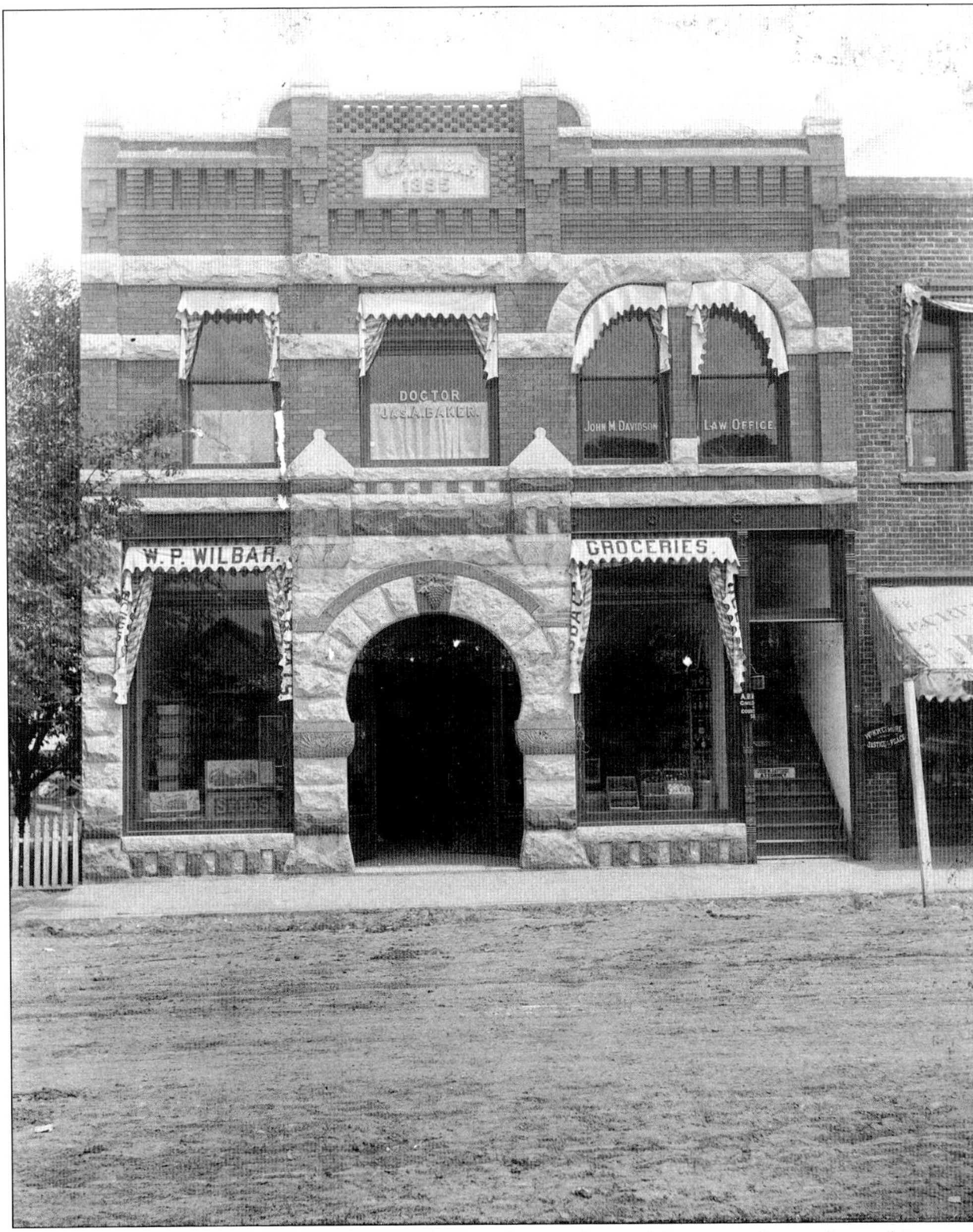

Florence's downtown business district soon became known for its elaborate and complex architecture. This photograph illustrates the success of the community and the boom economy it was experiencing. This building, constructed by William Peyton Wilbar, was completed to house his grocery store at 108 West Main Street in 1895. Still standing today, it has been significantly altered, but the base structure is still apparent. The ground floor contained W.P. Wilbar Groceries, and the upper floor accommodated various law and doctor offices. Wilbar constructed an addition to the building to the left, finishing it in 1897. Beginning with a grocery and household supply business in the cement production community of Portland, Wilbar became instrumental in providing supplies and services to Florence and surrounding communities. (Courtesy of John Wilbar.)

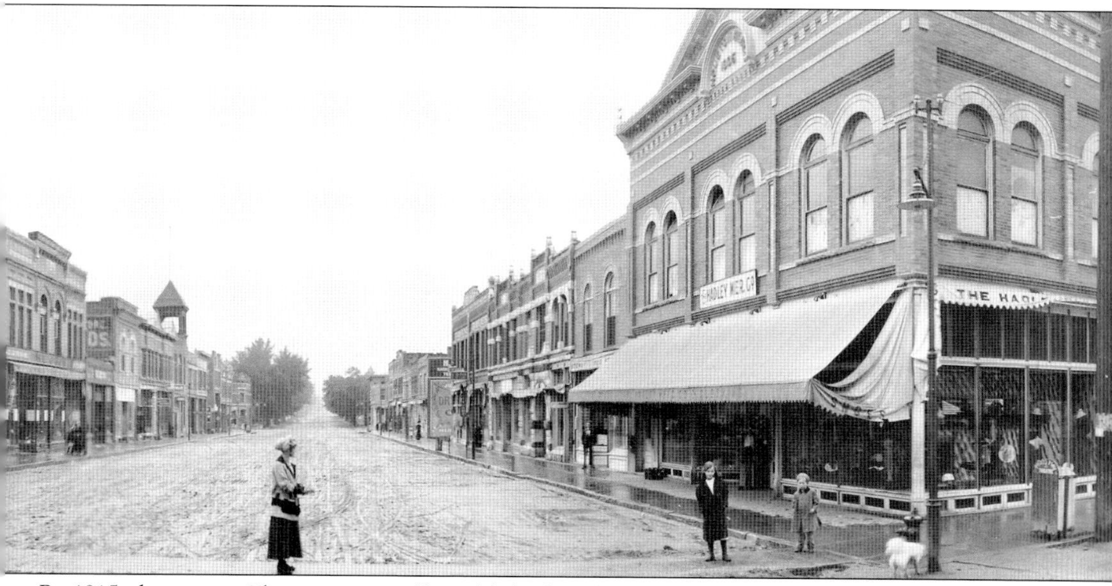

By 1915, downtown Florence was well established and bustling with business. The intersection of Pikes Peak Avenue and Main Street became the center of town, with commercial building growth in all four directions from there. New concrete sidewalks were installed in 1911, and finally, in 1923, the city awarded a contract for paving the streets. The ground floors of the buildings accommodated retail and service shops, and the upper floors contained business offices, doctor and law offices, and residential living space. This photograph of Florence's West Main Street was taken in 1914 from Pikes Peak Avenue. The large two-story building on the right is the Houston Building, constructed by Florence businessman Hughie Houston in 1905. It was originally occupied by the Hadley Mercantile Company on the ground floor and the Houston Opera House on the second floor. The building at left center with the bell tower housed the City of Florence offices upstairs and the fire department downstairs.

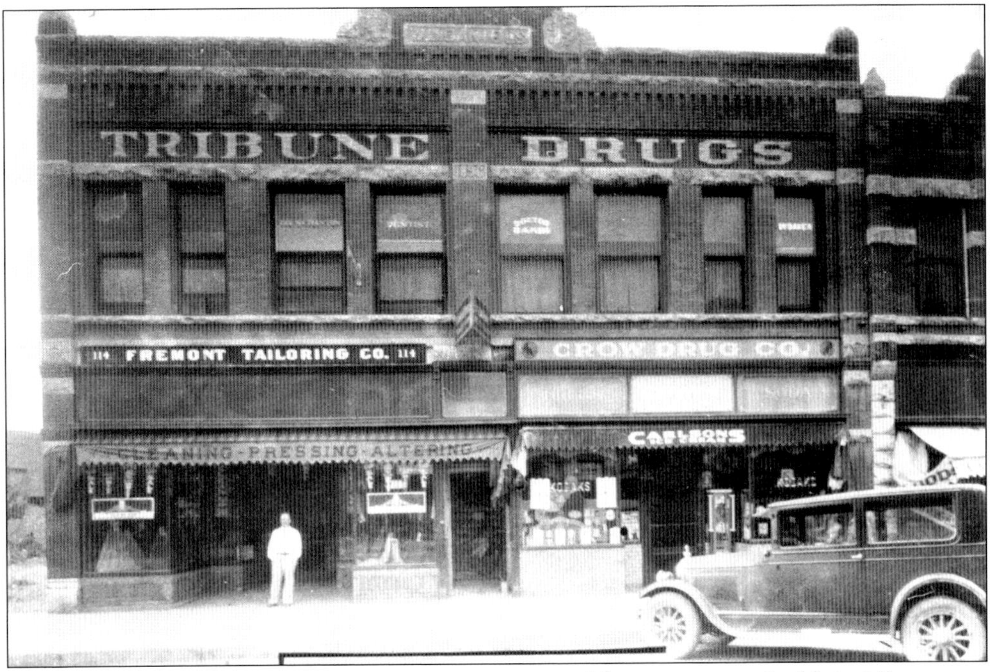

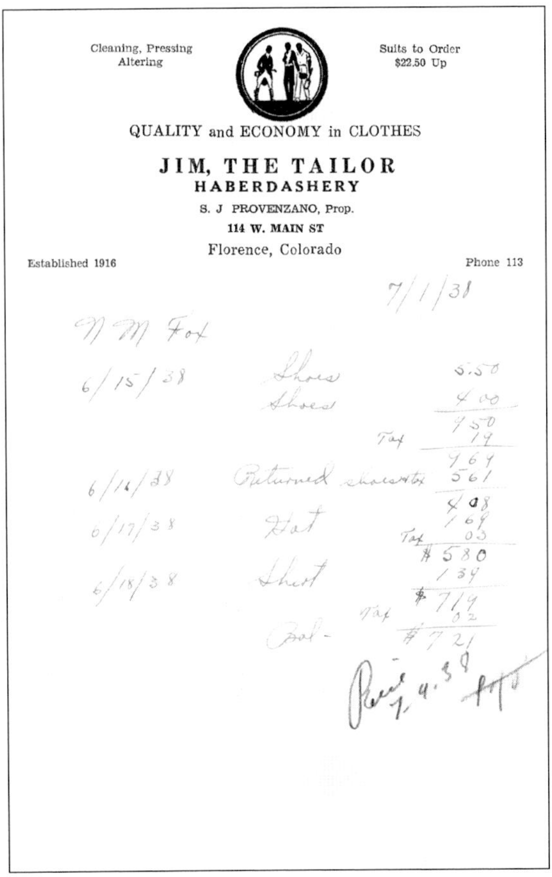

Cleaning, Pressing
Altering

Suits to Order
$22.50 Up

QUALITY and ECONOMY in CLOTHES

JIM, THE TAILOR
HABERDASHERY
S. J PROVENZANO, Prop.
114 W. MAIN ST
Florence, Colorado

Established 1916

Phone 113

7/1/38

N M Fox

6/15/38	Shoes	5.50
	Shoes	4.00
		9.50
	Tax	14
		9.64
6/16/38	Returned shoes + tx	5.61
		4.03
6/17/38	Hat	1.69
	Tax	05
		$5.80
6/18/38	Shirt	1.39
		$7.19
	Tax	02
	Tot-	$7.21

After arriving in the United States from Italy, Settimio Provenzano worked between Salida and Florence before settling into his own business in 1916 at the age of 20. Located at 114 West Main Street, Fremont Tailoring Company became an important supplier of men's and women's clothing. Pictured here standing in front of his store in 1927, Settimio became known to everyone as Jim the Tailor. (Courtesy of the Provenzano family.)

This monthly statement from Jim, the Tailor was made out to N.M. Fox on July 1, 1938. It shows the purchase of two pairs of shoes for $5 and $4.50 (one pair returned), a hat for $1.69, and a shirt for $1.39. (Courtesy of the Provenzano family.)

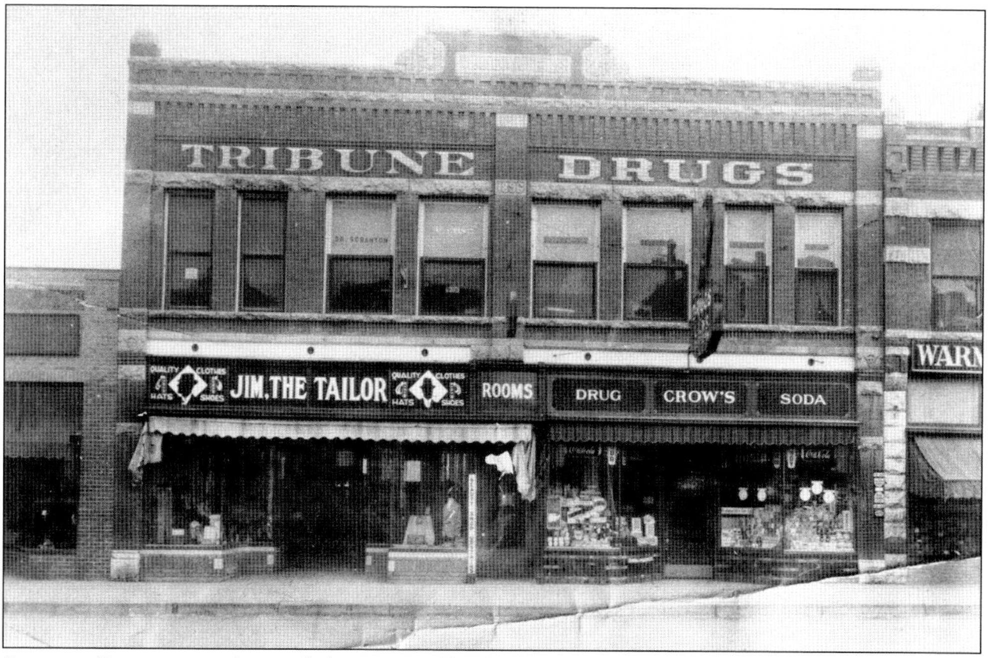

Settimio Provenzano changed the name of his business in the 1930s from Fremont Tailoring to Jim, the Tailor. He continued to build his business, expanding the products he carried including both men's and women's clothing and always perfecting the craft and skill of making fine clothing that he learned in Italy. (Courtesy of the Provenzano family.)

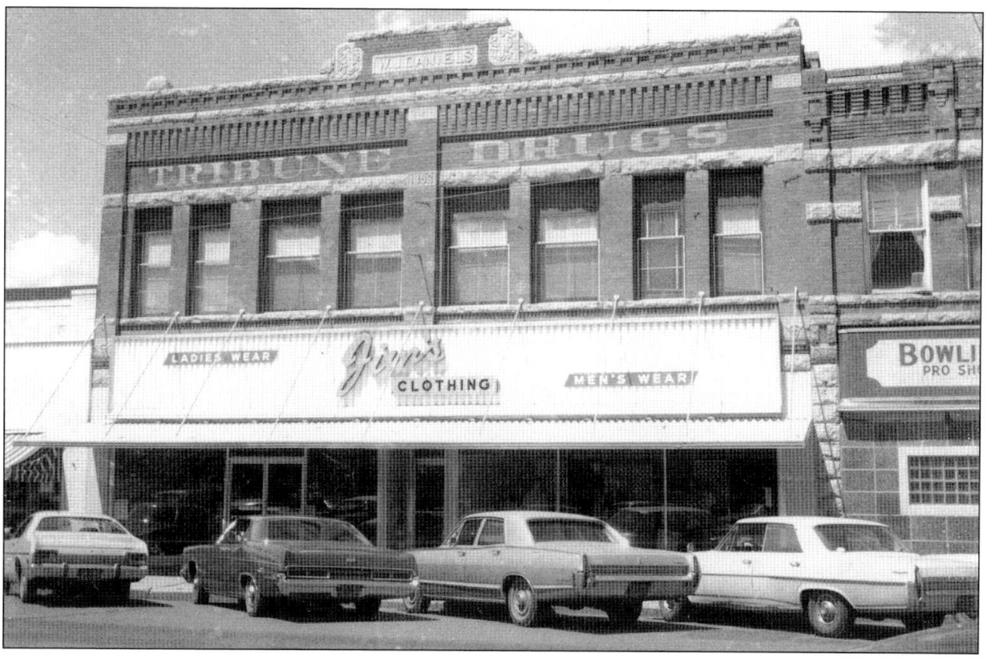

By the early 1960s, Settimio Provenzano, Jim the Tailor, had expanded into the east half of the building, renamed the business Jim's Clothing, and was joined by his son Jim. A fire completely destroyed the building on the night of March 22, 1975. The Provenzanos rebuilt (still standing at the same location) and continued the business into 2003. (Courtesy of the Provenzano family.)

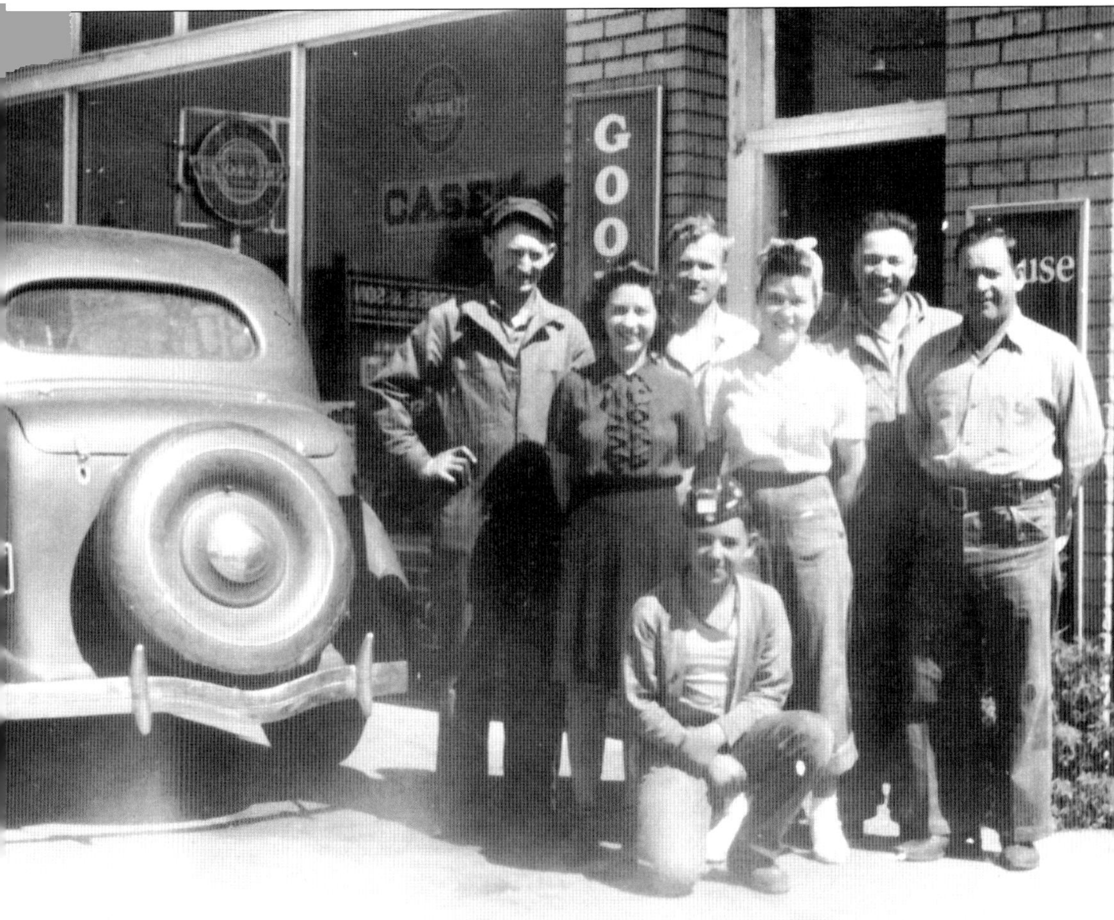

Augustos (Gus) Vendetti Sr. (far right) started work in 1930 as manager of Oil City Chevrolet Company in Cañon City. In 1933, he and his brother Nick purchased and opened Vendetti Chevrolet at 216 East Main Street in Florence, moving it across the street to 201 East Main Street in 1935. In 1937, he moved the dealership to 208 West Main Street, where he and his son Gus Vendetti Jr. (kneeling) operated the business as a Chevrolet dealership until 1968, and a used car dealership until 2005. From the date on the license plate, this picture was taken around 1945. Others pictured are, from left to right, John "Slim" Morello, Yolanda Zarlenga, Homer Ritter, Amy Del Monte, and Dom Senatore. (Courtesy of Sherrie Stille.)

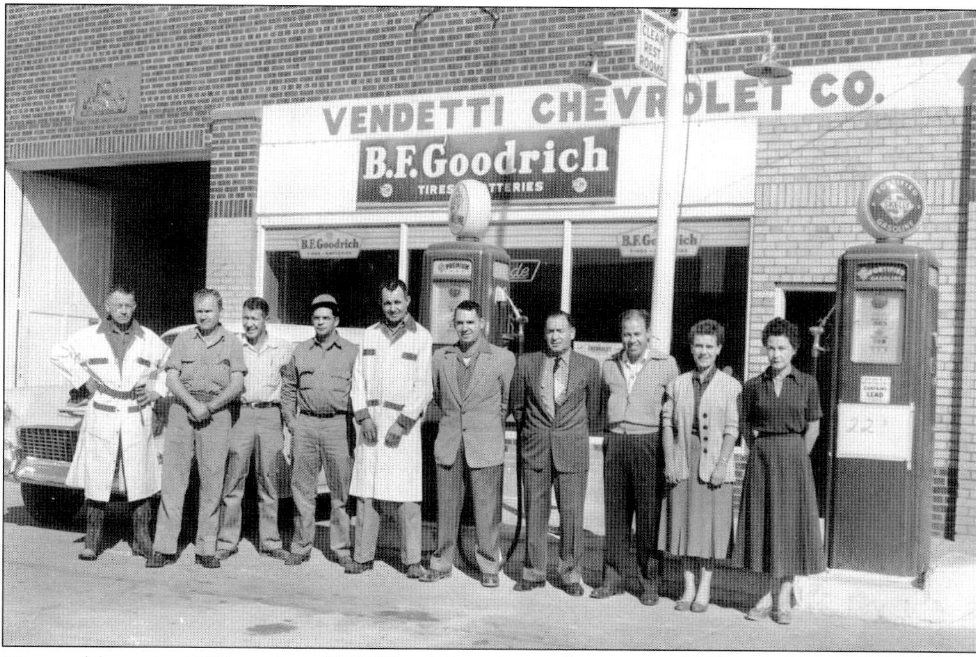

Pictured here in 1955 at their 208 West Main Street location, Vendetti Chevrolet Company employed, from left to right, Harry Daily, Homer Ritter, Sam "Bud" Bowman Jr., Harold Chadwick, John Morello, owners Gus Vendetti Jr. and Gus Vendetti Sr., Dom Senatore, Sylvia Perkins, and Amy Del Monte. The price for a gallon of gasoline was 22¢. (Courtesy of Gus and Barbara Vendetti.)

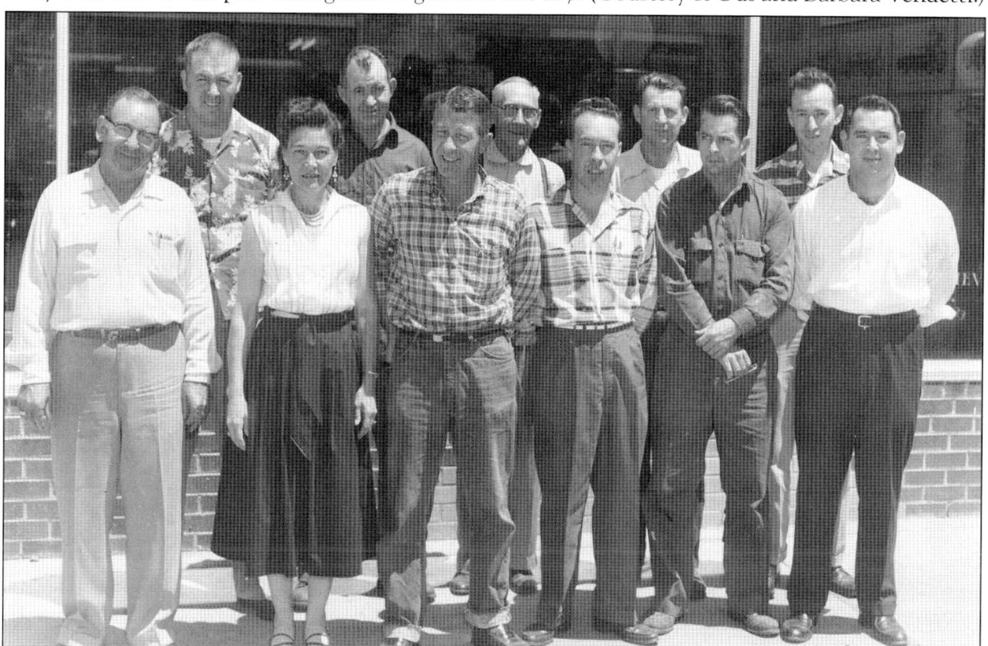

This picture was taken three years later in 1958. Vendetti Chevrolet Company employees included, from left to right, owner Gus Vendetti Sr., George Walk, Amy Del Monte, John Morello, Sam "Bud" Bowman Jr., Homer Redman, Harold Watkins, Bill Meigs, Harold Chadwick, John Sabe, and owner Gus Vendetti Jr. (Courtesy of Gus and Barbara Vendetti.)

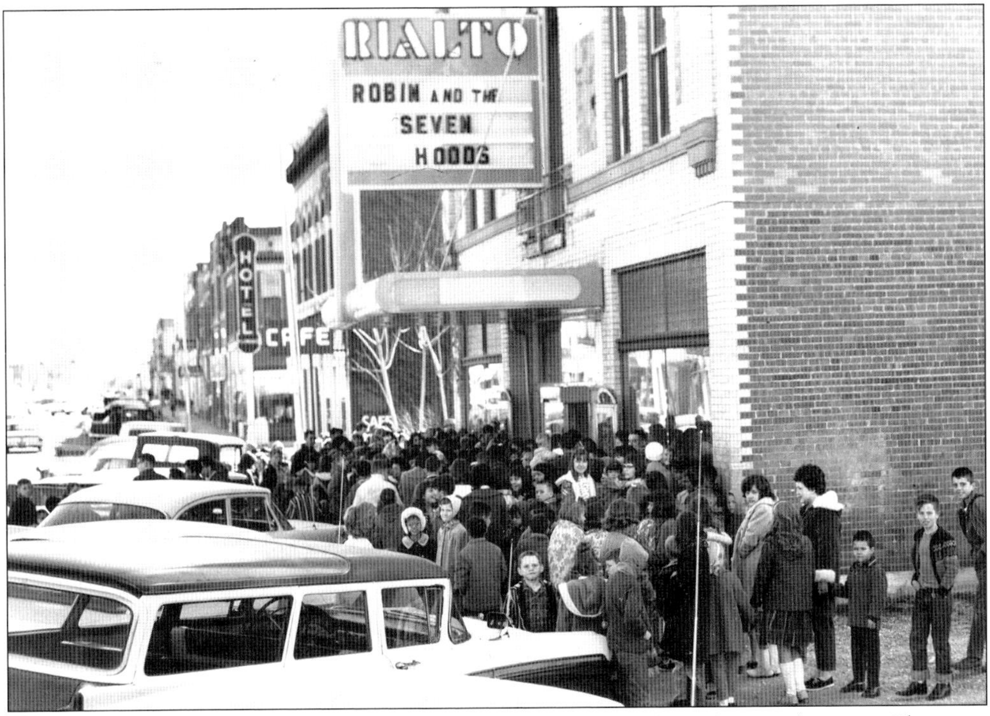

The Rialto Theater at 209 West Main Street was the first dedicated movie house in Florence. It was built in 1923, and shortly after completion was sold to the McCormick family of Cañon City. It was designed to accommodate live entertainment but primarily showed films, first silent films and then "talkies" beginning in 1929. As television gained popularity after World War II, patronage dropped until the theater closed in the early 1960s, about the time of this photograph.

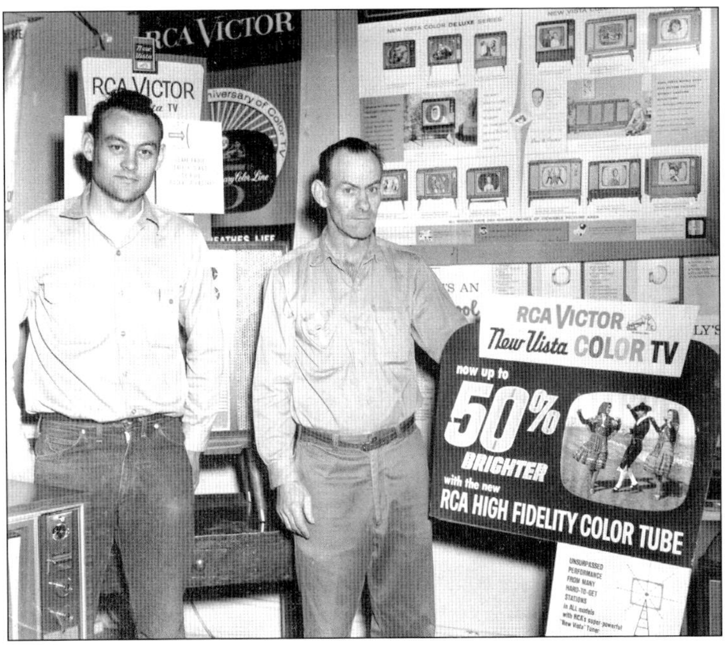

A new type of business began appearing in Florence with the growing popularity of the television after World War II. Larry's TV and Sport Shop, owned by Larry and Howard Gall, was at 220 West Main Street and was open from 1957 to 1993. Larry sold and serviced new and used television sets and other household appliances and was known for the quality fishing and outdoor supplies sold in the store.

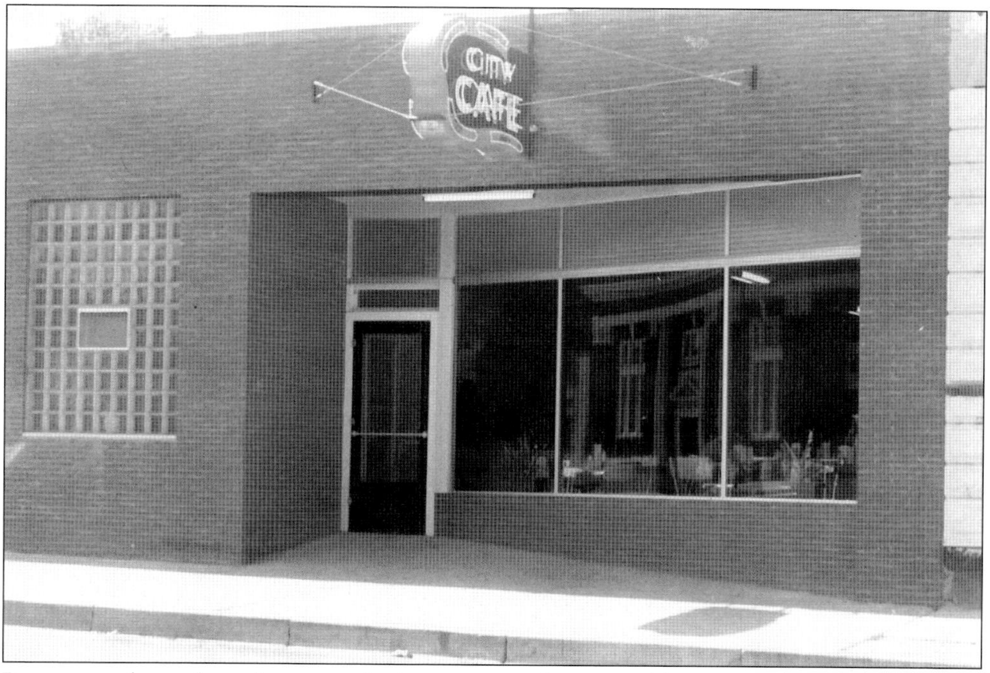

Restaurants have always been popular businesses in downtown Florence and surrounding areas. This is the City Café in 1956. Located at 103 West Main Street, City Café was in a section of the building rebuilt on the site of the Blunt Block, which had been destroyed by fire in December 1949. This same space was also occupied by the Florence Flower Shop under various owners until 2019.

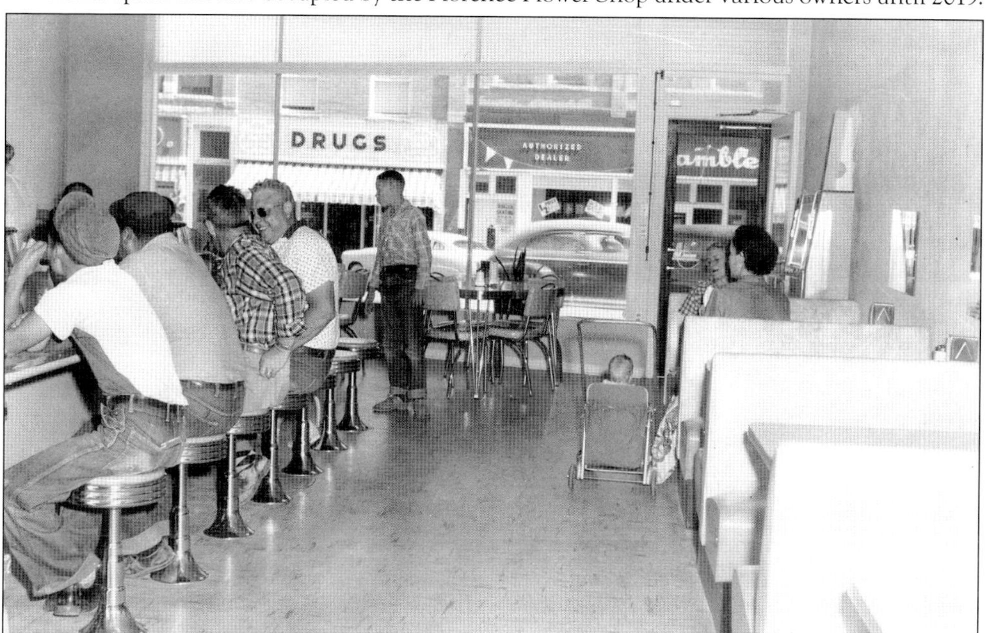

The interior of the City Café shows it to be the typical family-friendly restaurant of the 1950s, with counter and stools and booths along the wall. Through the windows, the Gambles Store and the entrance to the upstairs roller-skating rink (white double doors in center) can be seen across the street. Both occupied the Houston Building prior to it being razed in 1973.

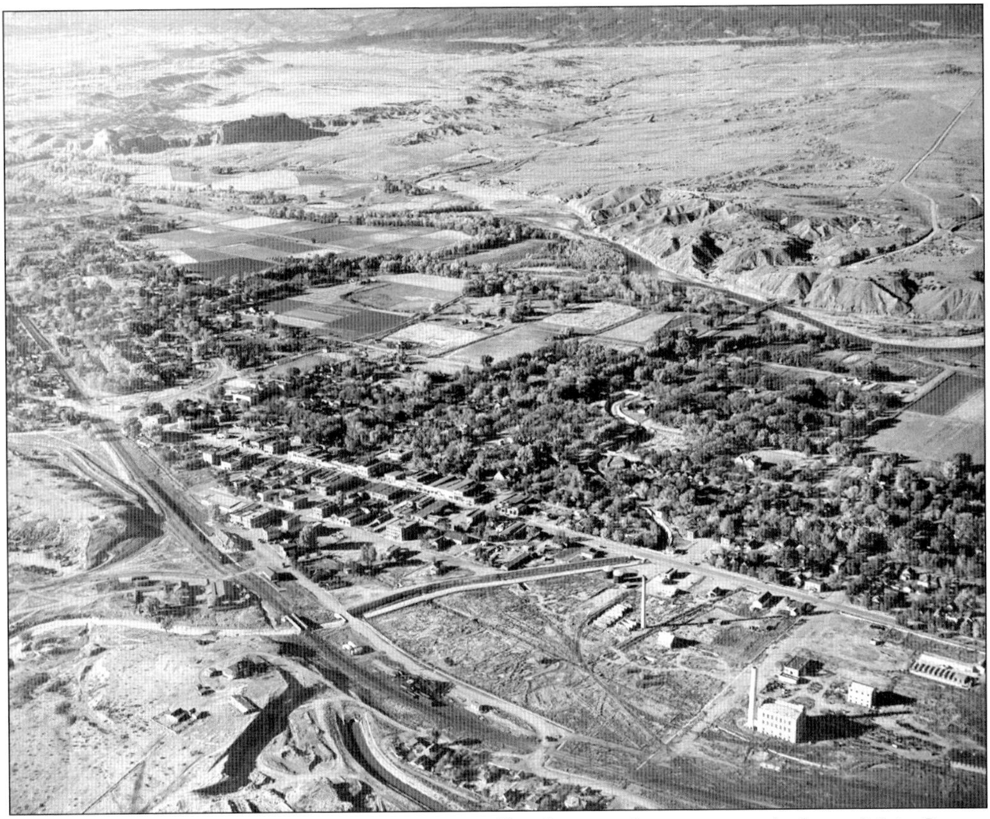

As Florence expanded on the Arkansas River valley floor, its downtown took shape. Main Street, seen here running east to west parallel to the river, served as US Highway 50 until 1948, when the highway was relocated farther north. Residential growth spread along either side of the main route, and although the downtown business district is concentrated at Pikes Peak Avenue and Main Street, evidence of past business can be found along the entire length.

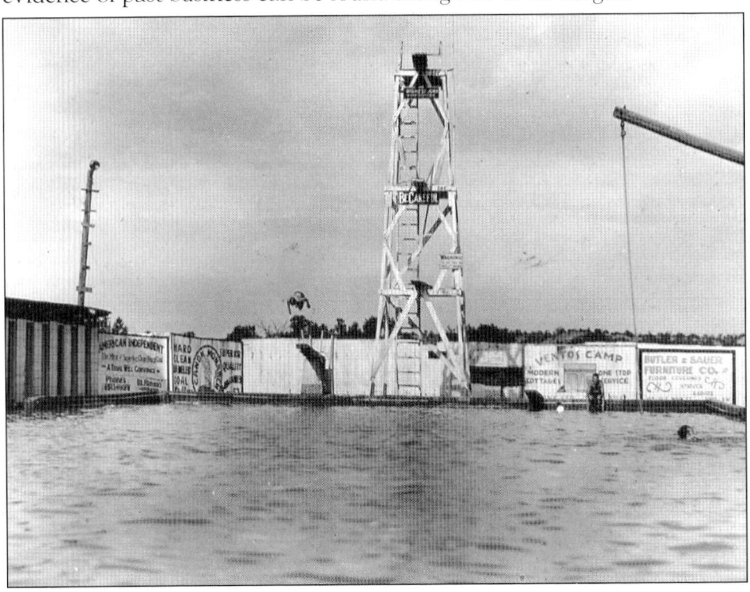

Attracting many visitors to the Florence area, the Hygienic Plunge hot springs swimming pool was a couple miles east of city limits in Rainbow Park. The pool was advertised for health benefits and entertainment until its closing in 1958.

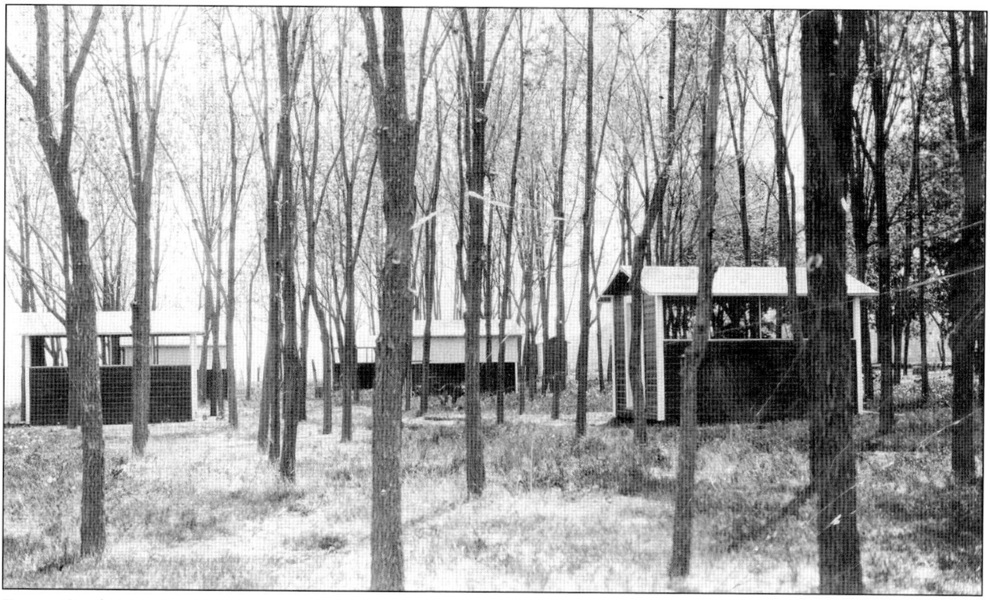

Evan Carl "E.C." Schmidt settled his family in Florence in 1918 with the purchase of 11 acres at the east edge of town. Initially farming the property, he eventually developed a section east of Gumaer Street between Second and Third Streets into a campground. Camp Mojada, with six one-room cabins and a common bath area, was a popular spot from 1925 up to the late 1950s. (Courtesy of Shimla Weare Basile, Dorothy Schmidt Weare collection.)

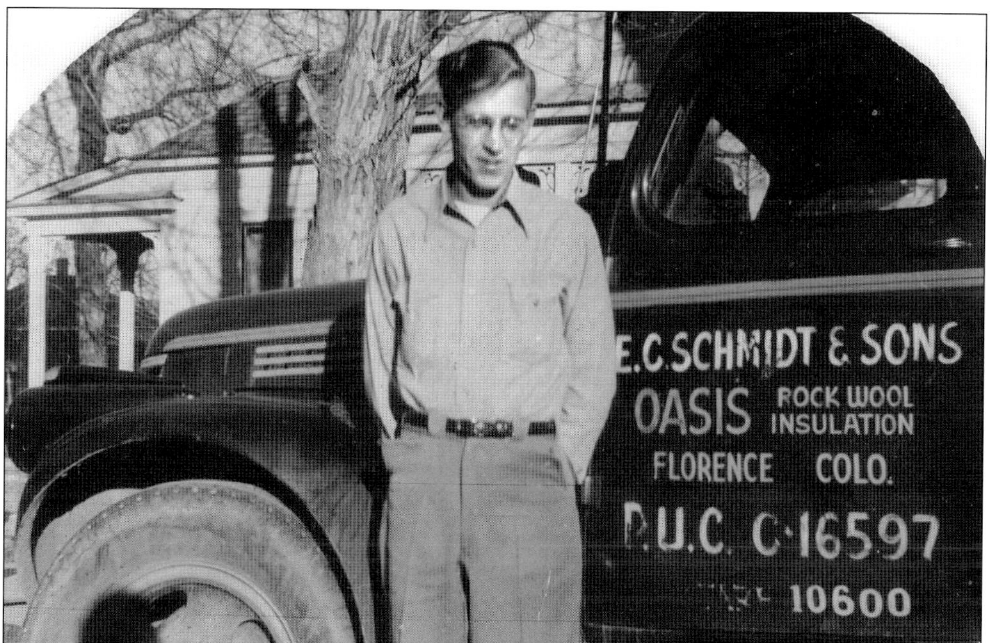

E.C. Schmidt and his two sons, Carl and Royal, owned and operated E.C. Schmidt and Sons Oasis Rock Wool Insulation in Florence in the early 1950s. Pictured here is Royal standing beside one of the company's trucks in 1952. Royal went on to work 27 years for Pueblo Rock Wool Insulation. (Courtesy of Royal and B.J. Schmidt.)

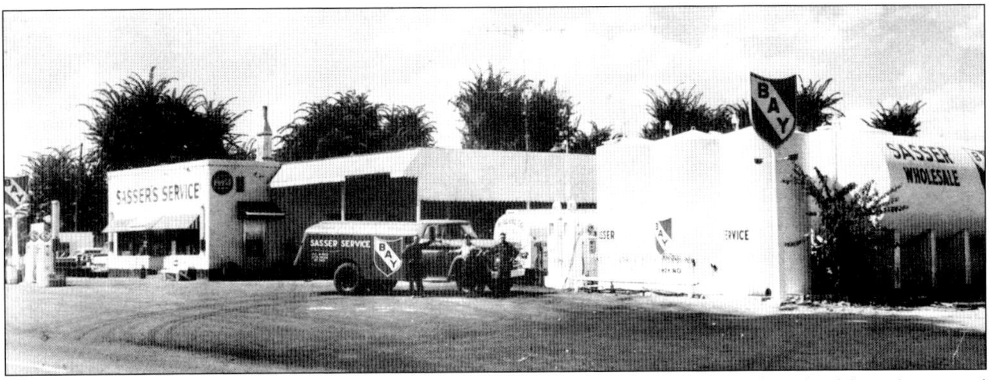

In 1945, Tom Sasser purchased land from Pius Greenwell and continued to build and expand the successful Sasser Service, which he began in Rainbow Park. Tom's son Jack joined him in the business upon returning from his service in World War II. Sasser Service, later Sasser and Nelson Service, became one of the largest fuel suppliers in the area, providing automotive fuel and service, home heating fuel, and wholesale products. (Courtesy of the Sasser family.)

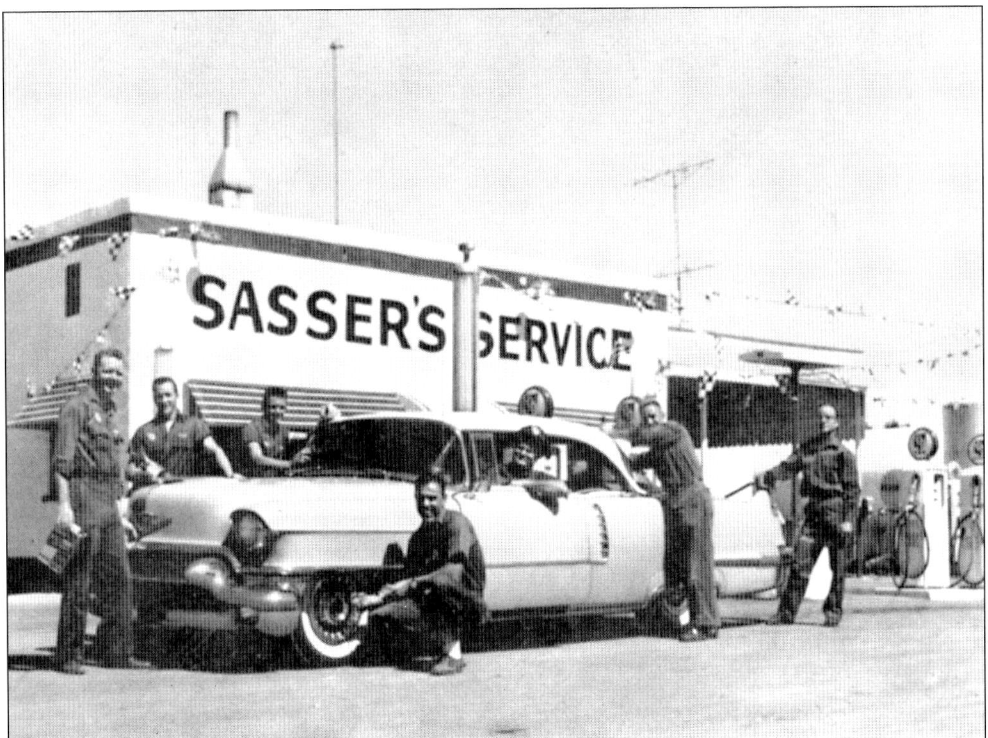

From humble beginnings in 1934, the Sasser family successfully grew its fuel and service business at 901 East Main Street into one of the largest in Fremont County. The Nelson family joined the business in 1957, and the station prospered until being sold upon Jack Sasser's retirement in 1980. Pictured here from left to right are Jack Sasser, Bill Robertson, Tom Nelson, Lee Nelson, Tom Sasser (in car), Clarence Nelson, and Leonard Perkins. (Courtesy of the Sasser family.)

Six

Civic and Community Groups

Throughout history, it is easily seen how people begin to gather in an area, first in small groups and mainly for survival. These groups begin to grow larger and larger as they find that the area can support their needs. Eventually, those small groups become large groups, and they realize they need to create some type of society that will make each individual life within the group better. Florence has done just that.

Beginning as a small group attracted to the abundant natural resources in the area, Florence grew. Early on, it began to create a society that would make life prosperous and beneficial to everyone. It created a government to organize streets and lots to build houses on. It found a way to collect and distribute water. It developed ways to make members of the group safe, to protect them from natural disasters, and to rebuild in case something did harm them. It created and supported areas to acquire the materials needed for survival, areas needed to educate children, areas needed so the group could gather as a community, and ways to enjoy what the group had created. Then it created organizations to ensure that everyone in the community was able to live the life that they desired.

That small group soon had the infrastructure it needed to become a successful society. Florence rose from the fertile soils of the Arkansas River to become a successful and prosperous community. The citizens of that first small group banded together to create a community that would thrive for years to come.

Most impressively, when exploring how this small group created the community of Florence, it becomes obvious that it was done through commitment, dedication, and the desire to make life better for everyone without expecting anything in return.

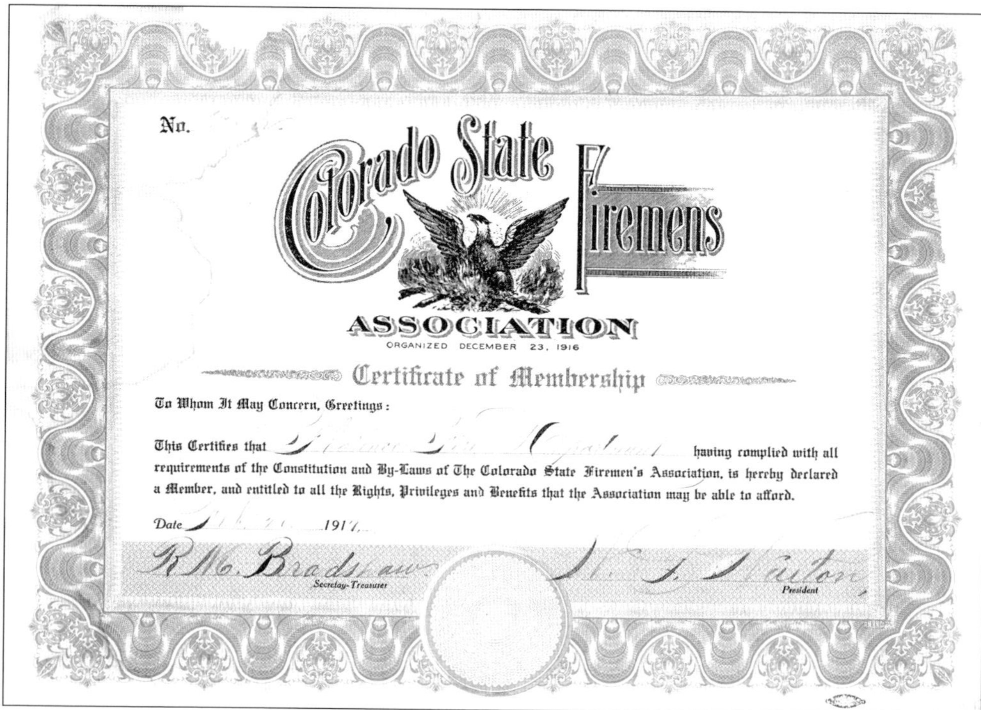

No.

Colorado State Firemens

ASSOCIATION

ORGANIZED DECEMBER 23, 1916

Certificate of Membership

To Whom It May Concern, Greetings:

This Certifies that Florence Fire Department having complied with all requirements of the Constitution and By-Laws of The Colorado State Firemen's Association, is hereby declared a Member, and entitled to all the Rights, Privileges and Benefits that the Association may be able to afford.

Date Feb. 21, 1917

R.M. Bradshaw
Secretay-Treasurer

President

The Florence Fire Department was established in 1890. It officially became the fourth member of the Colorado State Firemen's Association on February 21, 1917. The association was organized on December 23, 1916. (Courtesy of Florence Fire Department.)

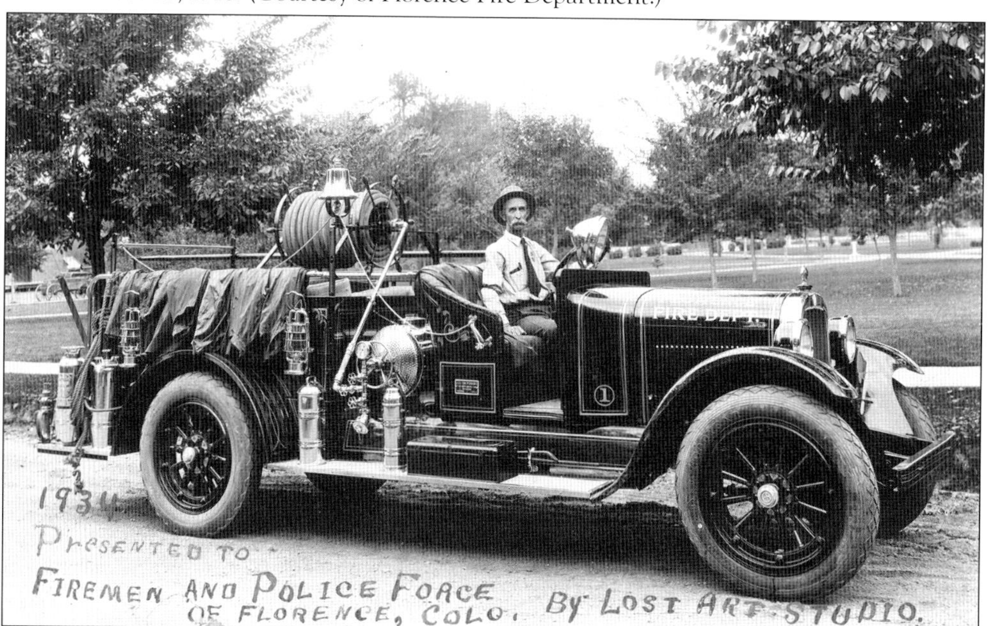

Fire chief John Ball proudly sits in the driver's seat of the new fire truck delivered to the Florence Fire Department in 1925 by the Julius Pearce Fire Department Supply Company of Denver. Marked as Unit No. 1, the truck is still owned and operated by the Florence Volunteer Fire Department and is used in parades and demonstrations. (Courtesy of Florence Fire Department.)

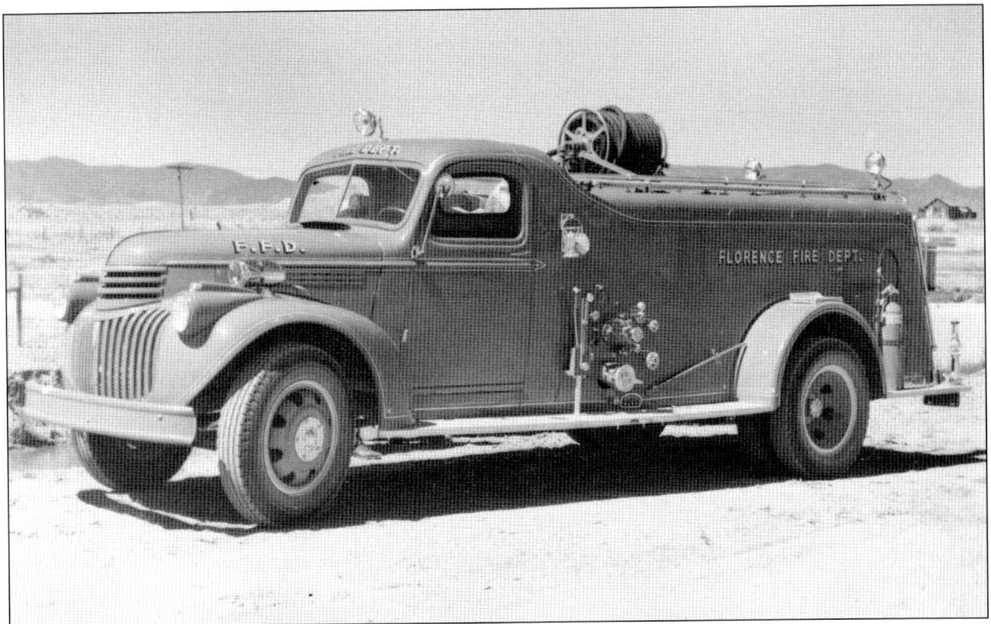

As an entirely volunteer organization since its inception, the Florence Fire Department has always prided itself on maintaining the most state-of-the-art and modern equipment it could afford. Its pride shows in this picture of a mid-ship pump fire truck built specifically for the department. (Courtesy of Florence Fire Department.)

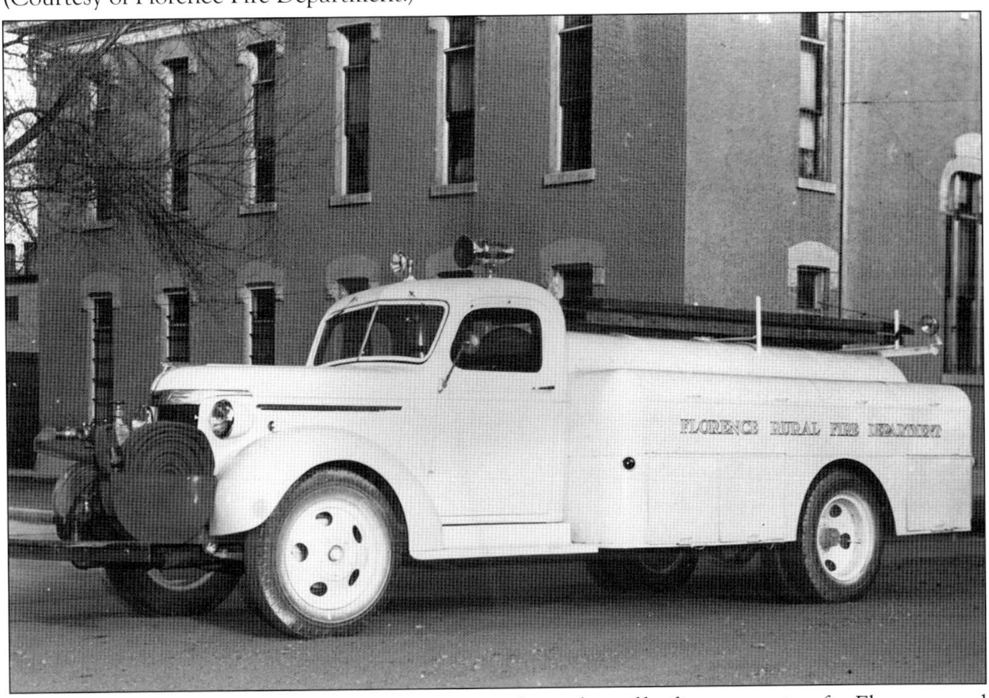

In 1954, the Florence Fire Protection District was formed to offer fire protection for Florence and the outlying communities of Rockvale, Coal Creek, Williamsburg, Portland, and Penrose. Each community has its own fire department supported by the newly created district. This tanker truck has "Florence Rural Fire Department" painted on the side. (Courtesy of Florence Fire Department.)

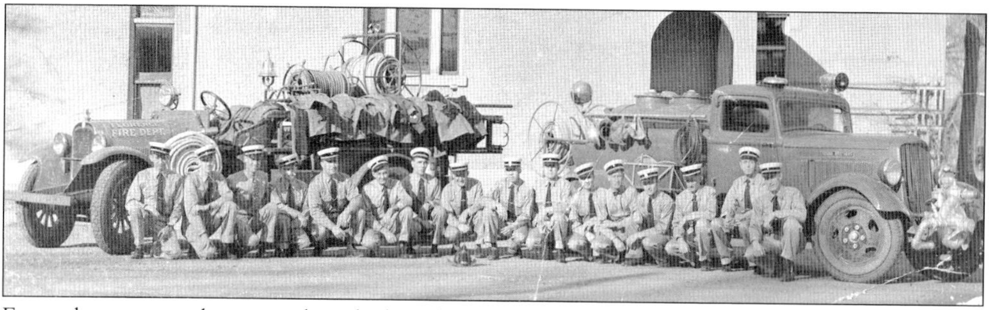

For as long as can be remembered, there has been an annual celebration of the Florence Fire Department. This was also an opportunity for a picture of the department's volunteers for the year. Here, the volunteer firemen gather in front of two of their fire trucks. This photograph was taken in front of the fire station and city hall at West Main Street and Maple Avenue. (Courtesy of Florence Fire Department.)

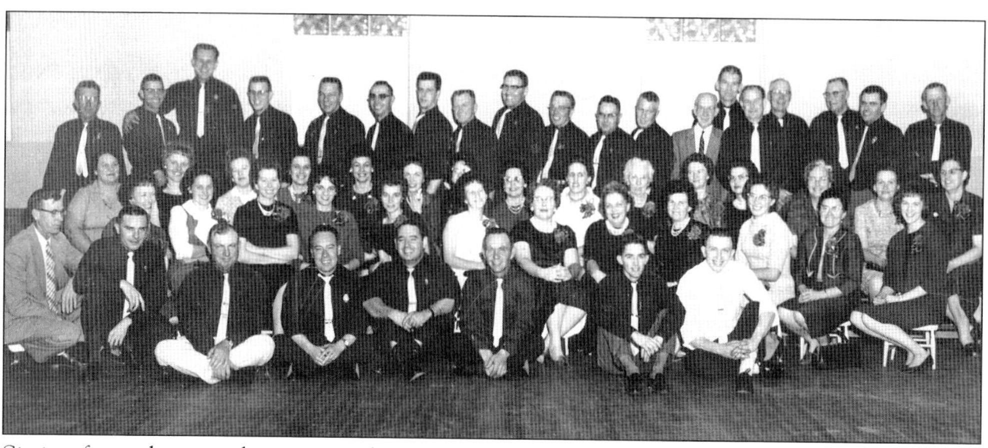

Sitting for a photograph in 1964, Florence volunteer firemen and their wives take part in the annual celebration. For many years, the celebration was a banquet honoring the volunteers followed by a popular department fundraiser known as the Annual Fireman's Ball. (Courtesy of Gus and Barbara Vendetti.)

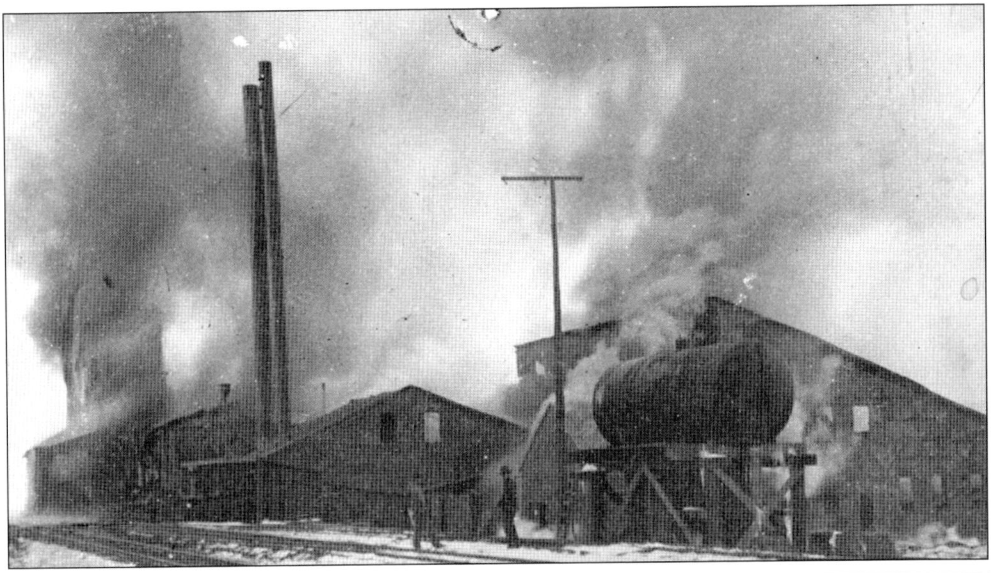

Like all communities, destruction by fire has been a part of the history of Florence since its beginning. Here, the Dorcas ore reduction mill burns to the ground in 1906. The Dorcas mill sat on the mesa to the north of Florence, served by the Vesta Branch of the Florence & Cripple Creek Railroad, which also served the Union and Beam ore reduction mills for processing ore arriving from Cripple Creek.

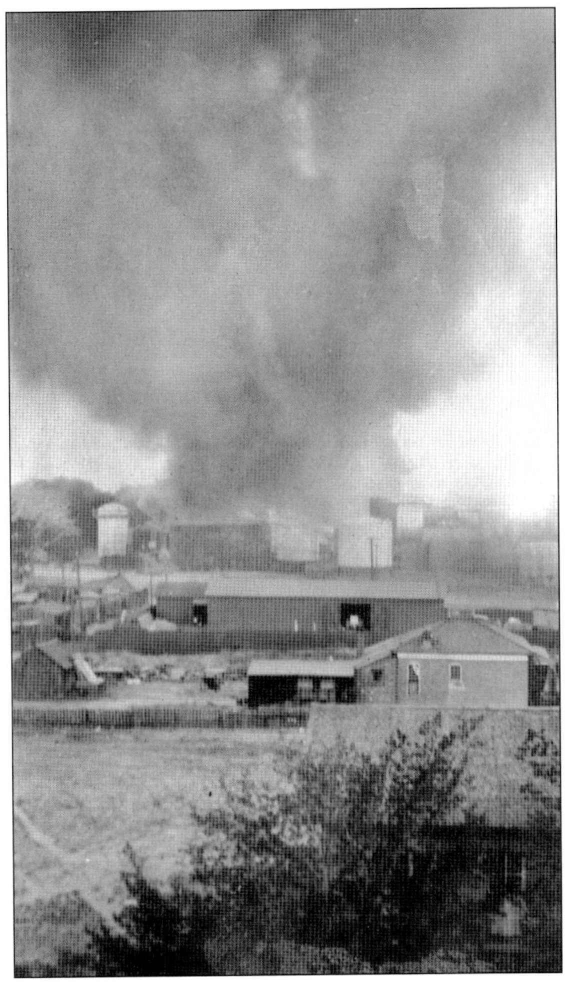

The Standard Oil Refinery, in the 600 block of East Main Street, exploded on the afternoon of Friday, June 26, 1925. Three workers died in the blast—Eugene Mattice, Lewis Stephens, and Frank Fox—as they were carrying out their duties of heating crude oil to vaporize it and cool the vapor down into gasoline.

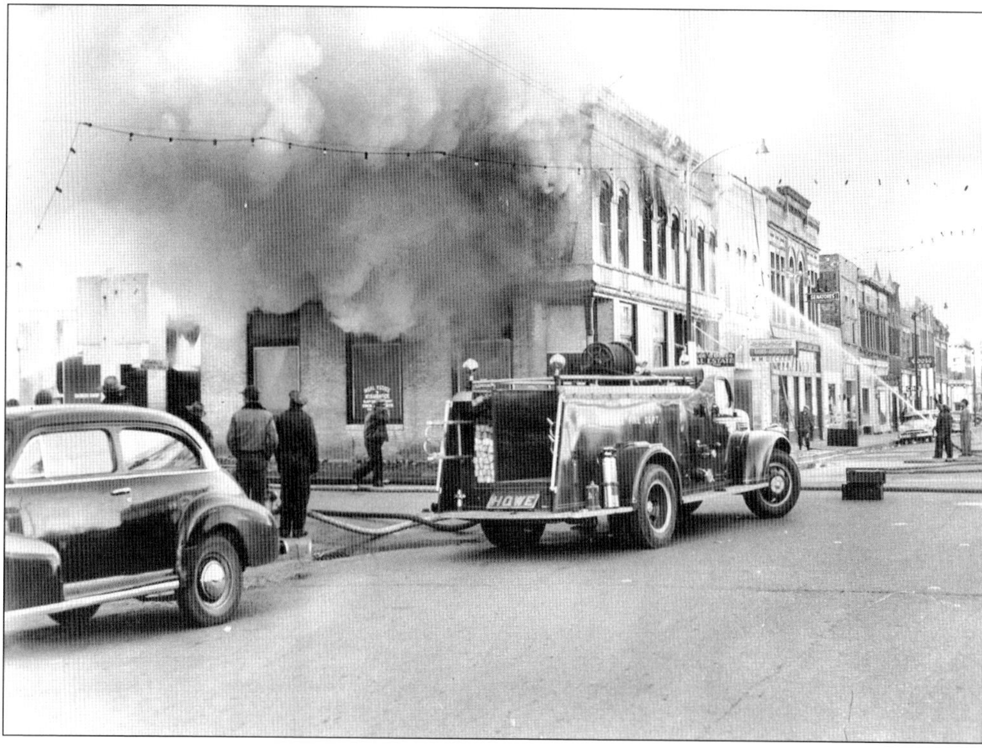

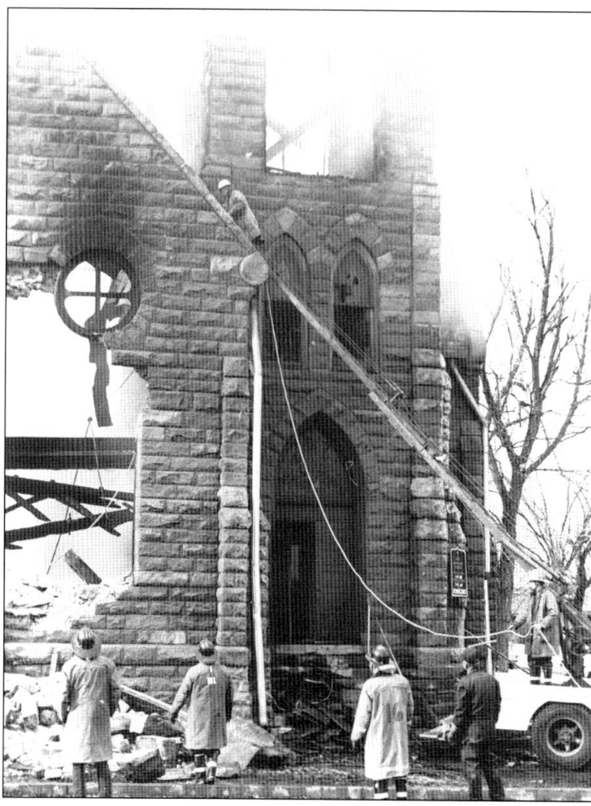

At 5:30 a.m. on Thursday, December 15, 1949, with temperatures near zero degrees, the Florence fire alarm went off for a fire at the Blunt Block on the southwest corner of Main Street and South Pikes Peak Avenue. Seven businesses and numerous upstairs residential apartments were completely destroyed by the fire. The current structure at the location was built shortly after. (Courtesy of Florence Fire Department.)

Fire totally destroyed the Frazer Methodist Church at the southwest corner of East Second Street and North Petroleum Avenue. On a Sunday morning, December 31, 1971, while warming the building up for services, the boiler exploded in the basement, engulfing the church in fire. The church was never rebuilt, and the lot remains vacant today. (Courtesy of Florence Fire Department.)

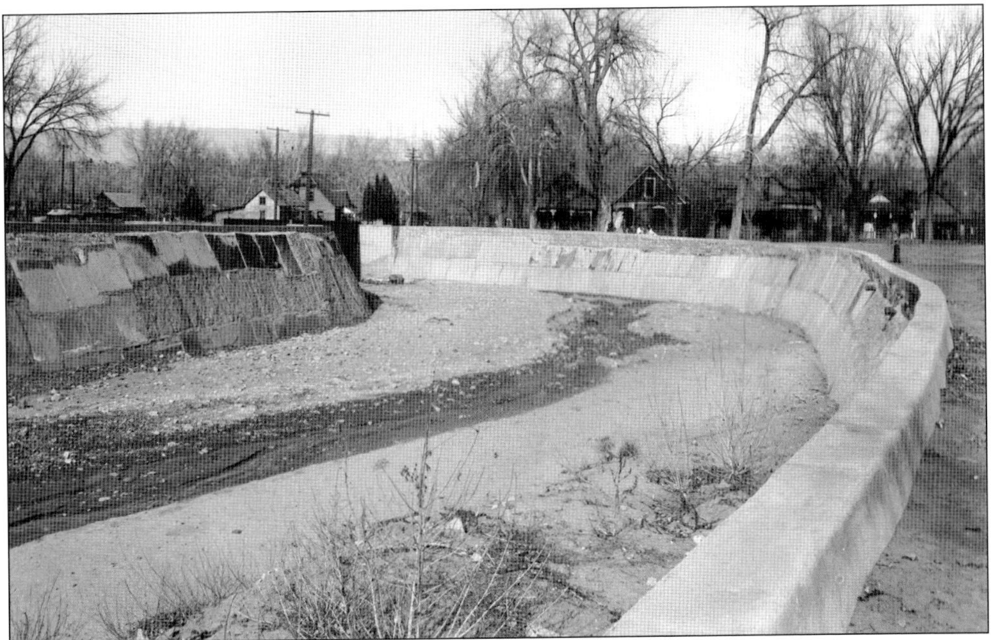

Natural disasters were also known to plague the growth of Florence. Summer cloudbursts in the hills to the southwest often quickly filled the usually dry creek beds running through town. Coal Creek, the original eastern boundary of Florence, was one of the effected streambeds. A major flood in 1932 led the federal government to step in to provide $20,000 in funding to build retaining walls along the banks of Coal Creek in 1938.

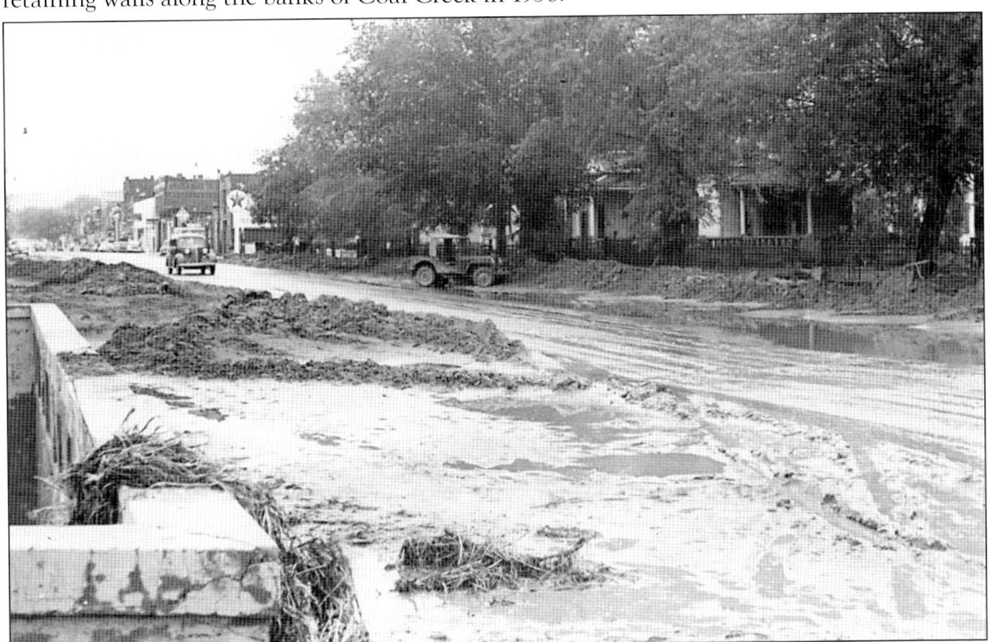

The retaining wall construction along the Coal Creek channel greatly reduced the damage caused by flash flooding, but it did not entirely eliminate it. This photograph, taken at the bridge of East Main Street near North McCandless Avenue, shows the sand and debris that overflowed the creek's retaining walls after a flash flood on June 6, 1948. (Courtesy of Gus and Barbara Vendetti.)

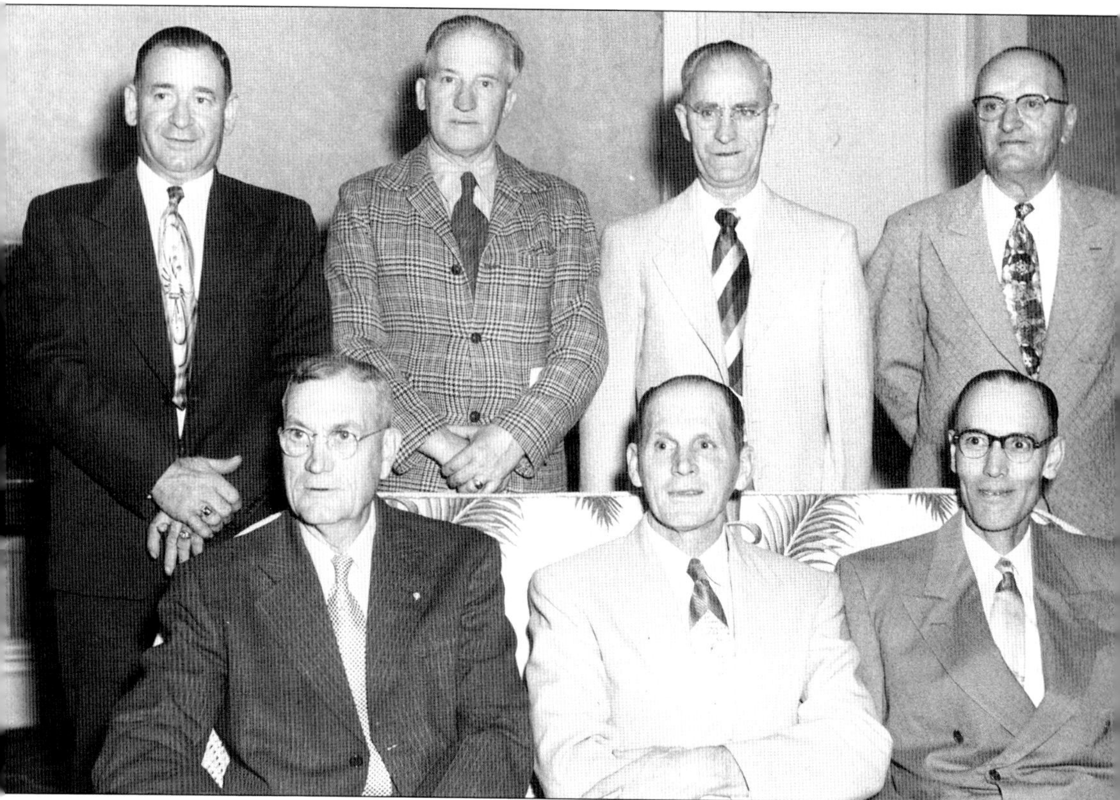

A dedicated and committed city council is the backbone to success in any growing and progressing community. Florence has been very fortunate to have such men and women who give their time, resources, and energy to serve their constituents in leading the community into the future. The infrastructure required by, and enjoyed in, the community to this day is a direct result of these many committed individuals. The ample safe drinking water, the safety and peace of mind enjoyed by citizens, the ability to drive on paved streets and walk on concrete sidewalks, and much more is all a direct result of these dedicated individuals. This photograph, taken during the 1950s, is an example of one such city council. From left to right are Mayor Gus Vendetti Sr., M.E. McDonald, C.W. John, Charles Largent, Judge Hugh Muir, Carl Dinnerline, and J.J. Fabrizio. (Courtesy of Gus and Barbara Vendetti.)

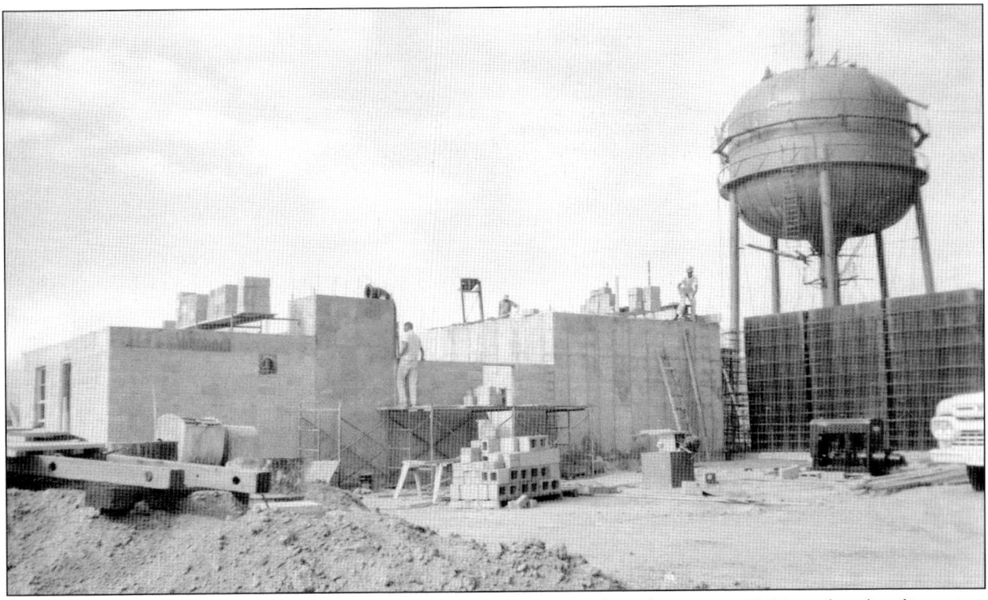

Construction of Florence's new water filtration and storage plant began in 1963 under the direction of city manager Frank Carochi Sr. The state-of-the-art facility cost the city $250,000 and was funded by issuing bonds. The facility continues to provide water to the community today, though it is only one part of a much larger system. (Courtesy of the Carochi family.)

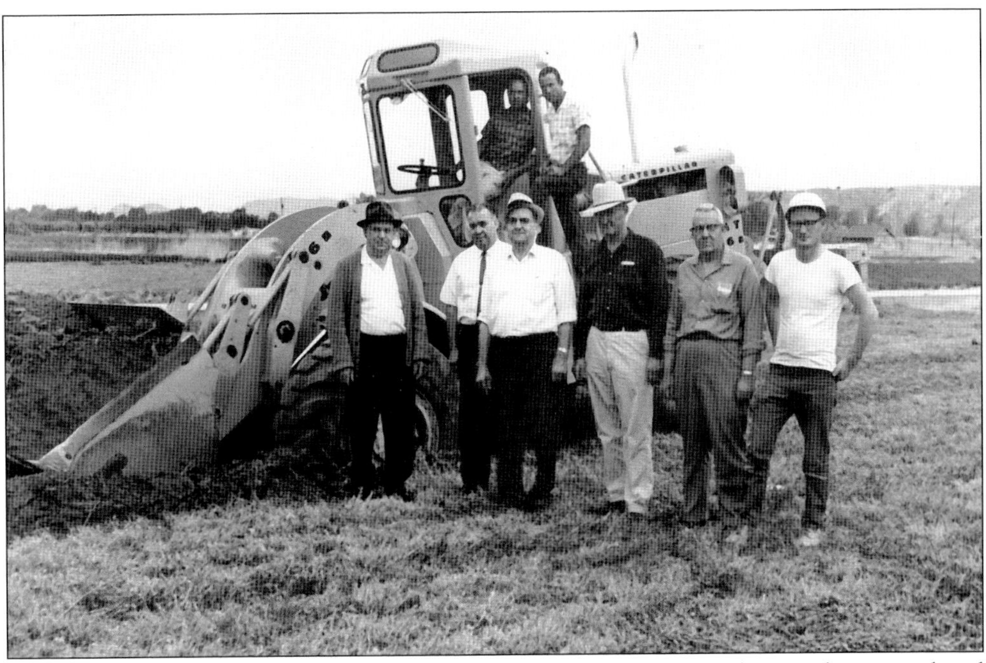

The Florence Sanitary Sewer Plant, constructed in 1959, was operational up until it was replaced by the much larger Fremont Sanitation Facility farther east. Here, at the location that is now the Wilcox Baseball Park, construction begins with Florence Sanitation District board members observing. From left to right are Henry Fox, Gene Senatore, Charles Cristelli, unidentified, and Paul Strickland. The men on the equipment and at far right are unidentified contractors.

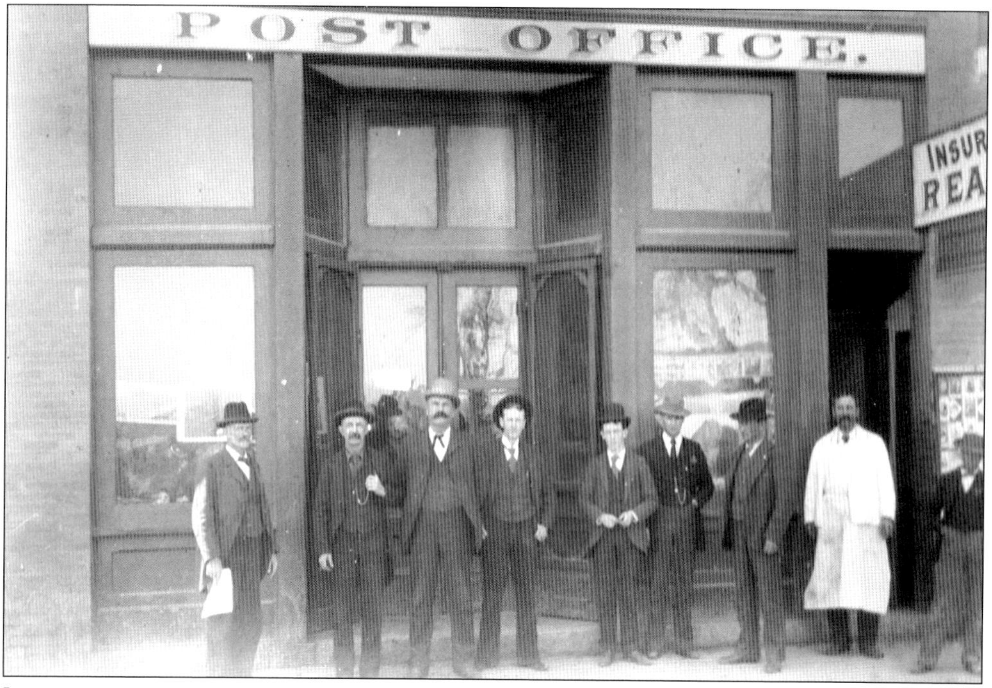

Just as in any community, the post office in Florence became a prominent location and served an important function. James A. McCandless served as the first postmaster in one of the first commercial buildings erected after Florence was incorporated. Over time, the Florence Post Office has sat in numerous locations under various postmasters and dedicated employees. The above photograph shows the post office in 1898, when it was in the 100 block of East Main Street. Postmaster Al Guilinger is third from left. The photograph below shows the Florence postal crew in 1970 with, from left to right, Harold Watkins, Chuck Watkins, Postmaster Walter Martin, Chuck Blankenship, and Darrel Lindsey. (Below, courtesy of Nancy Lindsey.)

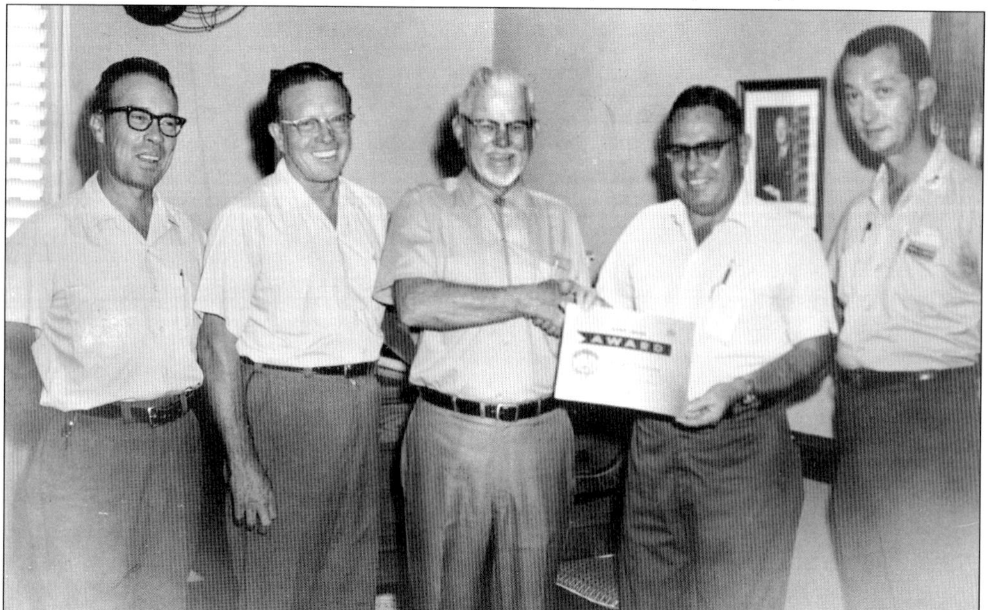

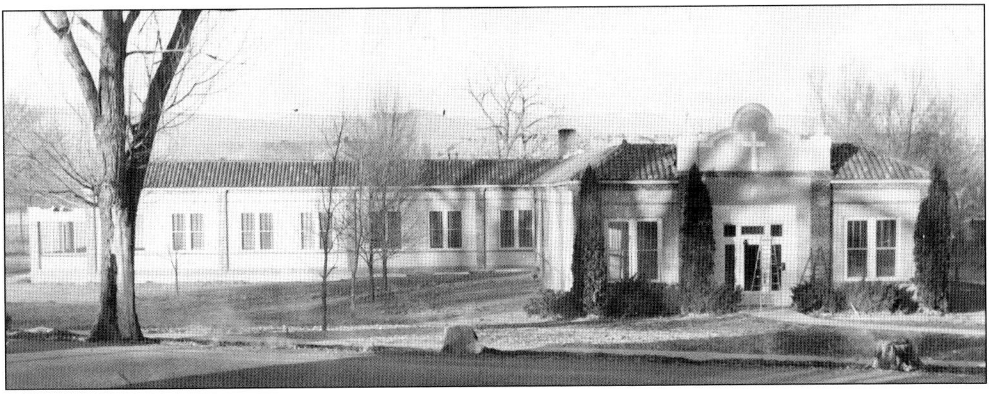

St. Joseph Hospital became Florence's first officially operational hospital in 1948. The Benedictine Sisters of Villa Madonna Convent of Kentucky took charge of the 30-bed facility. The building at West Third Street and Washington Avenue, which was once a chicken hatchery, was donated to the community by Mary Rankin, a local business owner. Through the volunteer efforts of the Florence Lions Club, which presented the original idea for a hospital in 1945, with a few doctors, a banker, a druggist, and many dedicated community members, the hatchery was transformed into a modern hospital at a cost of $200,000. The above photograph shows the front of the hospital near completion, and the photograph below shows the back with the emergency entrance at left. In 1971, again through community involvement, the hospital underwent a major expansion, increasing its size dramatically. St. Joseph Hospital closed in 1988.

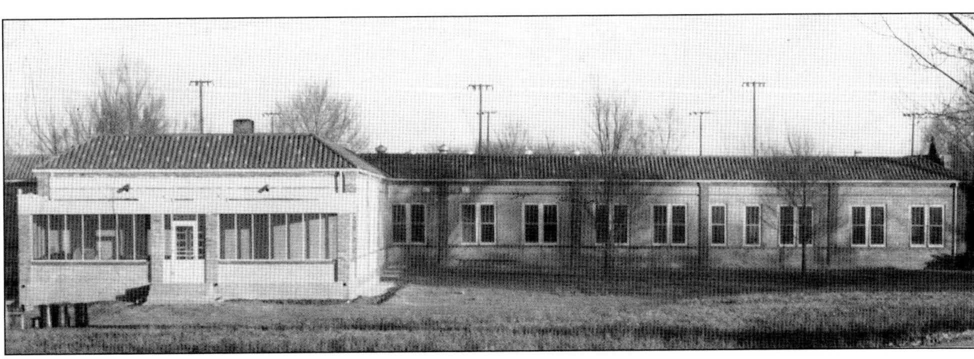

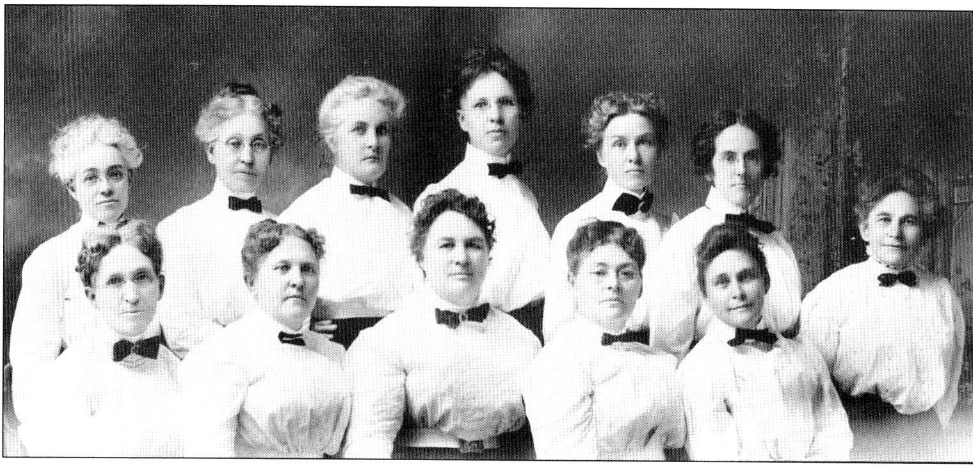

Known to everyone as "The Thimble Dozen," this group of women exemplified the spirit and meaning of volunteerism found in Florence. Between 1917 and 1925, they gathered regularly to unselfishly give of their time and skills in sewing and knitting items for servicemen stationed overseas during and after World War I.

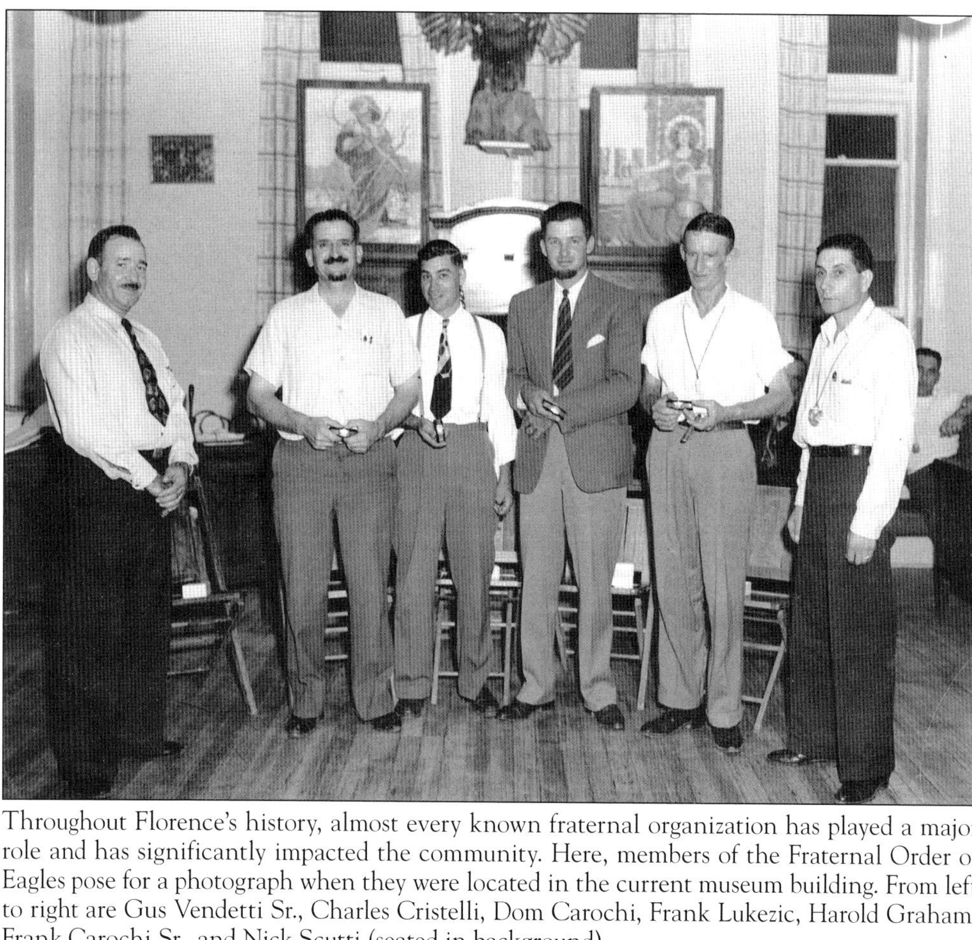

Throughout Florence's history, almost every known fraternal organization has played a major role and has significantly impacted the community. Here, members of the Fraternal Order of Eagles pose for a photograph when they were located in the current museum building. From left to right are Gus Vendetti Sr., Charles Cristelli, Dom Carochi, Frank Lukezic, Harold Graham, Frank Carochi Sr., and Nick Scutti (seated in background).

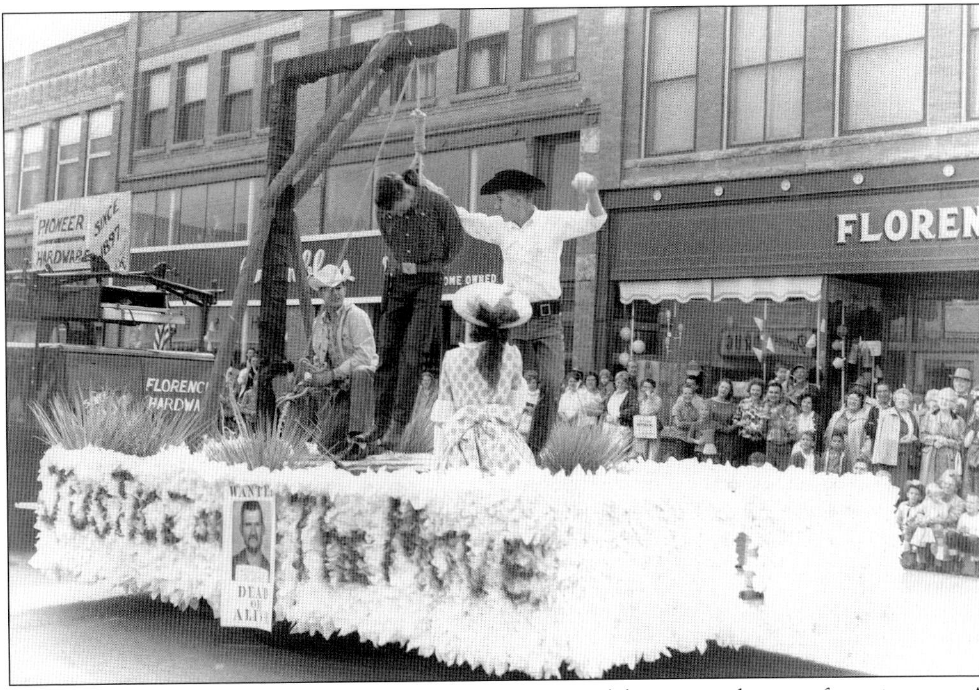

Since 1927, Florence has held the annual Pioneer Day celebration in honor of its pioneers. A highlight of the activities is a parade along Main Street. In 1963, a float entitled "Justice on the Move" depicted the capture and execution of a frontier fugitive. Actors included Carl Lancaster (outlaw), frontier law enforcement Jim Carochi (left) and Frank Carochi Jr. (right), and Hazel Lewis (center foreground) as the fugitive's sobbing girlfriend. (Courtesy of the Carochi family.)

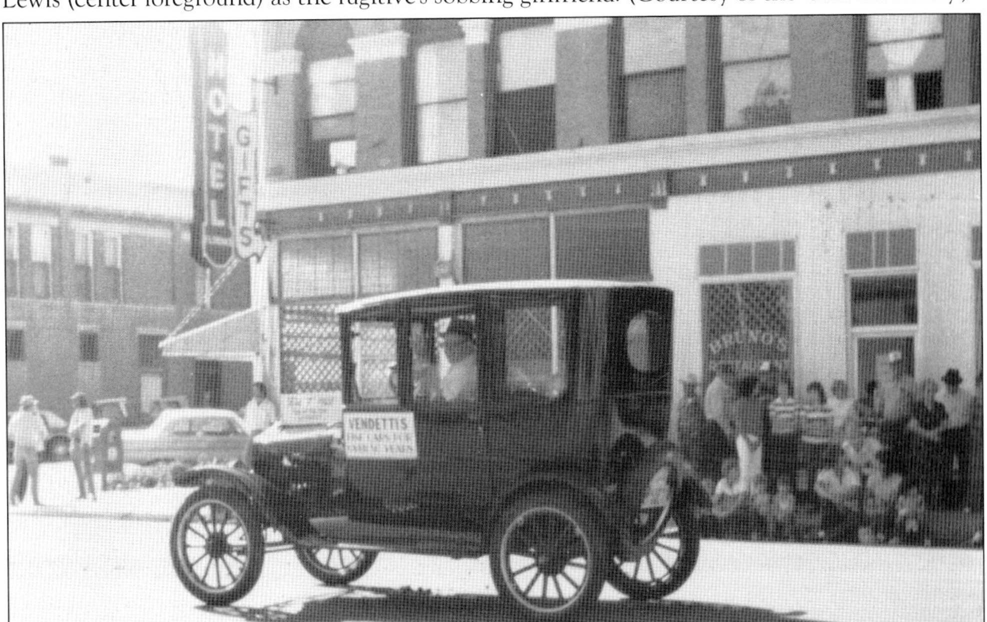

Gus Vendetti Sr. drives in the 1965 Pioneer Day parade, when he was selected as the chamber of commerce Outstanding Citizen of the Year. The car is Chopper Price's 1923 Ford Model A, which Gus did most of the restoration work on. (Courtesy of Gus and Barbara Vendetti.)

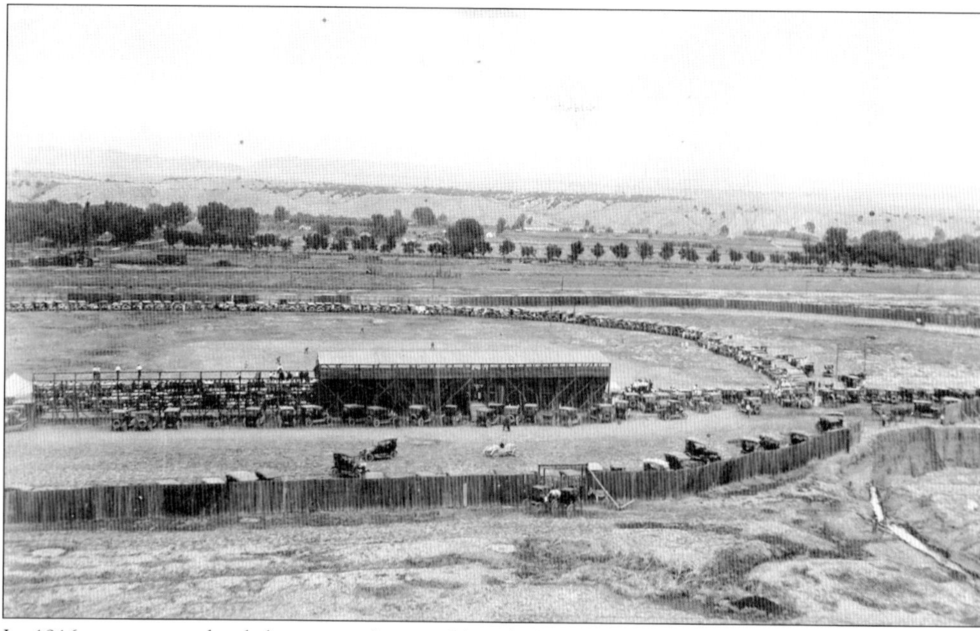

In 1916, a sponsored exhibition professional baseball game, with over 2,000 fans watching, was played at the Florence Ballpark south of town. After a two-hour delay due to the late arrival of Rio Grande train No. 4 from the west, the Denver Grizzlies went on to defeat the Chicago White Sox by a score of 4 to 1. The Coal Creek Band entertained the enthusiastic crowd during the wait.

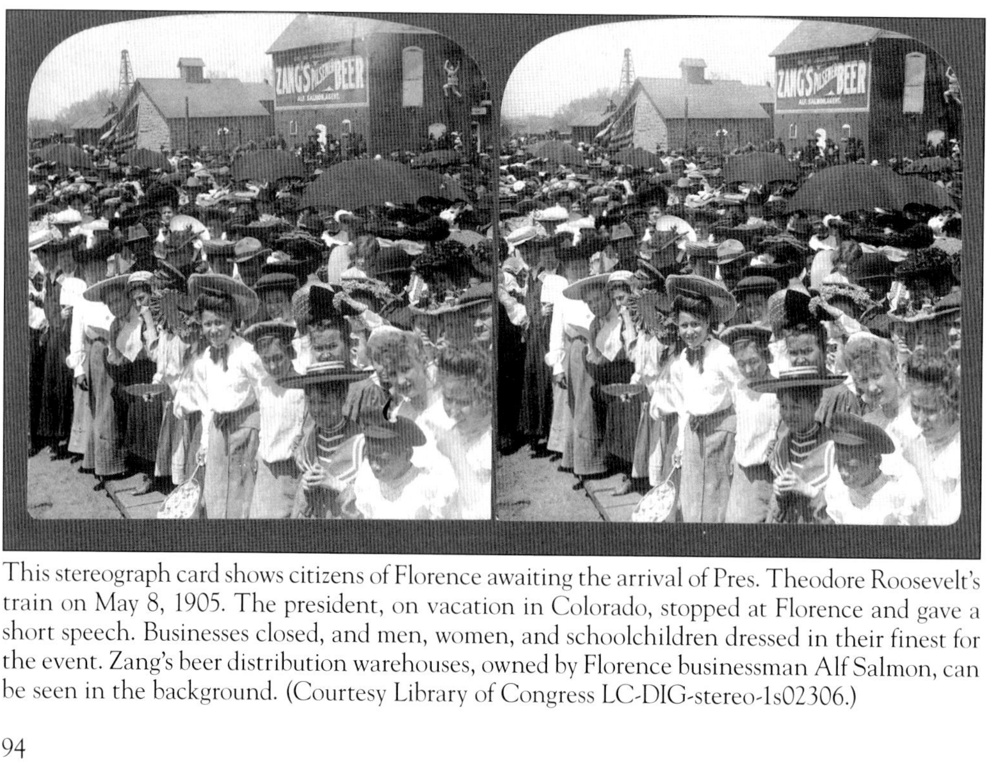

This stereograph card shows citizens of Florence awaiting the arrival of Pres. Theodore Roosevelt's train on May 8, 1905. The president, on vacation in Colorado, stopped at Florence and gave a short speech. Businesses closed, and men, women, and schoolchildren dressed in their finest for the event. Zang's beer distribution warehouses, owned by Florence businessman Alf Salmon, can be seen in the background. (Courtesy Library of Congress LC-DIG-stereo-1s02306.)

Seven

Home and Worship

With agricultural beginnings, the Arkansas River valley appeared very much like all Western frontier farmland: sprawling crop fields dotted with the occasional farmhouse and barn. The outlying coalfields had attracted the railroads with their demand for coal. Soon, paths and trails turned into streets, and the fields were transformed by expanding numbers of oil wells. A downtown area was developing with small shops and buildings to accommodate the distribution of supplies to the surrounding areas. Florence was incorporated, and the population began to grow. Housing for new families and workers was needed.

The first housing in Florence was, as was typical at that time, wooden structures, though a limited amount of adobe brick was being used. When it was found that kiln-fired bricks could be easily made here, the methods of construction quickly changed. The streets of present-day Florence are lined with single family and multifamily brick houses. An influx of workers for the coal mines, oilfields, and processing plants led to a rapid expansion of the residential areas, enlarging in all four directions from what had become the center of the community.

Housing in Florence is an interesting mix from just what is necessary for comfort to large multilevel structures. The greatest percentage of residents only had what was needed to support their family and what could be obtained with their wages. However, the more successful businessmen, speculators, and investors in the land and mineral industries employed more extravagant designs and construction.

With the growth in population came the need for spiritual gatherings and houses of worship. Florence is blessed with many large, finely designed churches reflecting the devotion and commitment of their attendees. Various architectural, aesthetic, and design methods are incorporated into these historic as well as modern facilities. For various reasons, some churches have been redefined and transformed for use in other private and public pursuits.

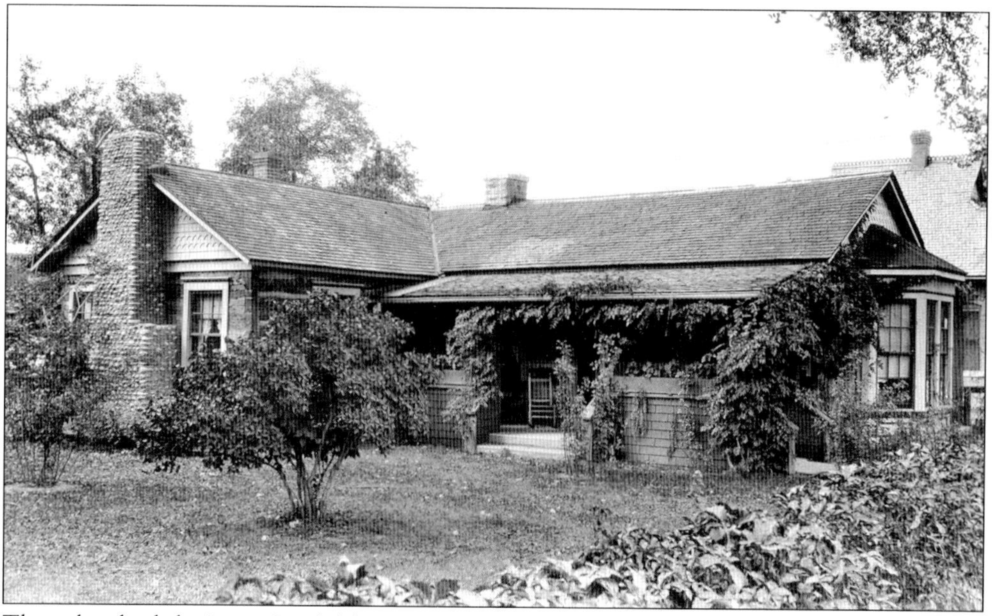

The cabin built by Isaac Canfield in 1869 has been slightly modified and relocated. James A. McCandless purchased land from Canfield, including the cabin, and had the cabin moved to what would become South Petroleum Avenue and East Second Street, its present location. McCandless lived in the cabin for 20 years, and later his son James Victor lived here until his death in 1938.

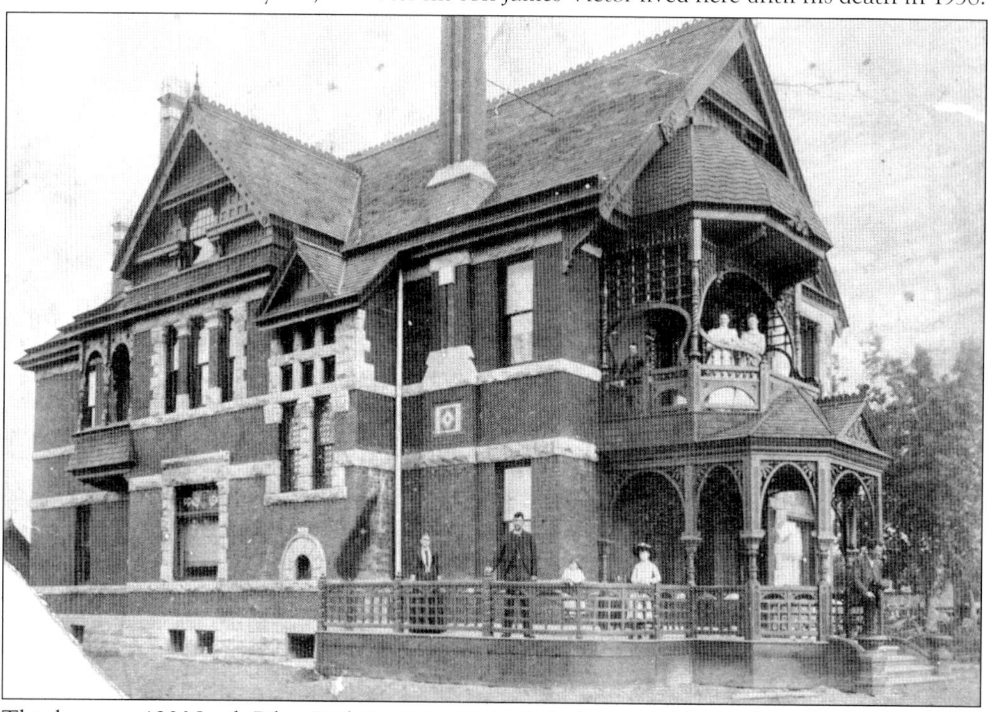

This home at 120 North Pikes Peak Avenue was built for James A. McCandless in 1889, two years after Florence was officially incorporated. The McCandless family lived in the house until shortly after James died in 1922. The Holt family of Cañon City purchased it in 1931, turning it into a funeral home. Frank and Irene Witty purchased it in 1952 and changed the name to Florence Mortuary.

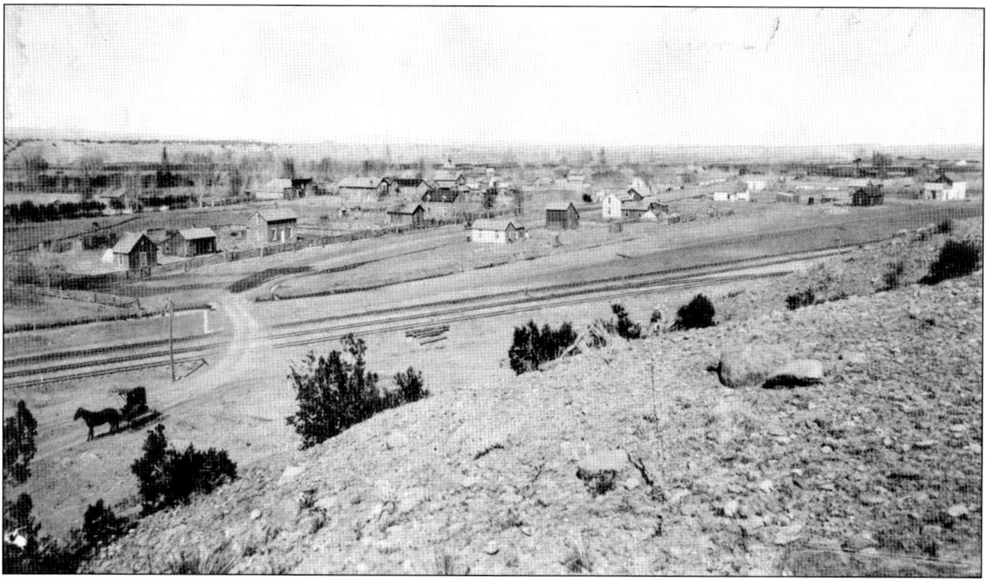

This photograph was taken in June 1877 from the mesa southeast of downtown. The date is just prior to Florence's incorporation but shows the platting of streets and blocks that was completed in 1872. The dirt road that the horse and buggy are on at lower left crosses the railroad tracks and moves onto Main Street about where present-day Church Avenue is.

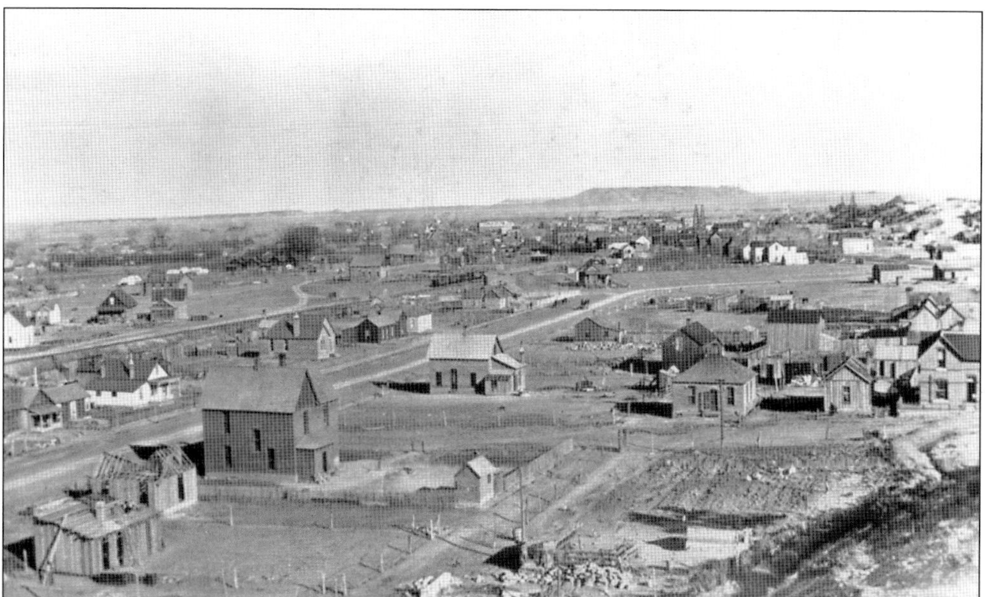

By 1900, the residential areas had expanded and spread out over the valley floor. The center of downtown was at top center and slightly to the right. Brick soon replaced wood as the preferred choice for home building, and because of that, many of the original residential structures are still standing.

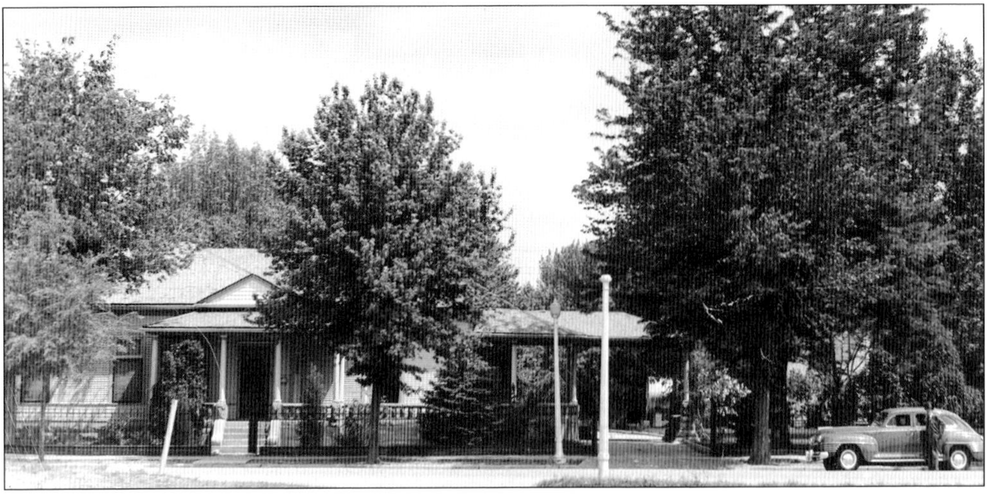

Augustus Gumaer built this home at 225 East Main Street in 1894. He came to the area in 1881 as a bank cashier and became a Florence businessman and founder of the Colorado Oil Company. Gumaer passed away in 1916, and the home was purchased by the United Oil Company and used as a men's clubhouse. In the 1920s, Florence businessman W.P. Wilbar purchased the house for his residence, and the Wilbar family owned the property until 1993. The above photograph shows the front of the residence from Main Street with W.P. Wilbar standing next to the car at right, with his wife in the driver's seat. Below is the back of the house, with the elaborate carport entrance to the left. (Both, courtesy of John Wilbar.)

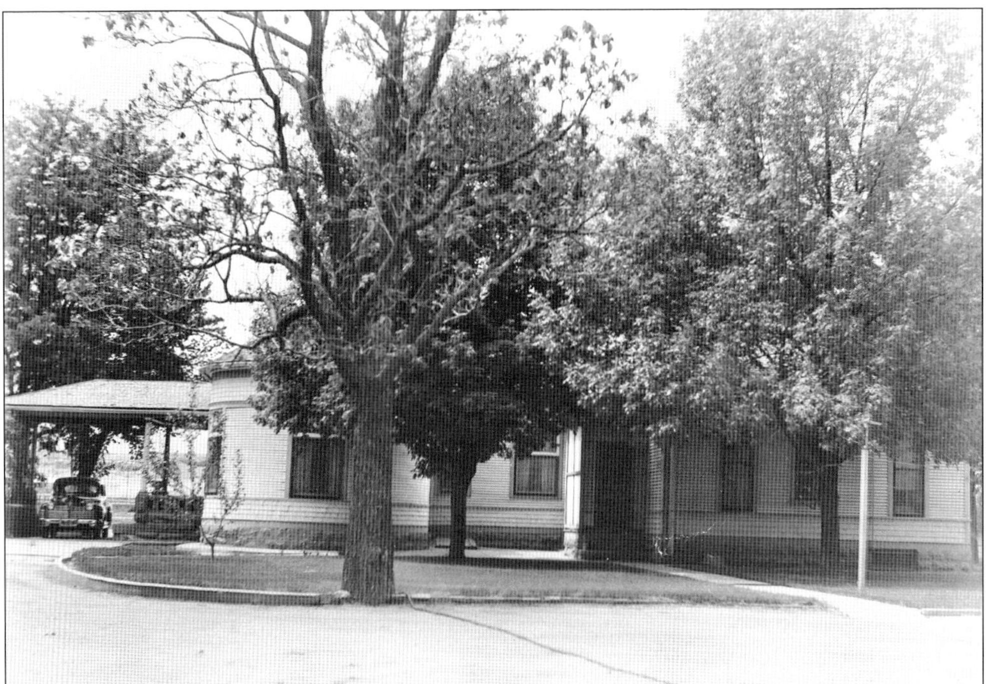

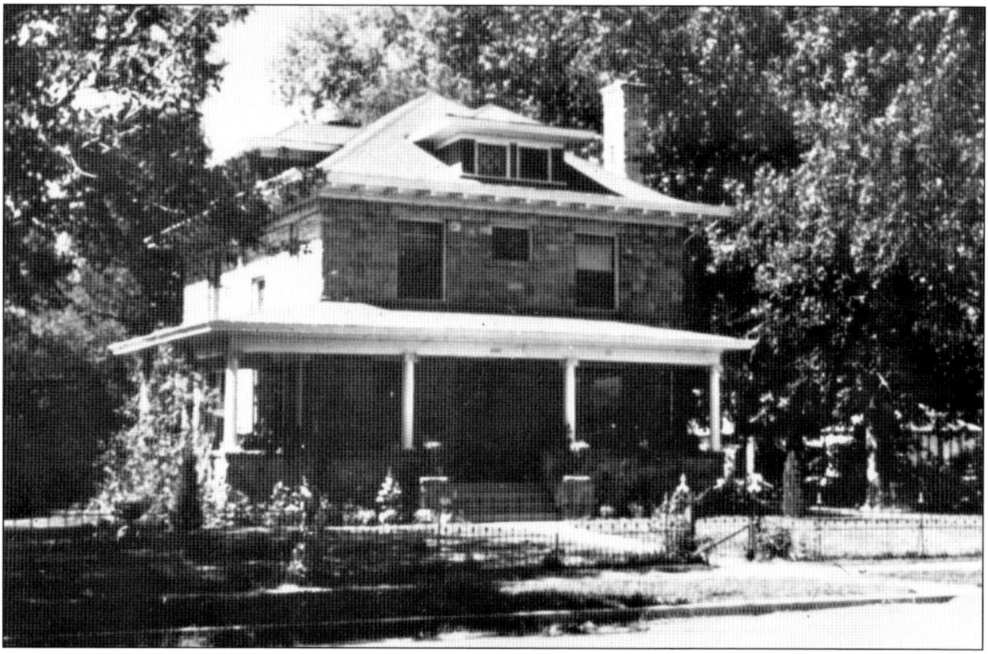

This home at 430 West Fourth Street was purchased by Phillip Griffith in 1910. He was a successful businessman of Florence and responsible for the construction of the current Pioneer Museum building. On the southwest corner of East Fourth Street and North Robinson Avenue, the house typifies the finer homes of the citizens who succeeded because of the opportunities in and around Florence.

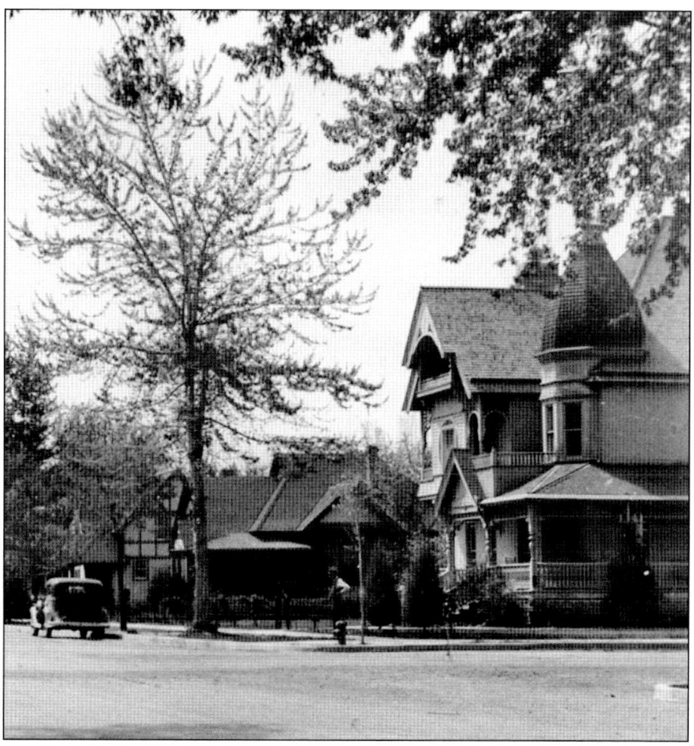

Another example of the success found in Florence, this residential block of East Second Street between Crawford Avenue and North Robinson Avenue is characteristic of the large two-story homes built for single families during the boom times. The home on the right, originally built for the Hadley family of the Hadley Mercantile Company, demonstrates the skills and abilities in architectural design and craftsmanship of the time.

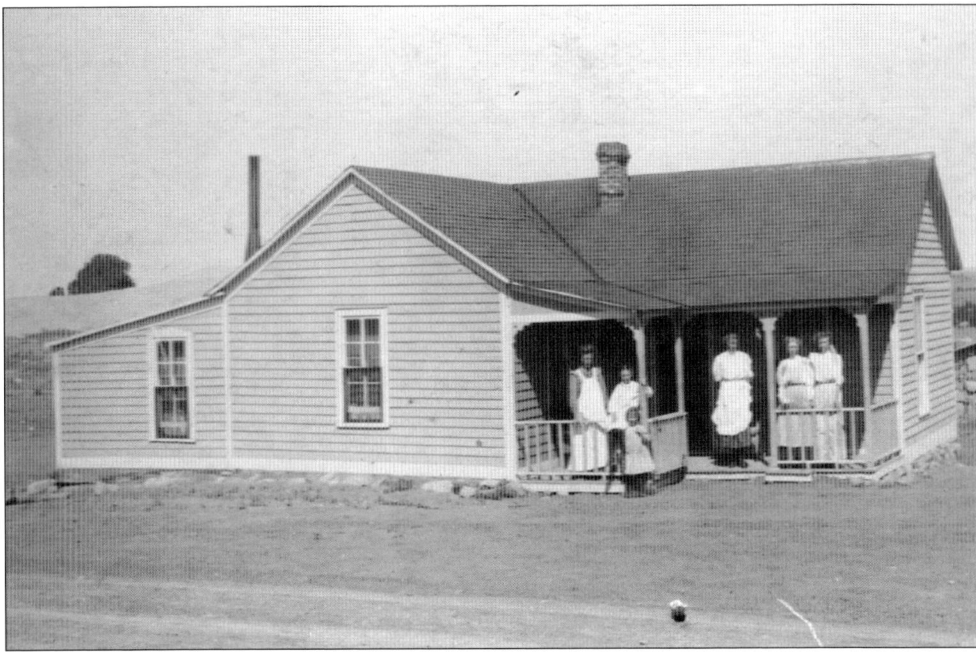

The largest percentage of Florence's population was working-class citizens. The many refineries, smelters, and other manufacturing companies, along with the oilfields, coal mines, and general supply companies, brought many families to the area for work. Wood-built structures such as this, as well as the later brick-built homes, can still be found throughout Florence.

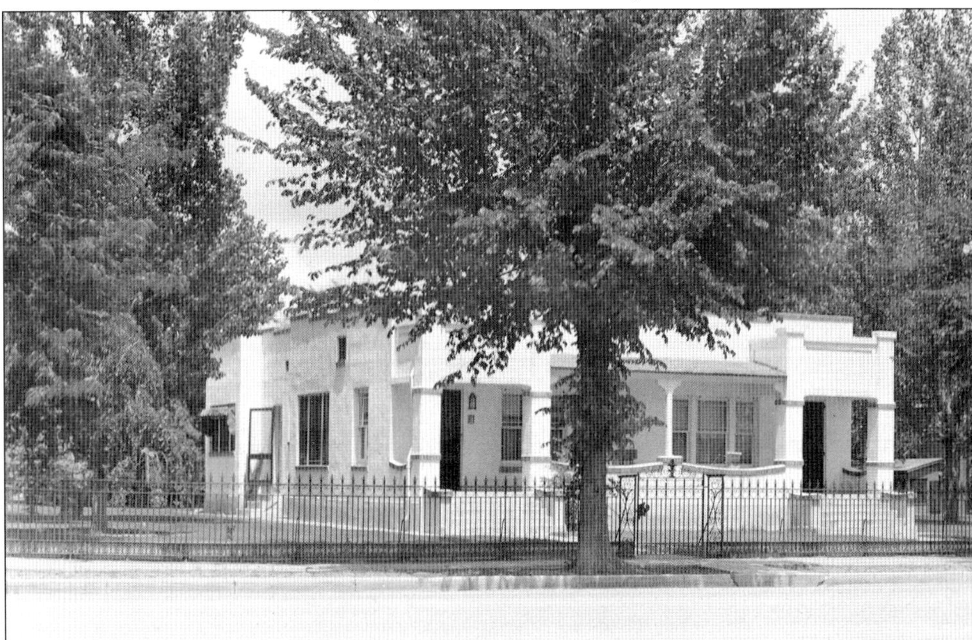

Duplex multifamily housing was popular as Florence grew. Sometimes built by investors to lease out and sometimes built by large families for their own use, multifamily structures were an economical way to provide a home. This example of a duplex was built by Florence businessman W.P. Wilbar in the 200 block of East Main Street. (Courtesy of John Wilbar.)

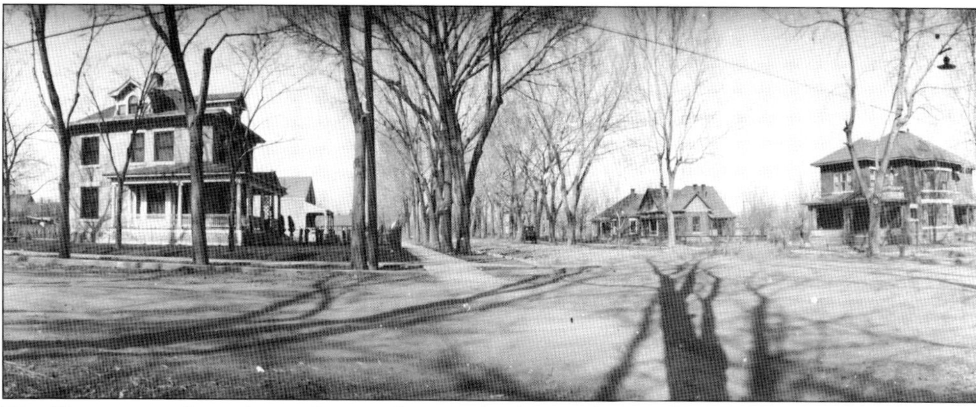

The Florence residential areas became known for their wide, tree-lined streets. This photograph, looking west at the intersection of East Third Street and North Robinson Avenue, is a good example of the early layout. Sidewalks were built through the formation of a sidewalk district in 1911, with a strip of land between the sidewalk and the street used for tree planting.

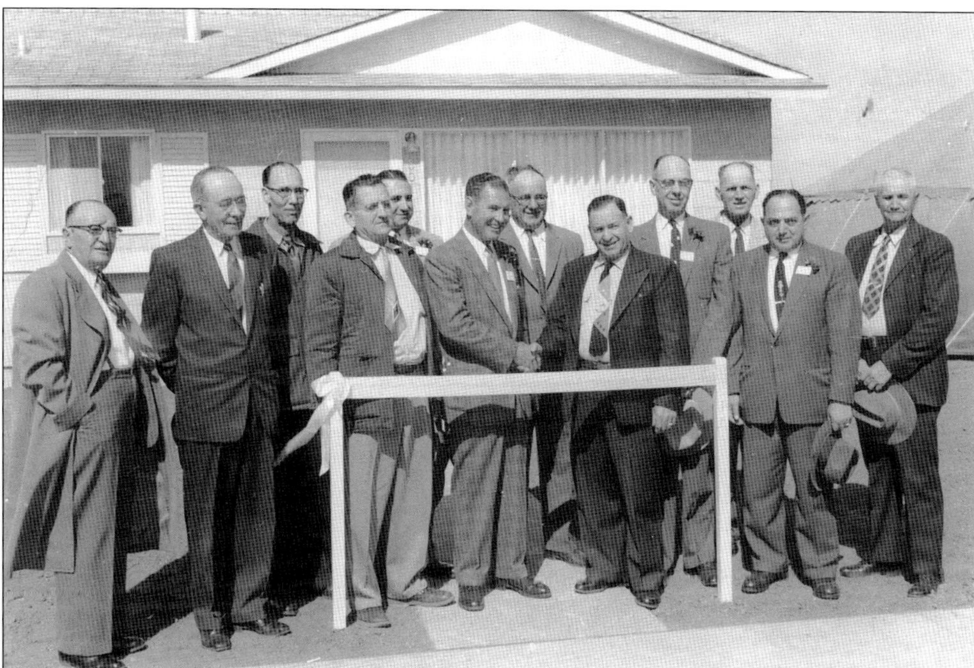

Like many communities, Florence saw a growth in housing construction at the end of World War II lasting into the 1950s. Florence expanded in all directions, although it was most notable toward the east. On March 10, 1956, this dedication ceremony for the first home completed in the Robin subdivision is attended by city officials, financiers, and the Alexander Construction Company. (Courtesy of Gus and Barbara Vendetti.)

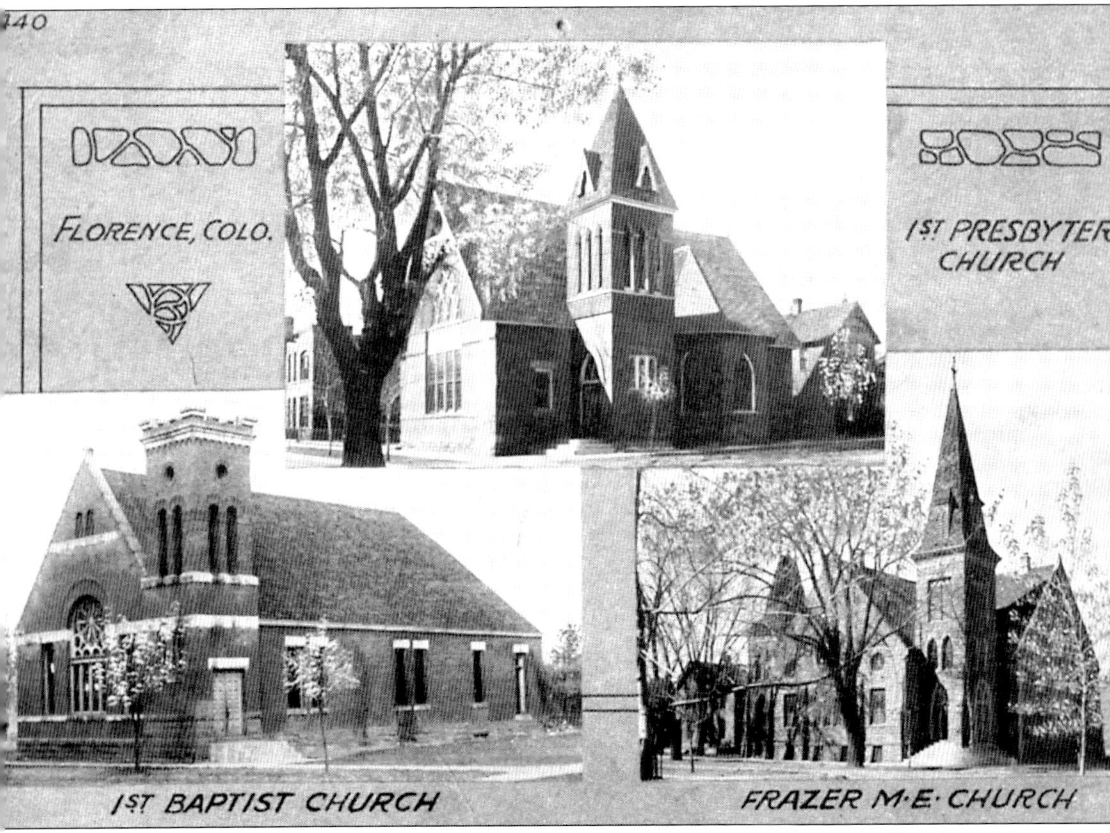

Religion has played a key role in the foundation and development of Florence. Churches were some of the first structures built as Florence grew, supporting various congregations. Frazer Methodist Church was organized prior to the incorporation of the town. This promotional postcard celebrates a few of the different institutions attended by citizens of Florence. The community has a history of welcoming diverse faiths and supporting their rights, a standard that continues to this day.

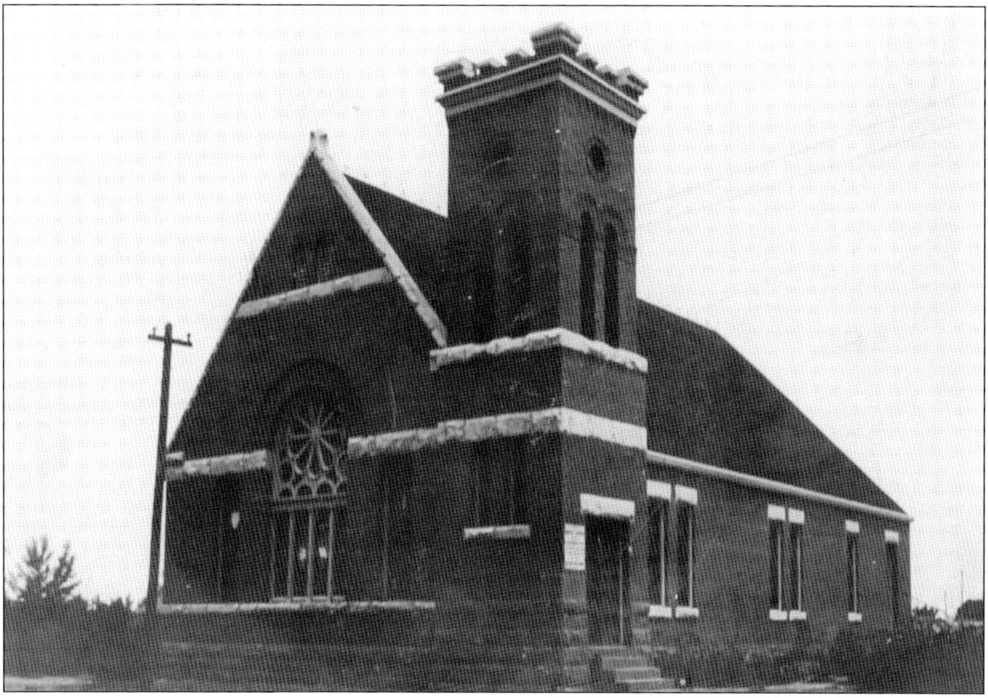

First Baptist Church was built in 1898 at the northeast corner of East Second Street and North Petroleum Avenue. This photograph was taken prior to the two-story addition that was constructed to the right rear of the building in 1956. The property has since been passed on to the Florence Arts Council by the congregation.

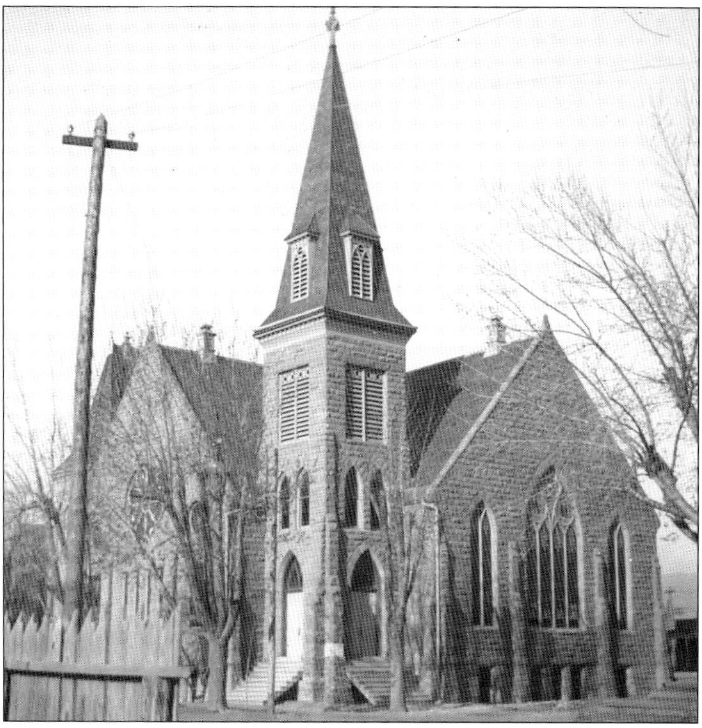

This photograph of Frazer Methodist Church at East Second Street and North Petroleum Avenue was taken not too long after construction was completed. The church sat kitty-corner from First Baptist Church. This structure was destroyed by fire in 1974.

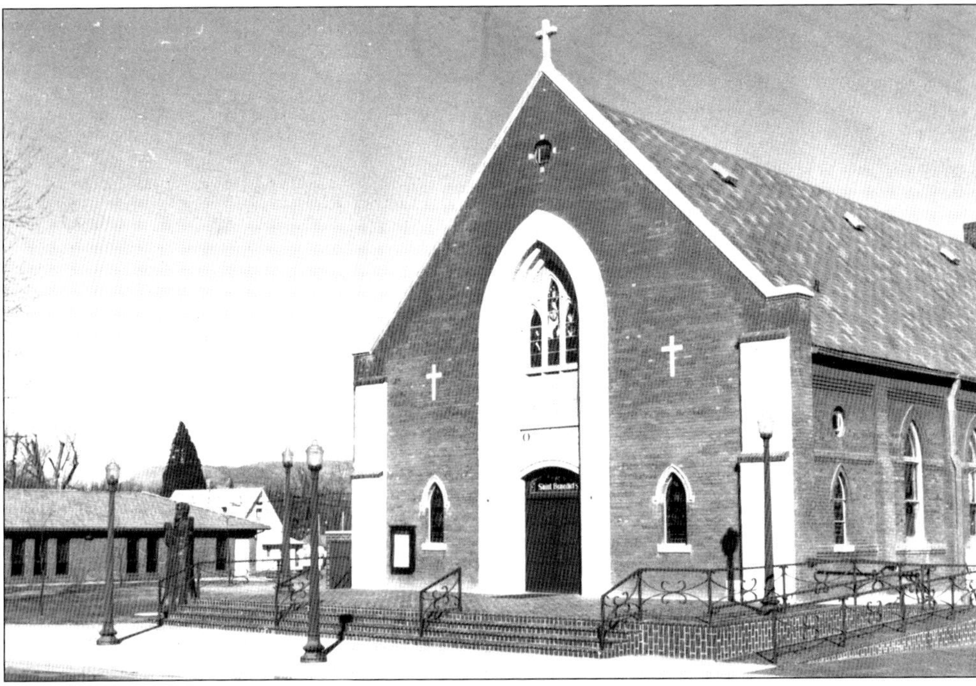

St. Benedict's Catholic Church at 622 West Second Street was built on the west side of Florence in 1906. Numerous modifications have been made to the structure, including the addition of the community meeting and classroom building at left. The parish is served through the Holy Cross Abbey in Cañon City.

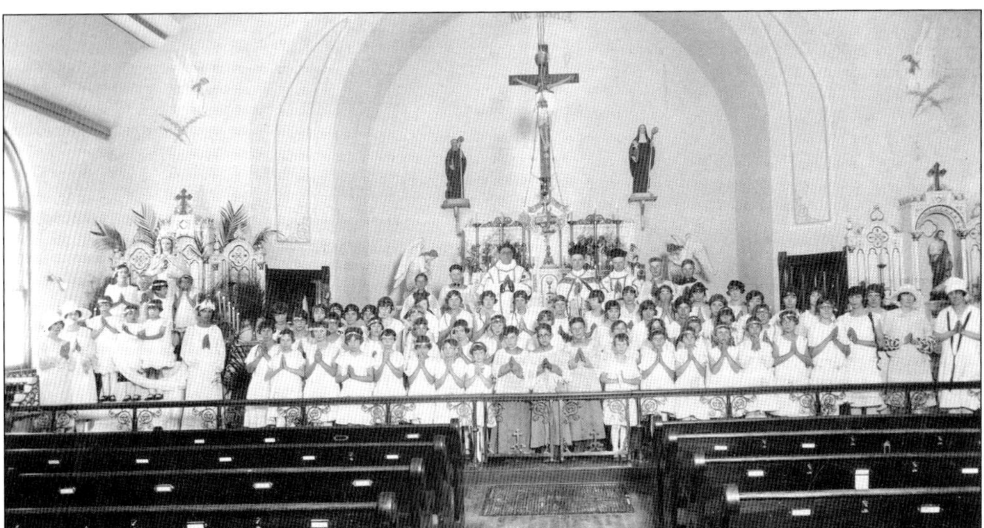

This photograph taken inside St. Benedict's shows the congregation, although the purpose of this gathering is unknown. The Catholic Church has been popular in eastern Fremont County since 1898, when St. Benedict's Abbey of Atchison, Kansas, was given charge of the mission here. (Courtesy of the Carochi family.)

Eight

Education

Public education, without question, has been the most significant concern of the citizens of Florence since the very beginning. The first building solely for education was constructed and was being used prior to incorporation. From the beginning to the present day, there have been 10 permanent, full-scale educational structures built within city boundaries and various less permanent facilities. Due to demographic changes, a school district was formed, and Florence integrated the areas of Rockvale, Coal Creek, Williamsburg, Brookside, Wetmore, and Penrose.

Florence has always offered kindergarten through twelfth grade, depending on what the contemporary system called for. Citizens have continuously supported the endeavors of the Florence educational organization, both financially and physically, constantly placing education as a priority of the community. The Florence school system's philosophy dictates that education is not textbook instruction alone but also encompasses extracurricular education as found in sports, the arts, and various other cultural environments and teachings.

Numerous families in the community can boast multigenerational participation in the Florence educational organization. It is not uncommon for students to sit in the same building as their parents, or in a few cases even have the same teacher. One in particular, the E.C. Schmidt family, is able to claim over 100 years of continuous attendance in a Florence school.

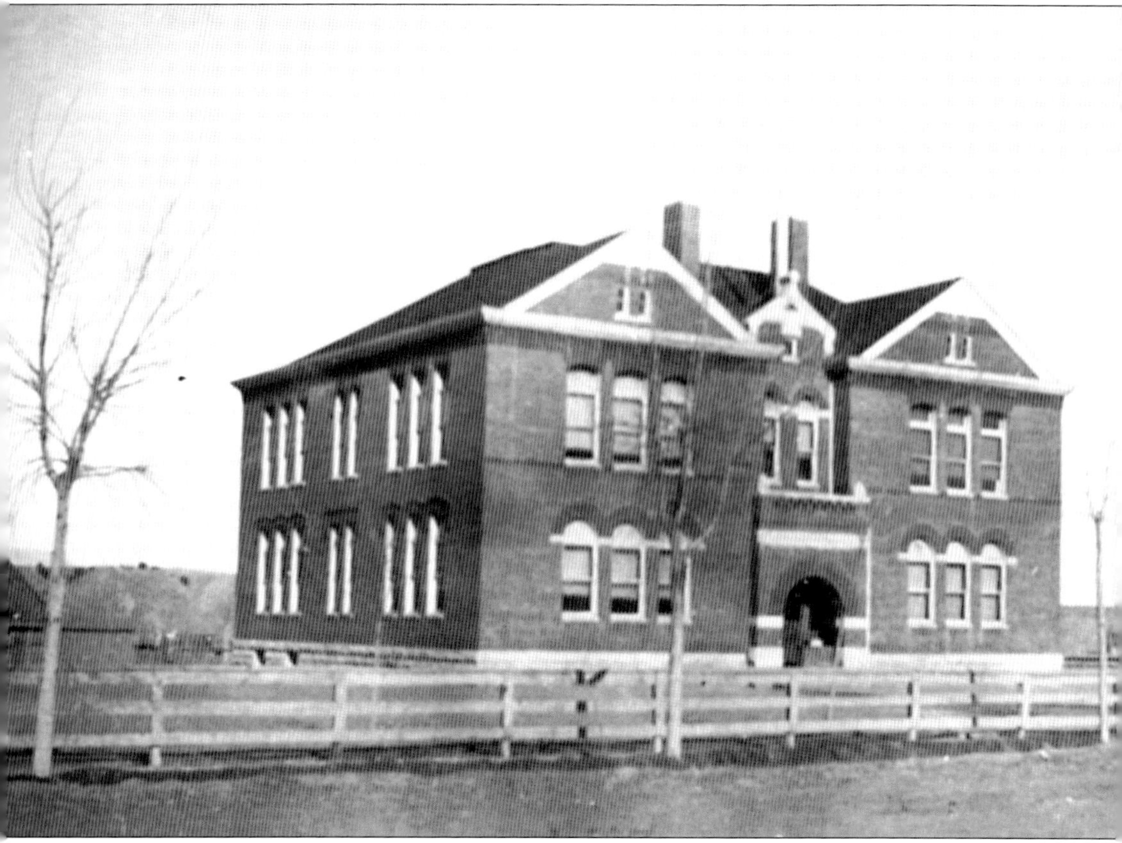

McCandless School was on East Third Street between Midland and McCandless Avenues. Built in 1895, it served as Florence's only school for a time, followed by the high school and eventually the elementary school. This building was demolished in 1964 due to its deteriorating condition, and the location has become the property of First Southern Baptist Church.

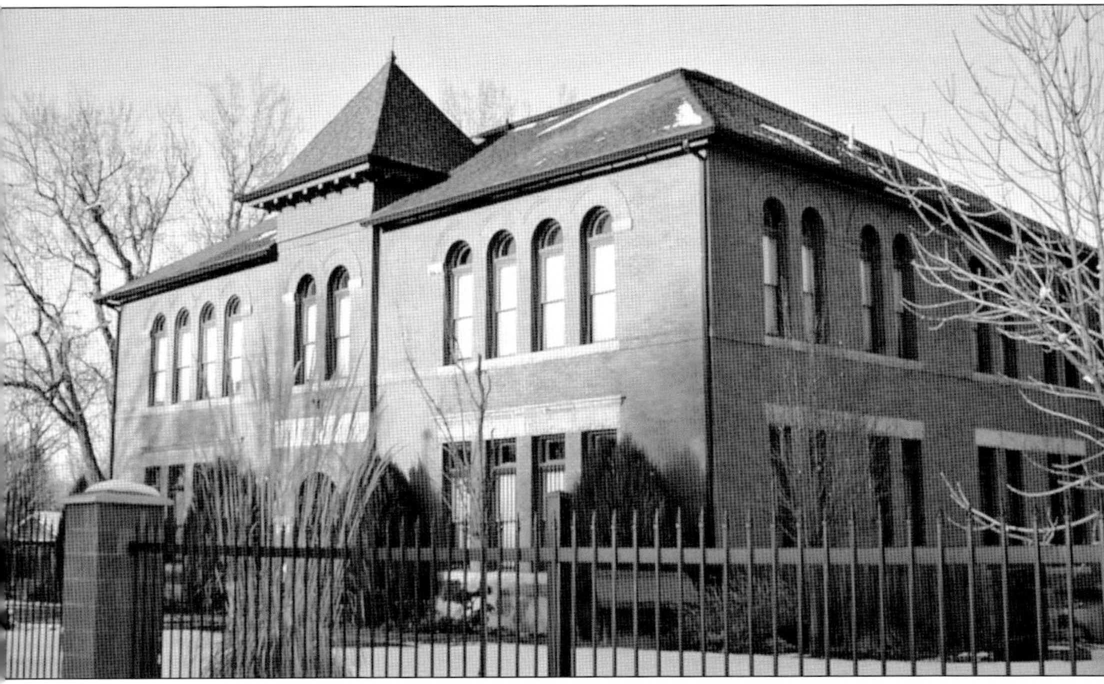

Emerson School was on West Second Street between Houston and Lobach Avenues. This modern photograph of the building suggests what the bustling school once looked like. It was originally built to house an elementary school and was well attended by Florence families. Emerson School became unsafe due to age and the deteriorating condition of the structure and was replaced in 1963 by a new elementary school.

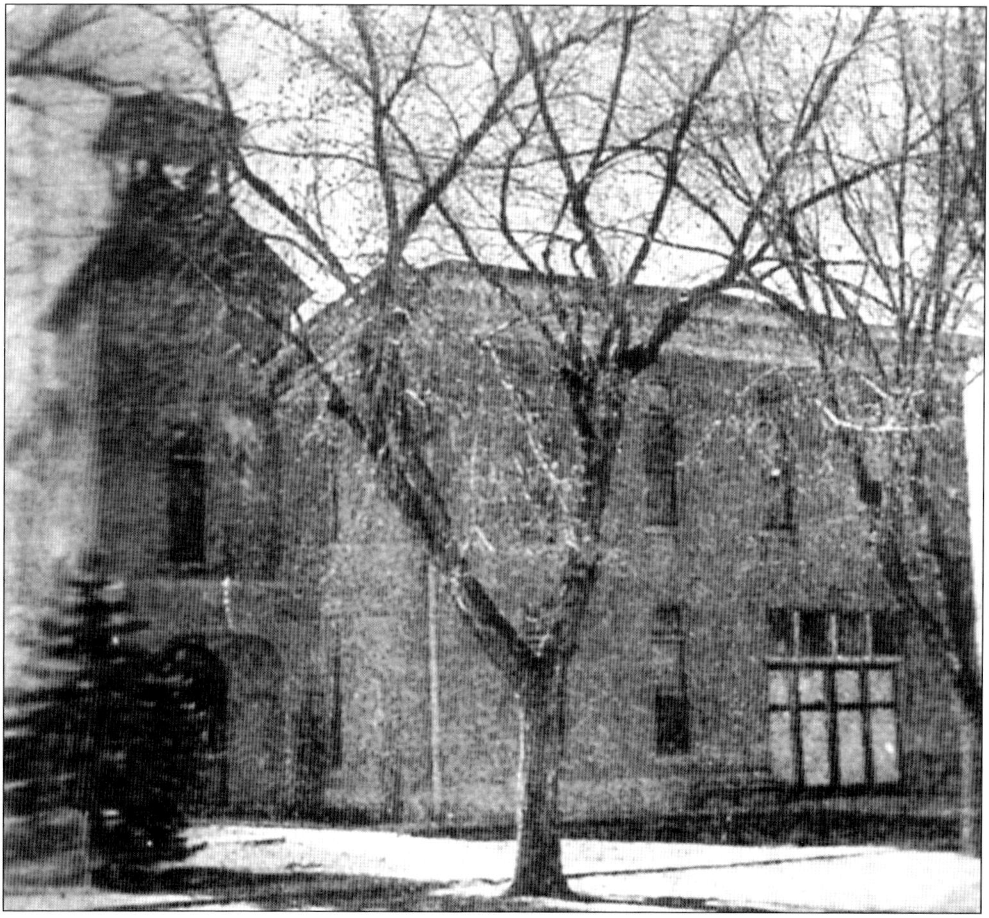

Central School was at the corner of West Main Street and Maple Avenue. The structure was constructed in 1887 as the second school in Florence with the closure of Front Street School on East Front Street and Petroleum Avenue. This school was in use until 1926, when it became the city hall and fire department. It was demolished in 1977 when the present structure was built, also housing both city departments.

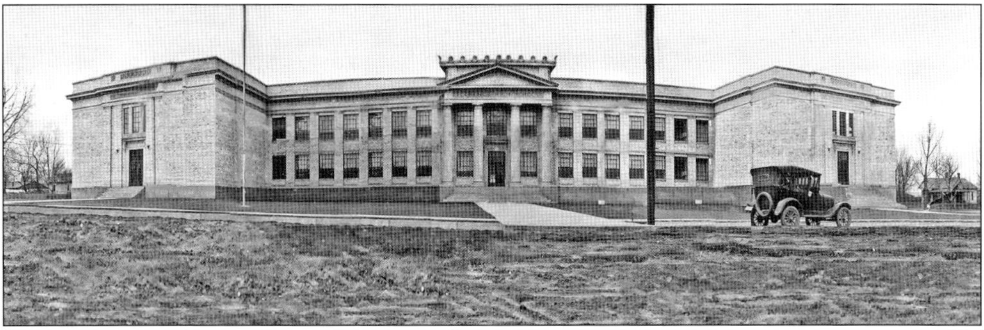

Florence High School was at 215 North Maple Avenue. The classical-style building was completed in 1921 with a bond issue of $100,000. Florence High School was planned to serve students of Florence for many years, and it succeeded in providing that service. Three generations of Florence families attended and graduated from this school. This building became the fourth of five total high school structures in the history of Florence, the fifth being built in 2006. This facility closed its doors as an educational institution in 2019. Taken shortly after construction was completed, the above photograph shows the front of the building with the main entrance at center, the auditorium at left, and the gymnasium on the right. The smaller building at far right below had various uses over time, including an eighth-grade classroom, cafeteria, and band room.

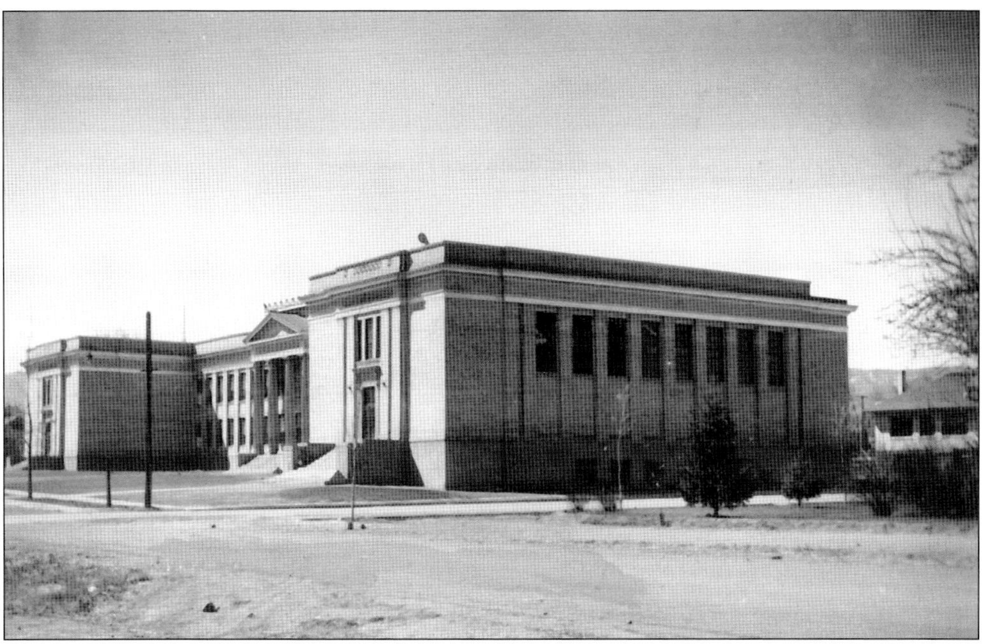

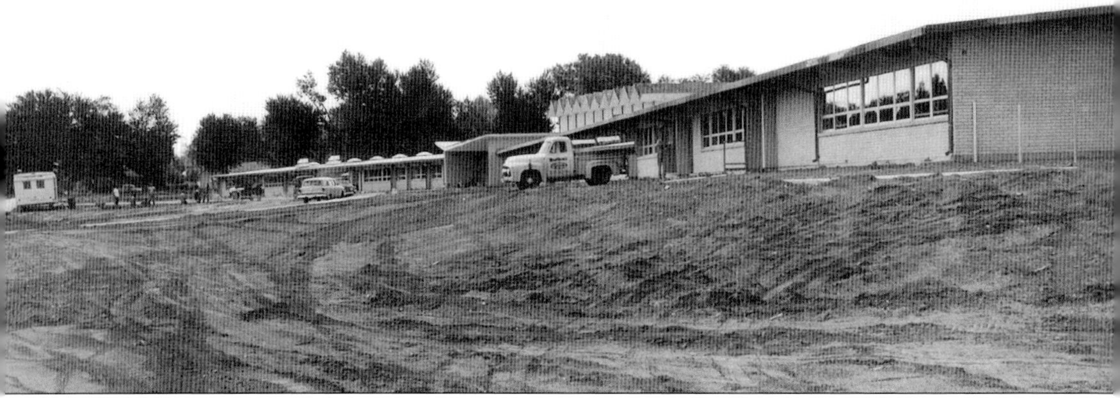

Eastern Fremont Elementary School is at 500 West Fifth Street. The school was built in 1963 for slightly less than $100,000. It originally served kindergarten through eighth grade. The new school building was required because of the closures of McCandless School and Emerson School, which had exceeded their useful lives. Fremont Elementary School continues to serve as an elementary school, with kindergarten through the sixth grade.

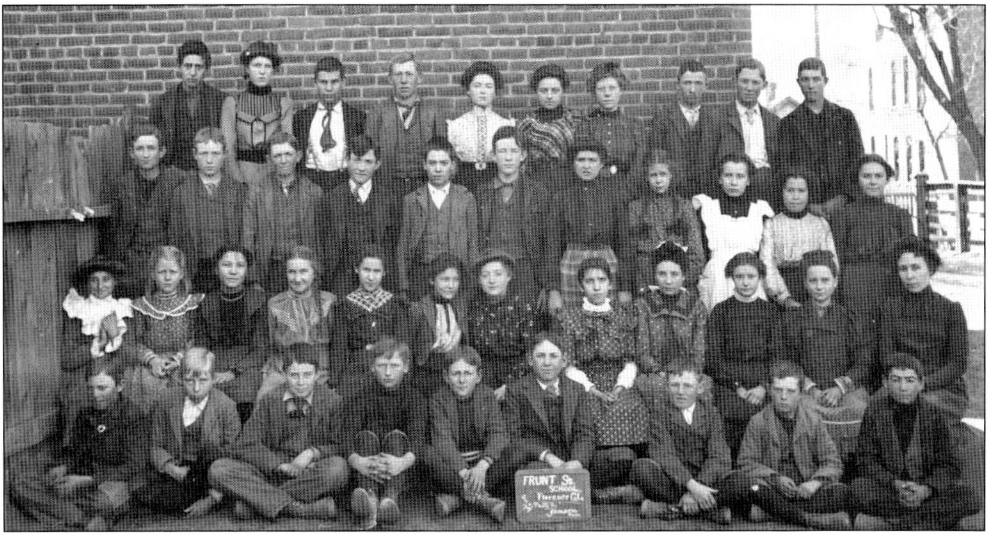

This is one of the first known photographs of the entire student body of the Florence educational system. It was taken in 1877 outside the first school in Florence, at East Front Street and South Petroleum Avenue. The sign reads, "Frunt St. School. Florence Colo Photo by Jansen Photo Dec '77."

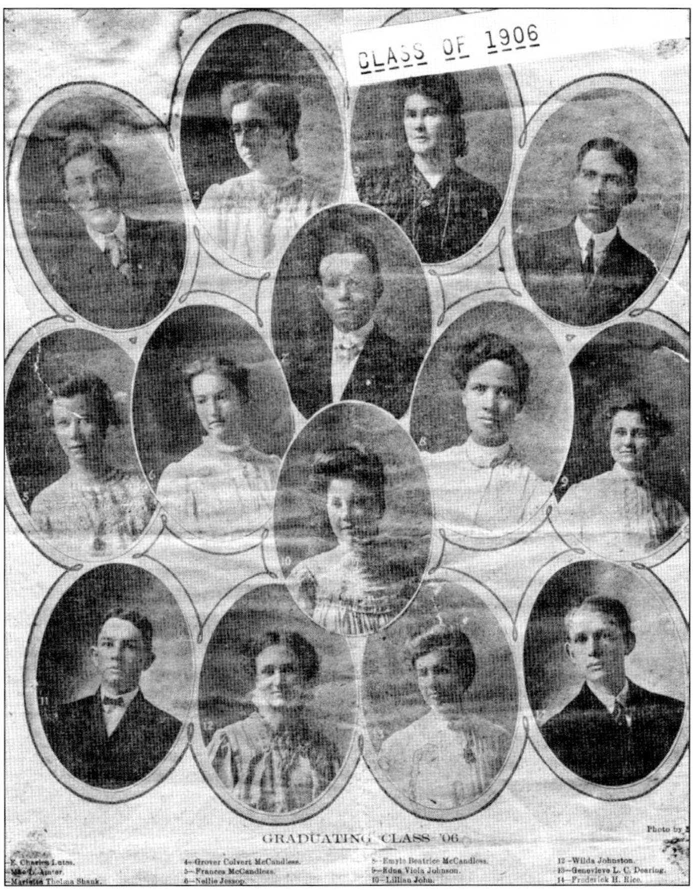

The 1906 graduating class of Central School is pictured here. A total of 14 seniors graduated that year, with three of them being from the McCandless family: Grover Colvert, Frances, and Emyle Beatrice.

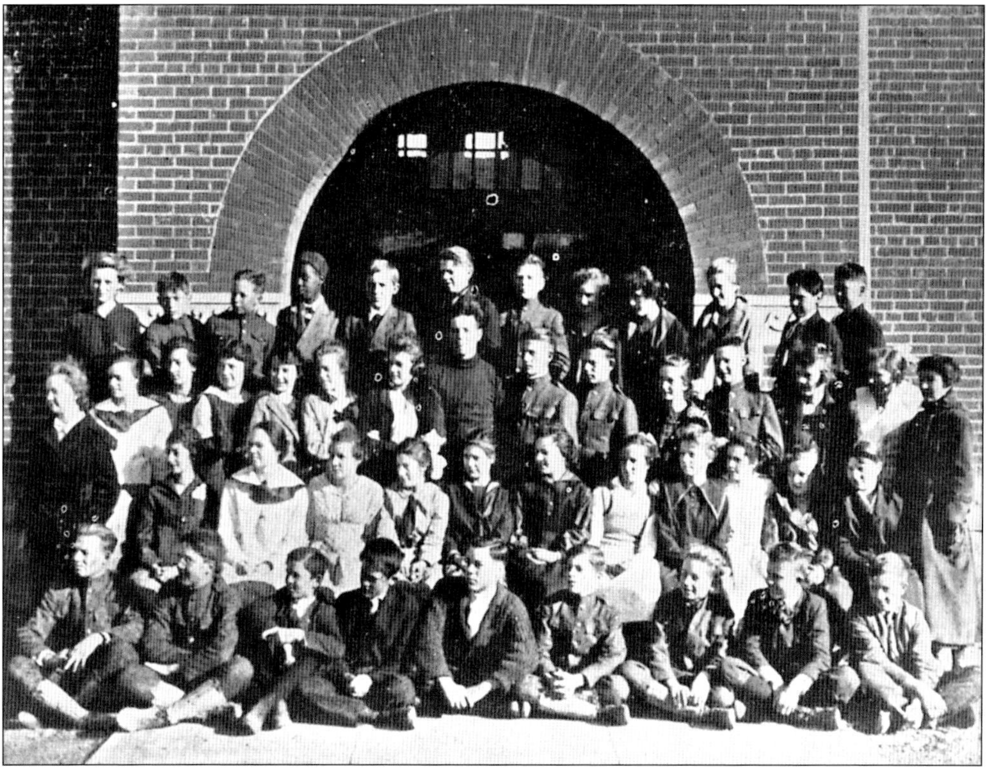

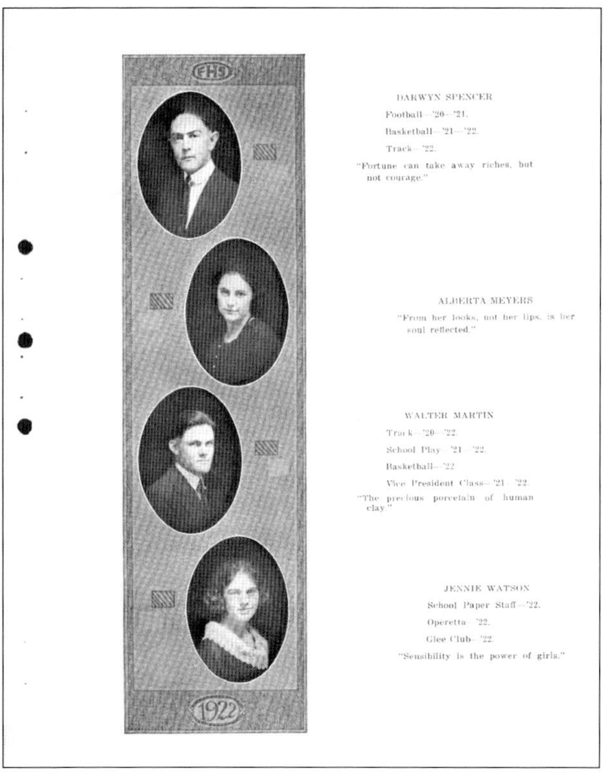

DARWYN SPENCER

Football—'20—'21.

Basketball—'21—'22.

Track—'22.

"Fortune can take away riches, but not courage."

ALBERTA MEYERS

"From her looks, not her lips, is her soul reflected."

WALTER MARTIN

Track—'20—'22.

School Play—'21—'22.

Basketball—'22.

Vice President Class—'21—'22.

"The precious porcelain of human clay."

JENNIE WATSON

School Paper Staff—'22.

Operetta—'22.

Glee Club—'22.

"Sensibility is the power of girls."

The Florence High School class of 1922 sits for its class picture outside McCandless School. This picture, taken in 1918, shows one of the last high school–level classes to attend McCandless School before moving into the newly completed Florence High School. This class became the first to graduate from the new building.

This page out of the 1922 senior class section of the Florence High School yearbook shows four students of the first class to graduate from the new school. The third one down, Walter Martin, served as the class vice president and later went on to become postmaster of the Florence Post Office. He was commonly known throughout Florence as "J. Walter Martin" and was quite involved in the community.

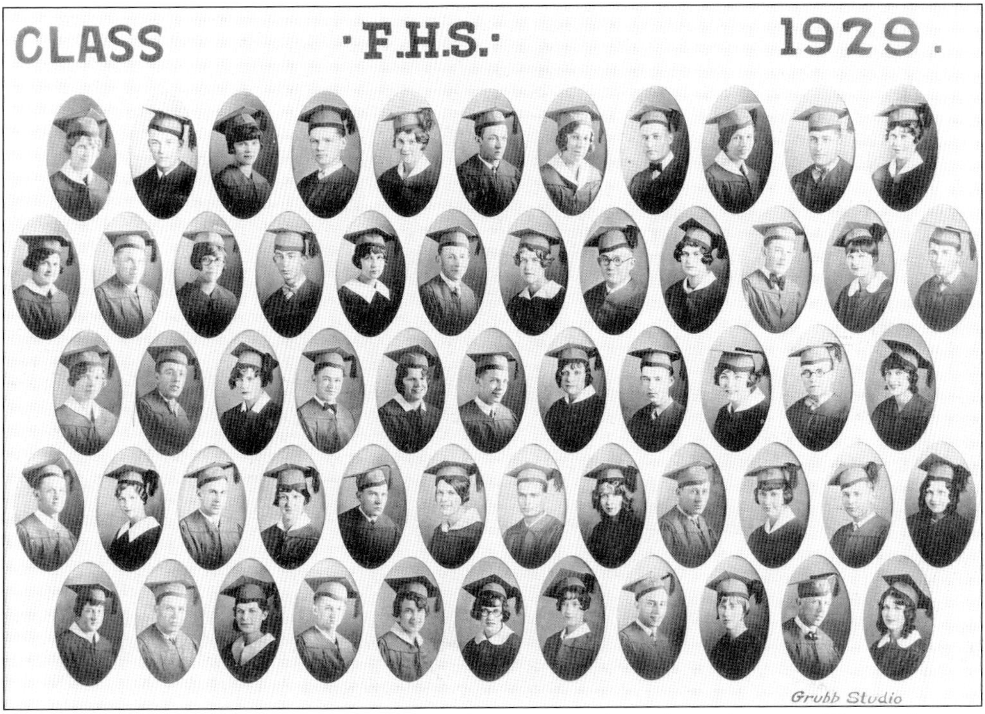

Class sizes at Florence High School continued to increase throughout the years. The graduating class in 1929 had 57 students from Florence and surrounding areas of the school district. Chopper Price was one of them; he is in the second row from the top, third from right.

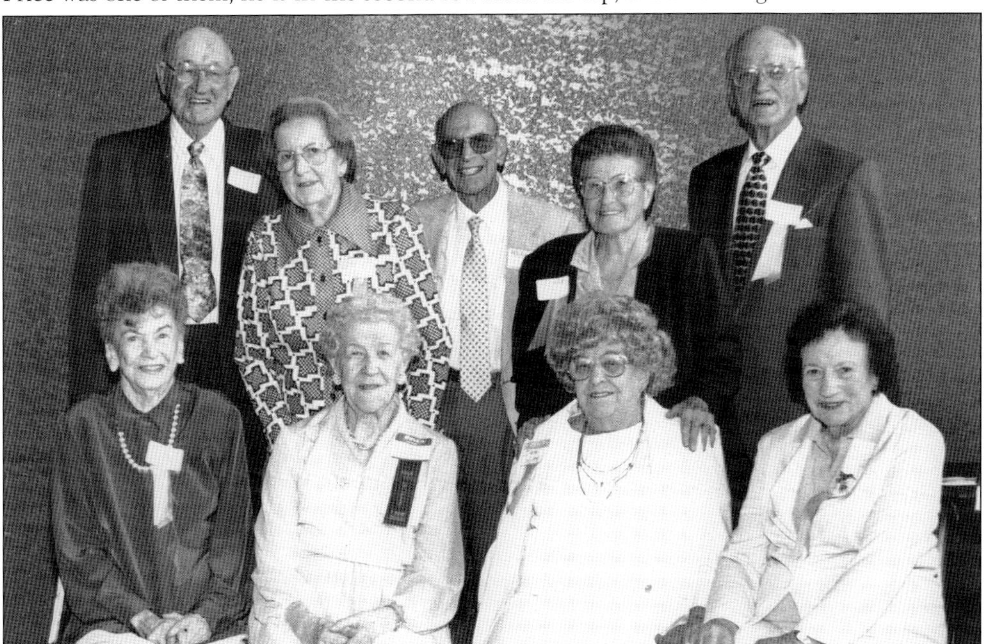

In 1979, the class of 1929 held its 50th reunion. Those in attendance included, from left to right, (first row) Jane Cantrell, Louis Mitchell, Irene Witty, and Florence Kelly Lobach; (second row) Chopper Price, Edith Nats, Bob Fritz, Thelma Tedesko, and Howard Poteet.

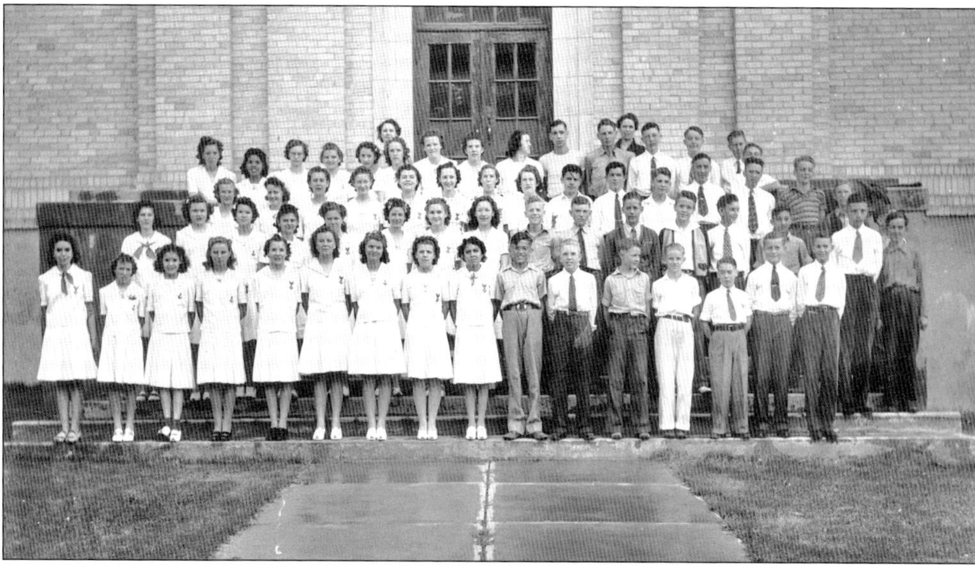

Pictured in 1941 is a gathering of various grade levels. The girls on the left wear matching uniforms with anchor or eagle emblems, and the boys on the right wear ties. Among those pictured are eighth graders Harold Watkins (first row, fifth from right) and Jack Sasser (first row, third from right). (Courtesy of the Sasser Family.)

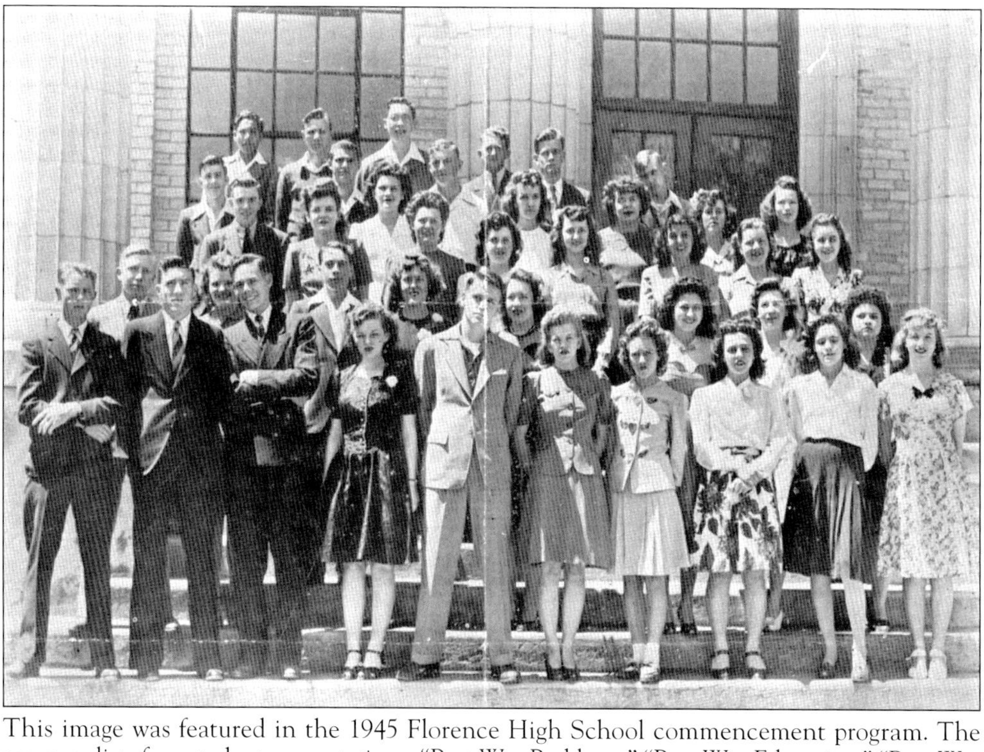

This image was featured in the 1945 Florence High School commencement program. The program lists four student presentations: "Post War Problems," "Post War Education," "Post War Employment," and "Rehabilitation of the Service Man." Jack Sasser (first row, far left) was drafted and left for service in the Pacific shortly after graduation. (Courtesy of the Sasser family.)

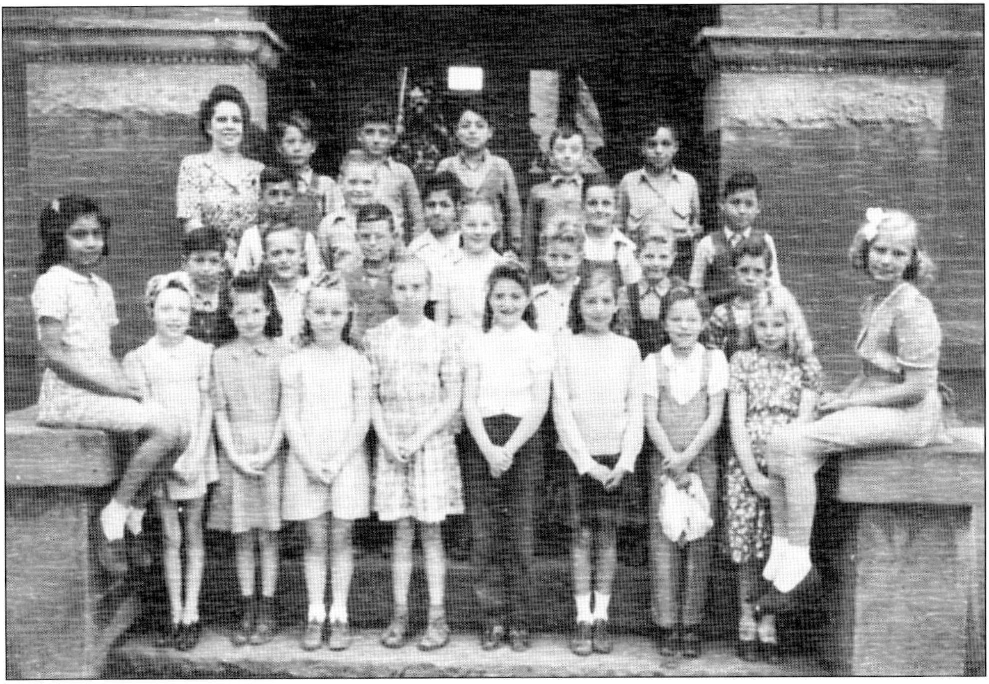

This class picture shows third-grade students of Emerson School in 1944. They went on to become the graduating class of Florence High School in 1954. (Courtesy of the Provenzano family.)

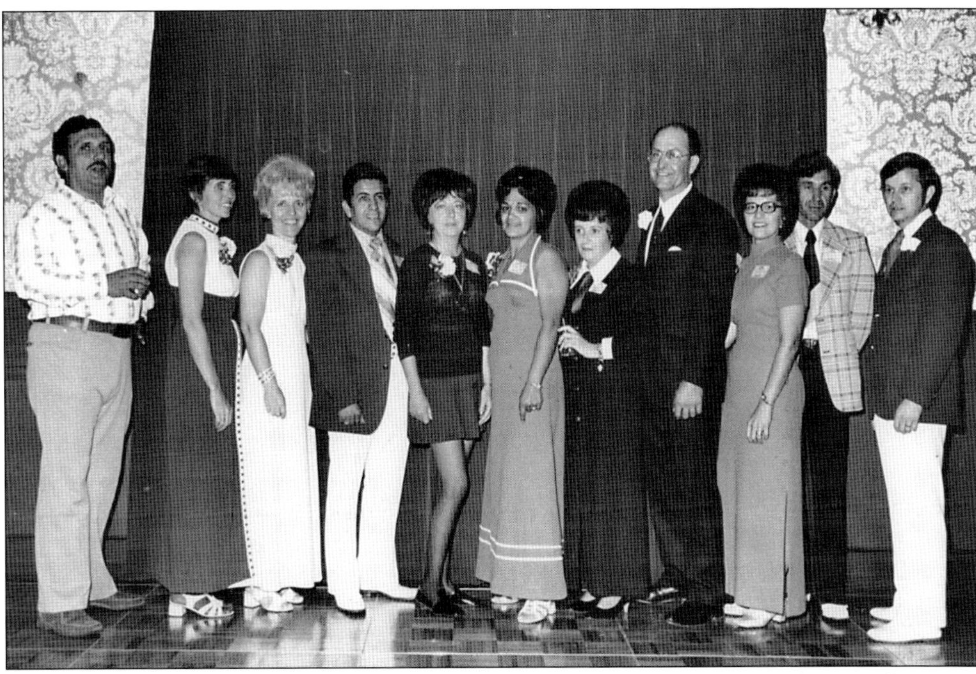

Celebrating their 20-year reunion, 11 members of the class of 1954 gather for a photograph in 1974. At the time, they had children of their own attending Florence schools, making them the second or even third generation of families in Florence schools. (Courtesy of the Provenzano family.)

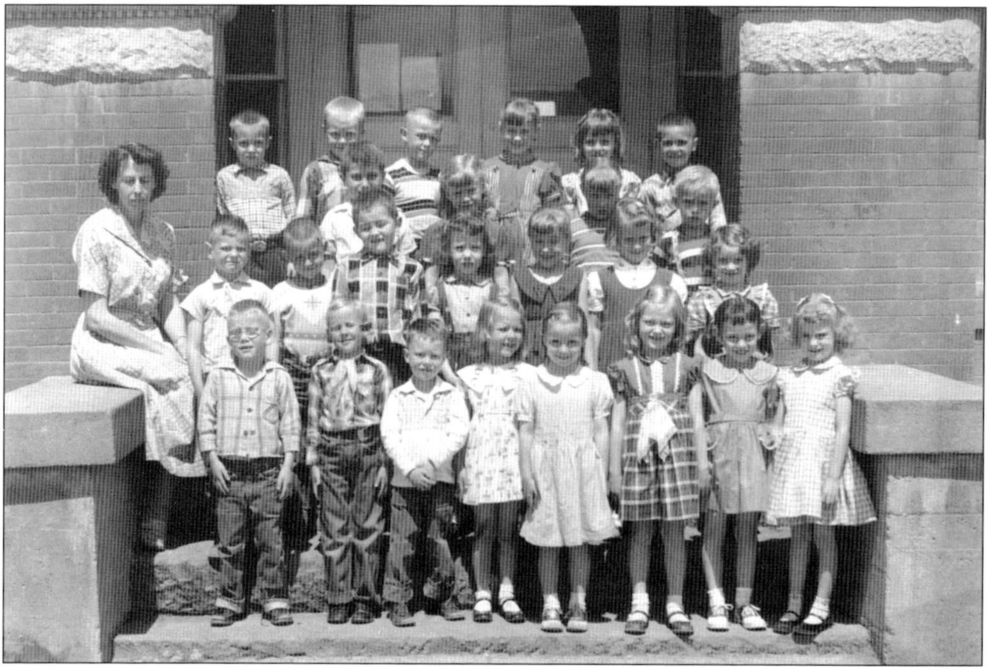

This and the following three photographs follow Marsha Sasser and Joanna Schmidt through their elementary years in Florence schools. These two, like many of the other students in these images, were the second generation of their families to attend Florence schools. This photograph shows kindergarten at Emerson School in 1956. Sasser is at far right in the first row, and Schmidt is fifth from right in the first row. (Courtesy of the Sasser family.)

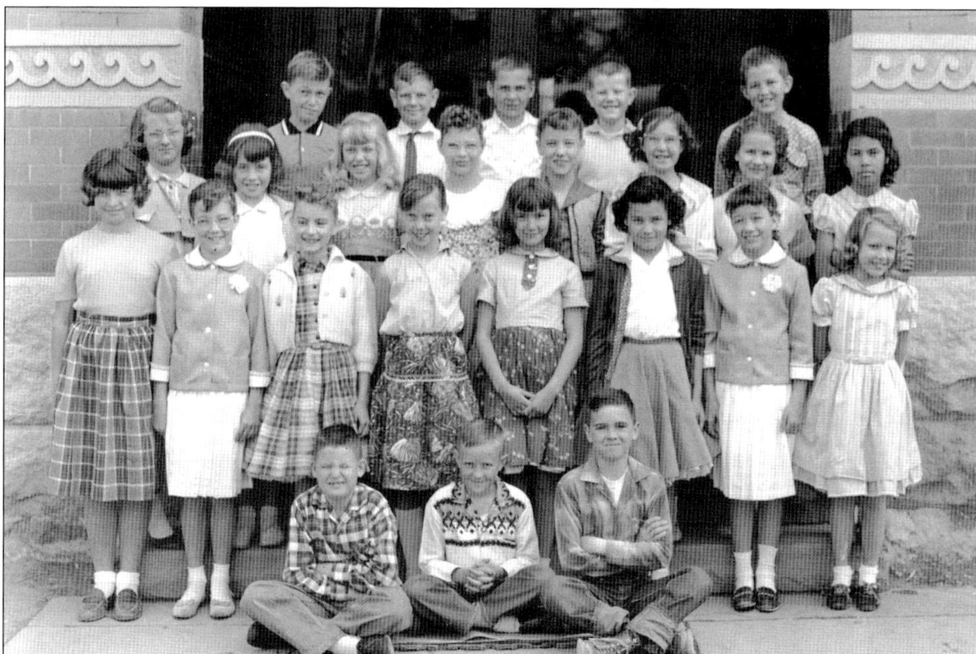

This was the third grade class at McCandless School in 1959. Schmidt is at far right in the second row, and Sasser is sixth from right, also in the second row. (Courtesy of the Sasser family.)

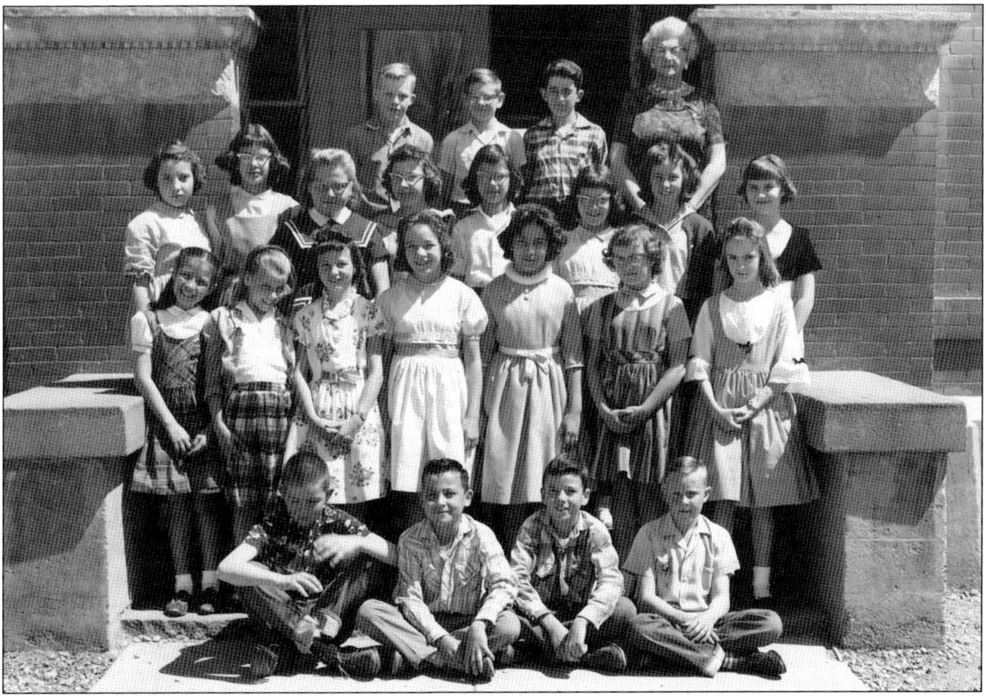

This photograph was taken in 1961, after the class was moved back to Emerson School. Now in fifth grade, Sasser is at far right in the second row, and Schmidt is sixth from right in the second row. (Courtesy of the Sasser family.)

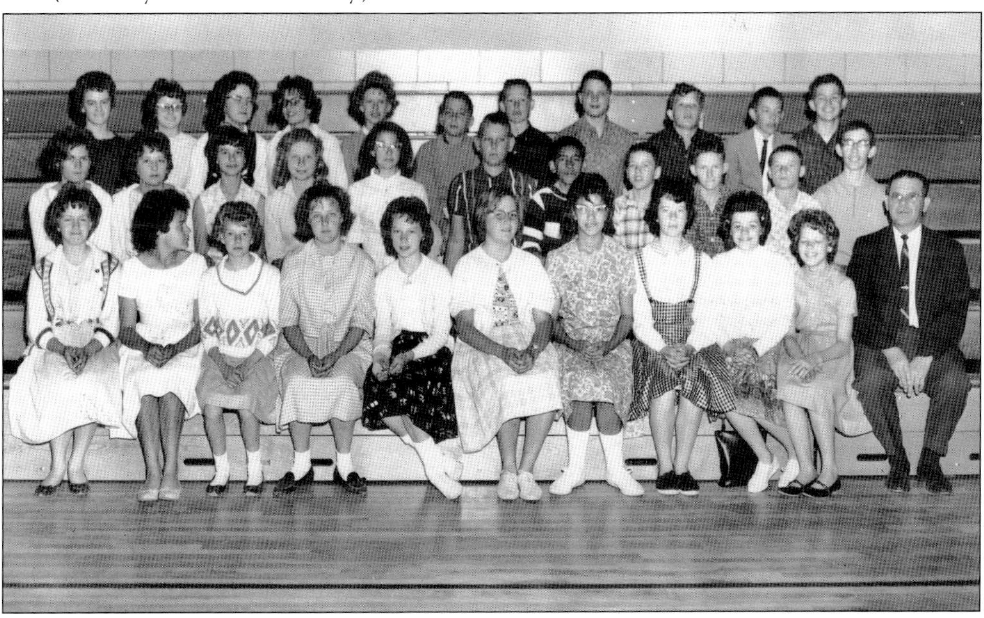

In this photograph, taken in the new Eastern Fremont Elementary School in 1963, Marsha Sasser and Joanna Schmidt are in seventh grade. Schmidt is at far right in the first row, next to the teacher, and Sasser is at far left in the third row. They went on to graduate in 1969, and each had children who have graduated from Florence High School, becoming the third generation to attend Florence schools. (Courtesy of the Sasser family.)

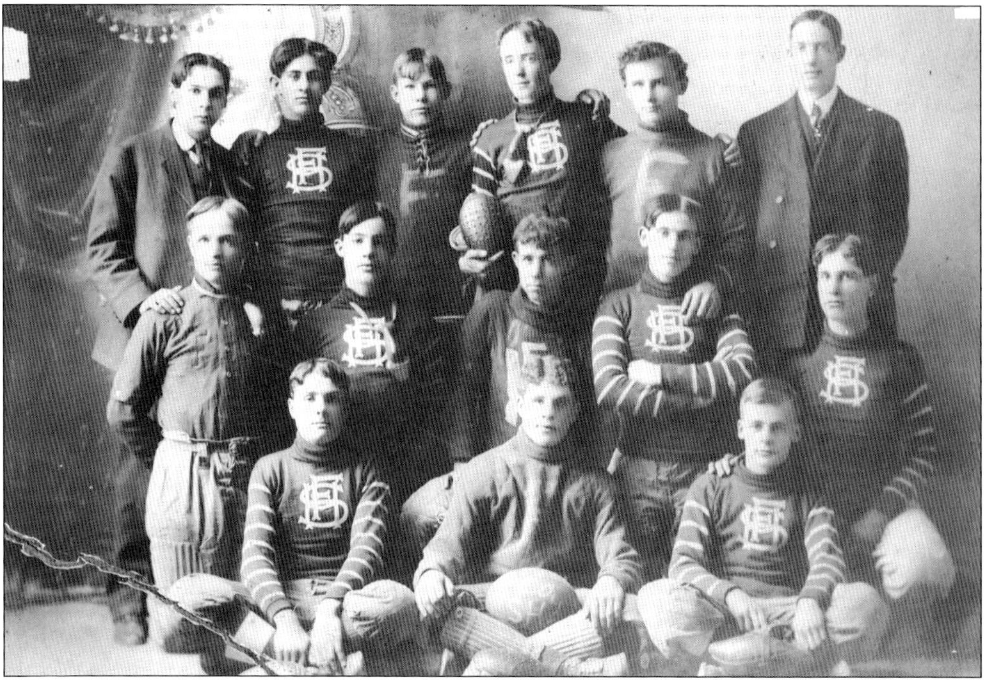

The Florence school system, with the support of the community, has always emphasized that a well-rounded education involves more than just classroom study. This photograph of the 1907 Florence High School football team illustrates that commitment, especially considering that the first high school football game was played just 13 years earlier, in 1894.

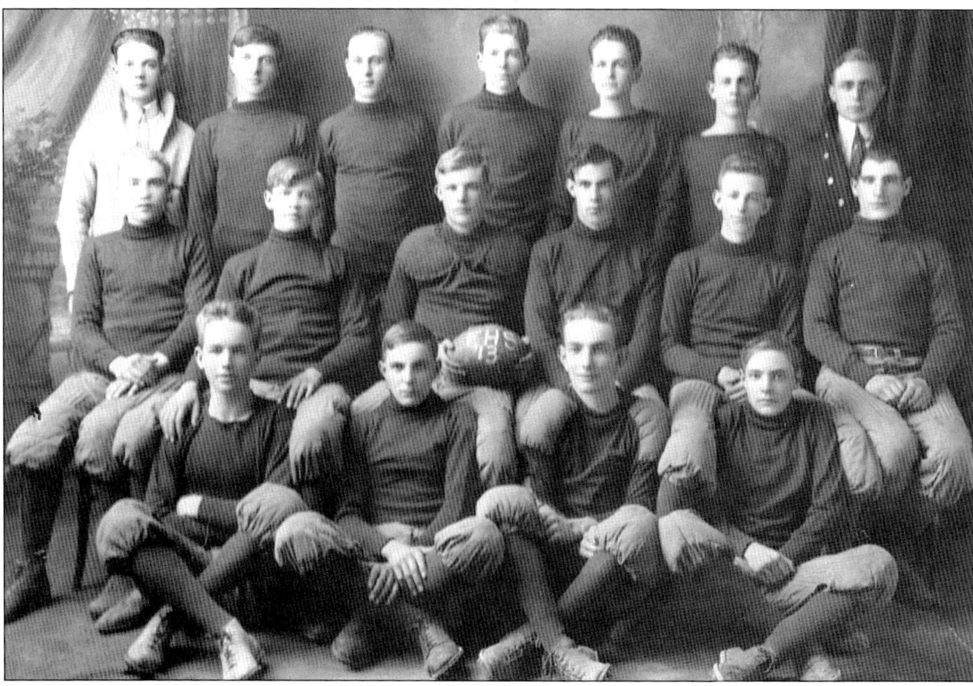

The 1913 football team poses for a team photograph. The players' padding and safety equipment slowly improved over time. It appears that only one player was afforded the luxury of shoulder pads.

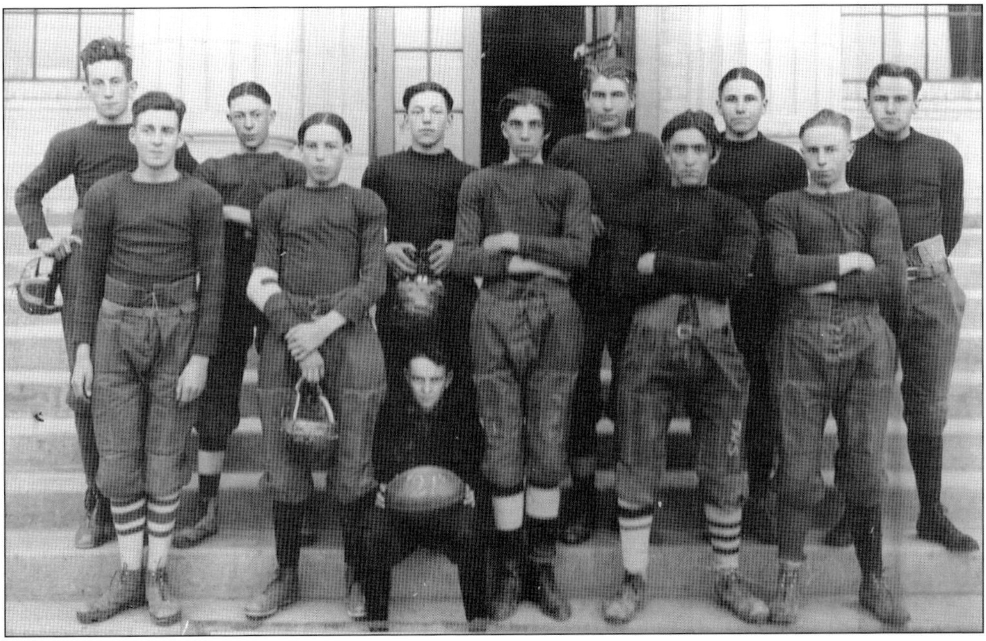

The 1921 football team stands on the steps of the new Florence High School building. It is unknown if some of that year's players were unavailable for this photograph or if there were only 11 players on the team that year.

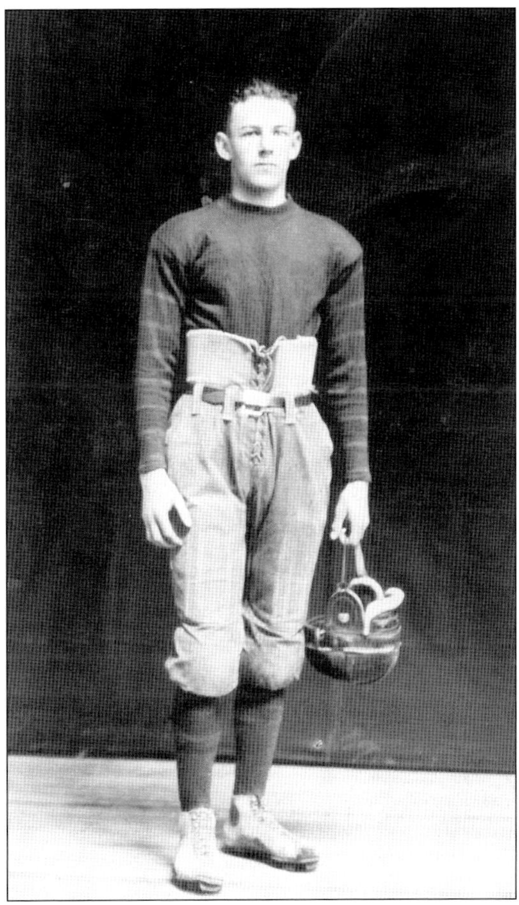

After graduating in 1922, John Camerlo accepted a football scholarship from Regis College in Denver, earning the nickname "Twin Six" after a speedy car from that time. He returned to Florence after a year and went on to become a successful businessman, Florence police chief, and county commissioner, along with numerous other community roles.

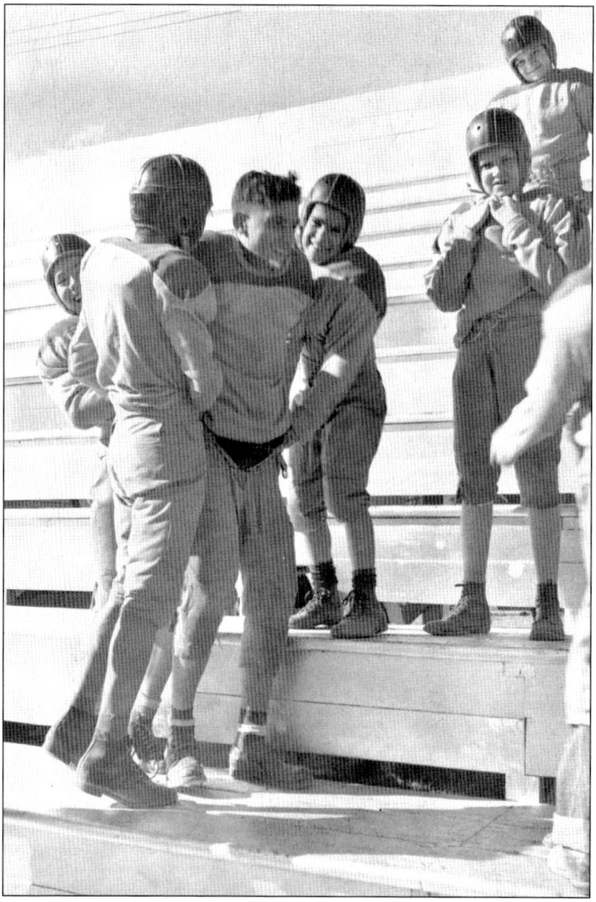

This photograph of typical junior high school boys and their horseplay was taken before a football game in 1949. Standing on the bleachers of the high school football field, young Jim Provenzano appears to be getting assistance from his eighth-grade teammates in suiting up for the game. (Courtesy of the Provenzano family.)

The Florence Lions Club invited the senior members of the 1953 Huskies football team to lunch. From left to right are (seated) Lions Club president Paul Strickland and Huskies head coach Don Richards; (standing) Jerry Del Monte, Dave Adair, Jim Provenzano, Pete Del Duco, Carl Huerta, and Bill Alley. (Courtesy of the Provenzano family.)

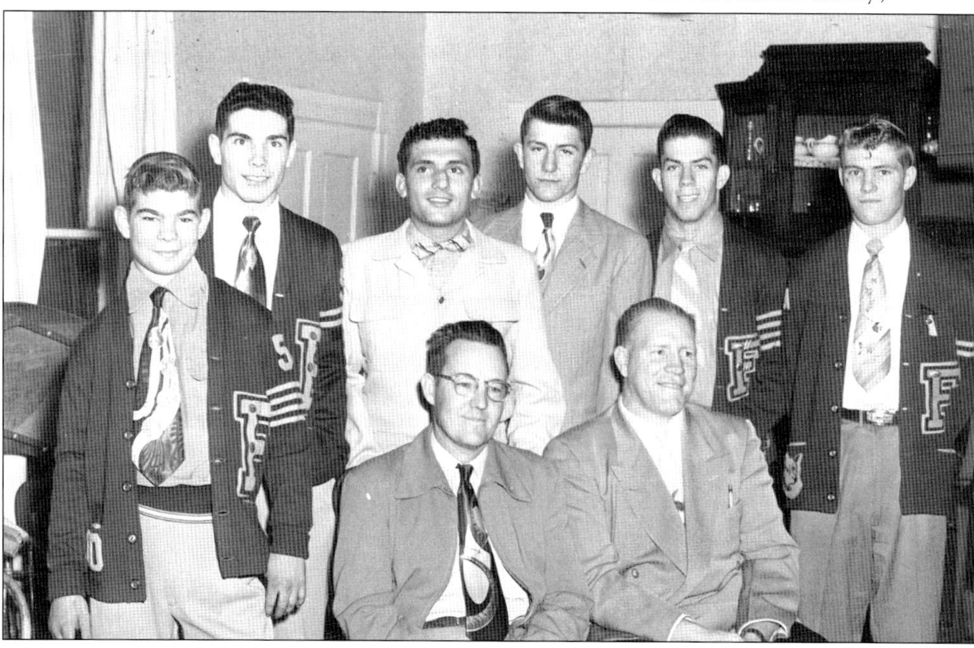

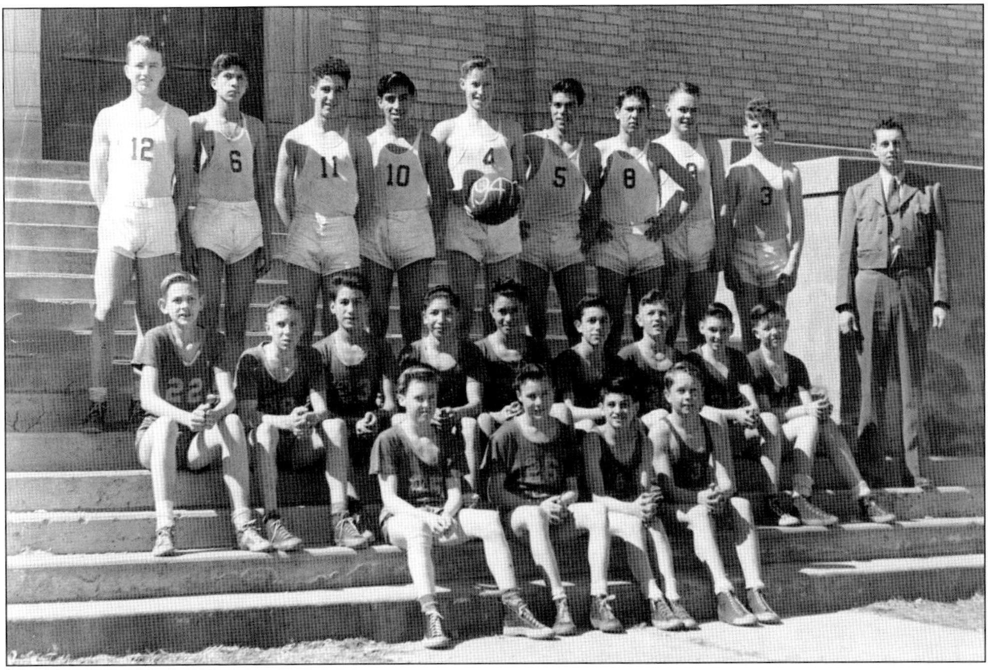

Outside the gymnasium of Florence High School, basketball players pose in 1947. Basketball practice at that time included all teams, freshman, junior varsity, and varsity. Throughout Florence's history, the school sports programs and the athletes who participated in them have always been closely followed by the entire community. (Courtesy of the Provenzano family.)

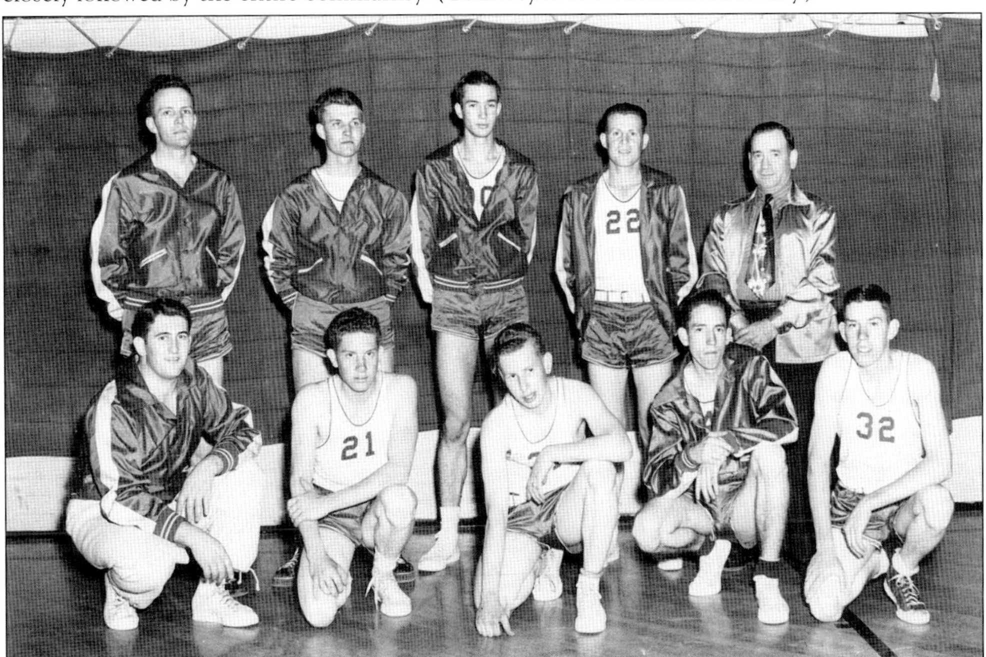

This 1950s intramural basketball team was sponsored by Vendetti Chevrolet. From left to right are (first row) Pete Cresto, Bob Orton, and three unidentified; (second row) Jim Core, Roy Hoza, Felix Lukezic Jr., Bill Meigs, and coach Gus Vendetti Sr. (Courtesy of Gus and Barbara Vendetti.)

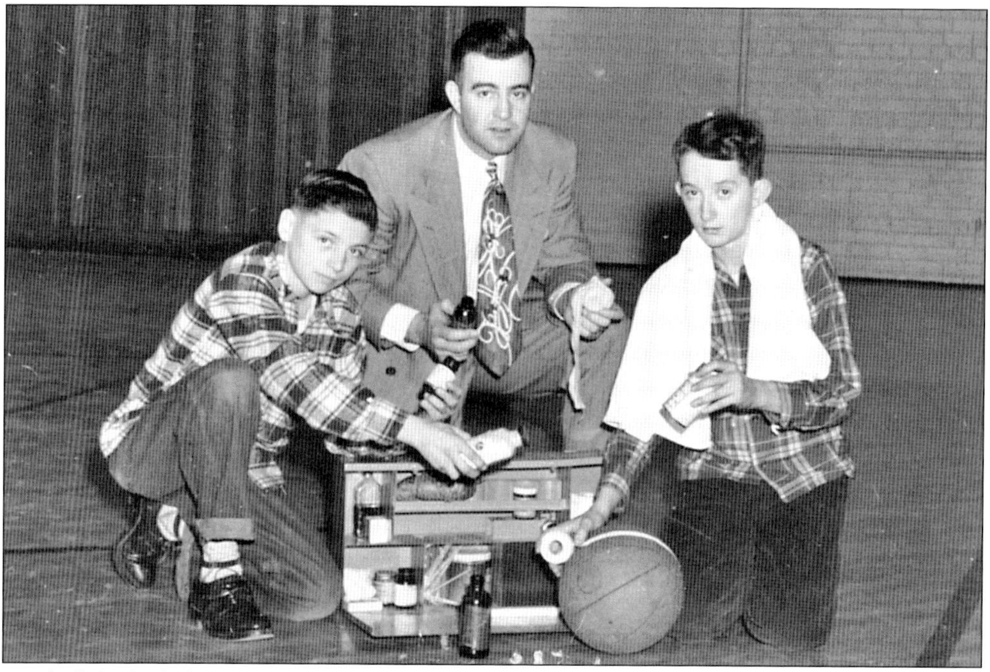

Football, basketball, and baseball teams rely heavily on equipment managers and assistants. They become essential to the coaches and players alike and have a vital function on the team. Here, in 1951, assistants Frankie Rochio (left) and Darrell Lindsey assist Coach Trujillo with preparing for an upcoming game. (Courtesy of Nancy Lindsey.)

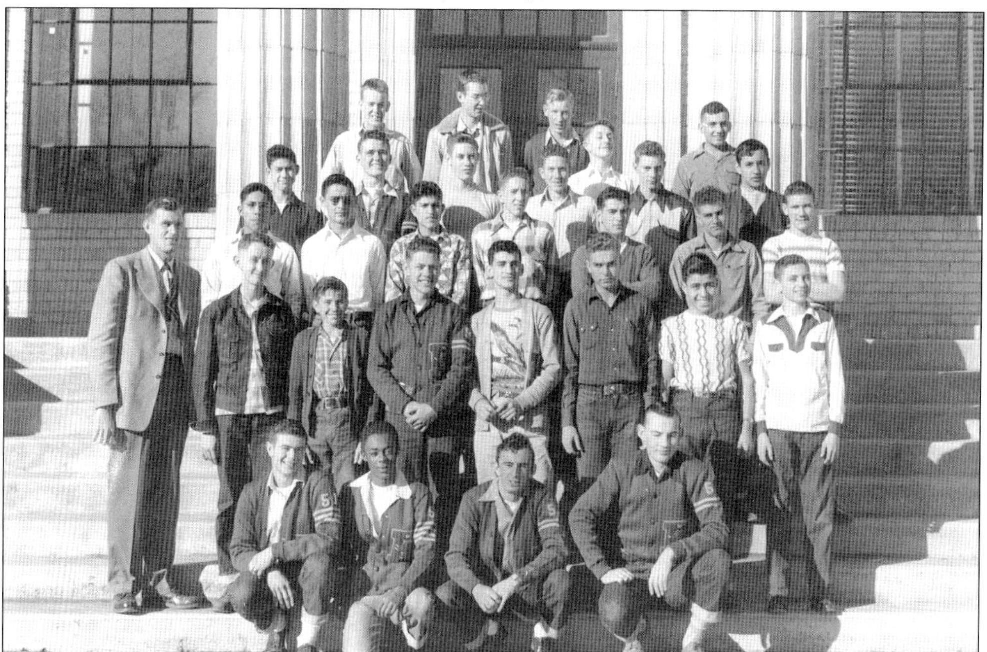

The F Club of Florence High School is made up of students who have earned their letters in school athletics. This photograph, taken on the front steps of the high school, shows the 1951 F Club with 29 members and sponsor John Core. (Courtesy of Nancy Lindsey.)

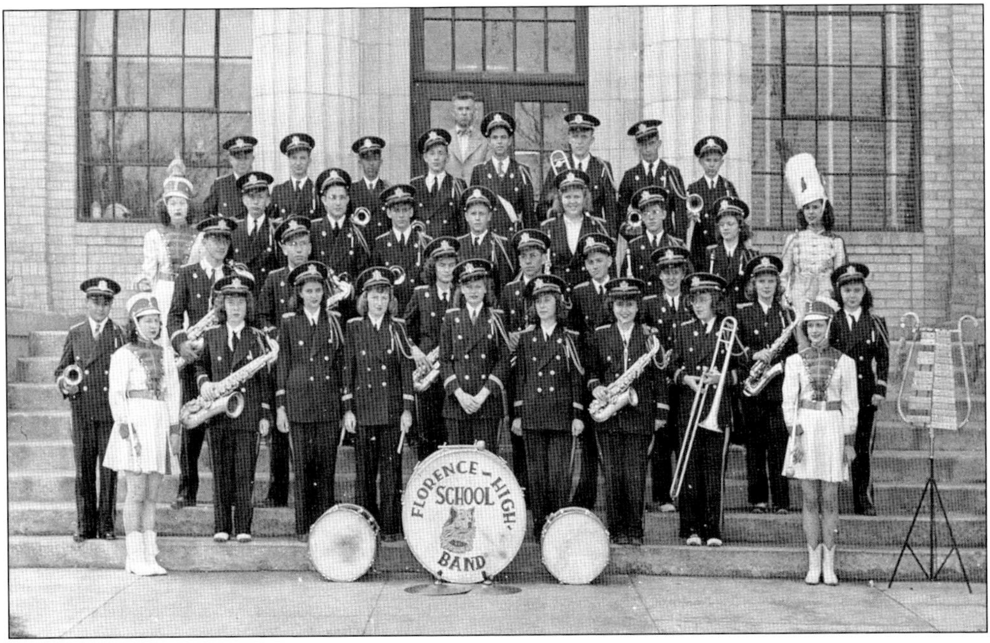

These two photographs showing the Florence High School band (above) and the Florence Junior High School band (below) were found deep inside the archives of the Florence Pioneer Museum and Research Center. Extensive research was completed in an effort to determine the exact date of the pictures, but no specific information could be found other than the fact that it was most likely 1948. They are included here to demonstrate the important role that the school band has in achieving a comprehensive education and the significant value that the citizens of Florence have always placed on extracurricular activities.

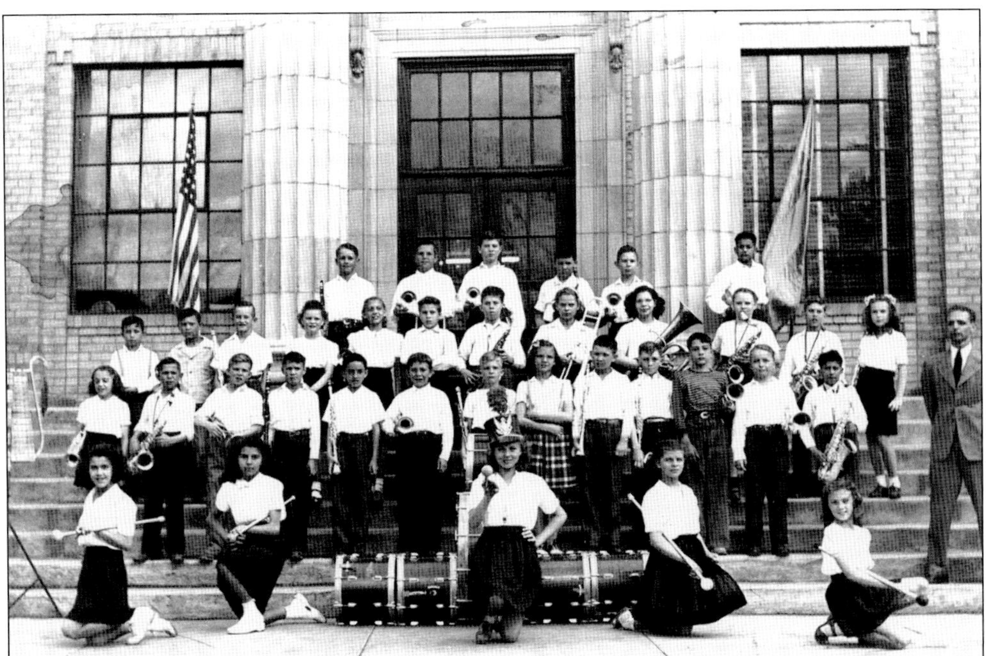

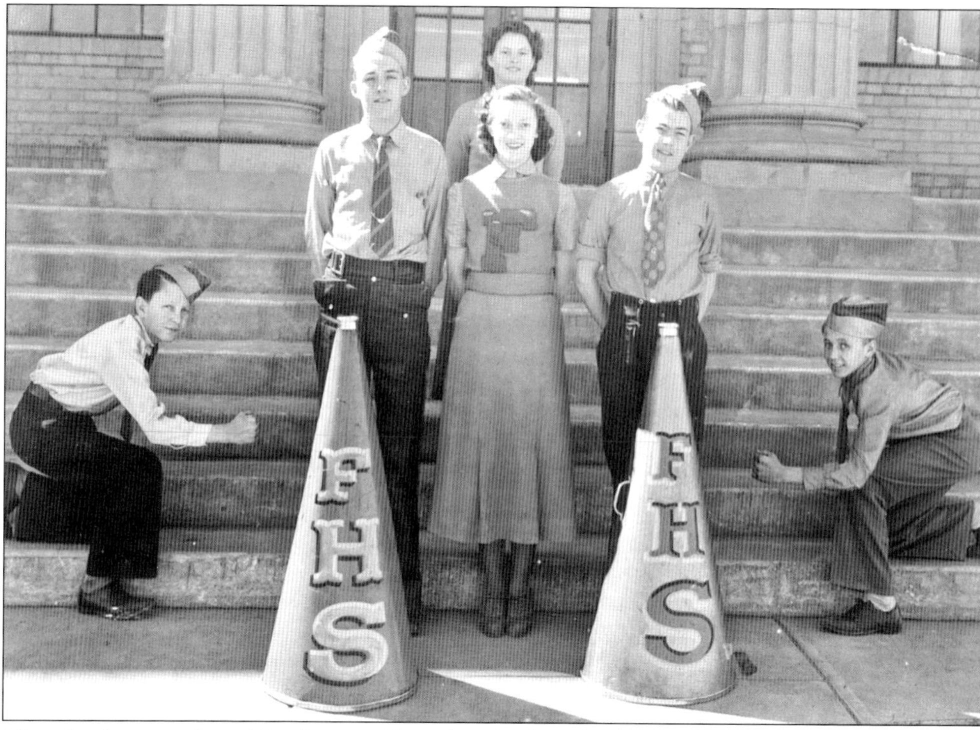

Cheerleaders are elected by the overall student body to lead the school in cheers at all athletic events. For the 1938–1939 school year, the cheerleaders were, from left to right, Vernon Price, Ivan Aeton, Sunta Albricos-Mossberger, Lynn Wilcox, and Amos Syock. Standing in the back is Jessie Blankenship-Grisenti.

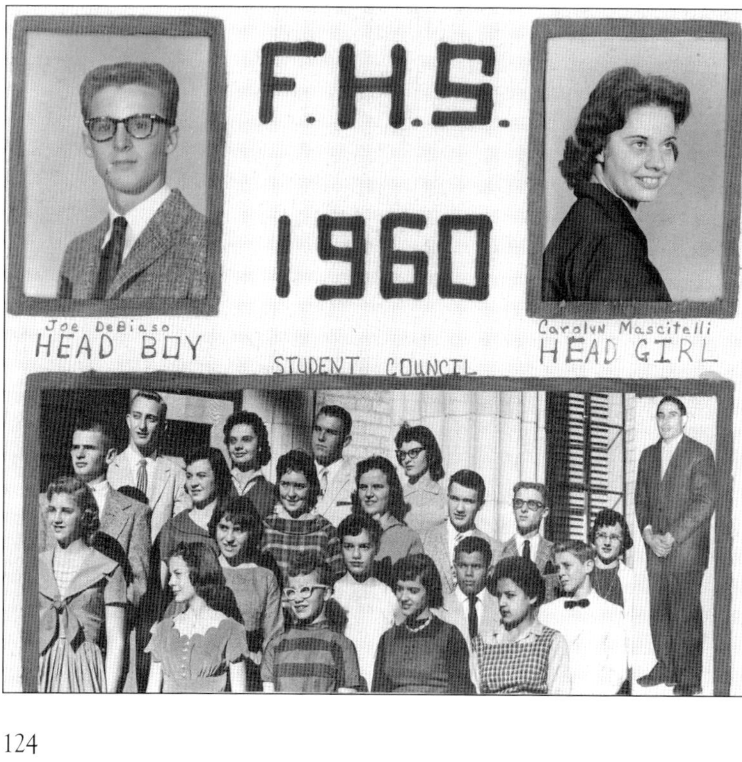

This handmade plaque was once in the Florence High School trophy case. The 1960 student council poses on the front steps, with insets of head boy Joe DeBiaso and head girl Carolyn Mascitelli. Another inset shows sponsor Frank Morelli.

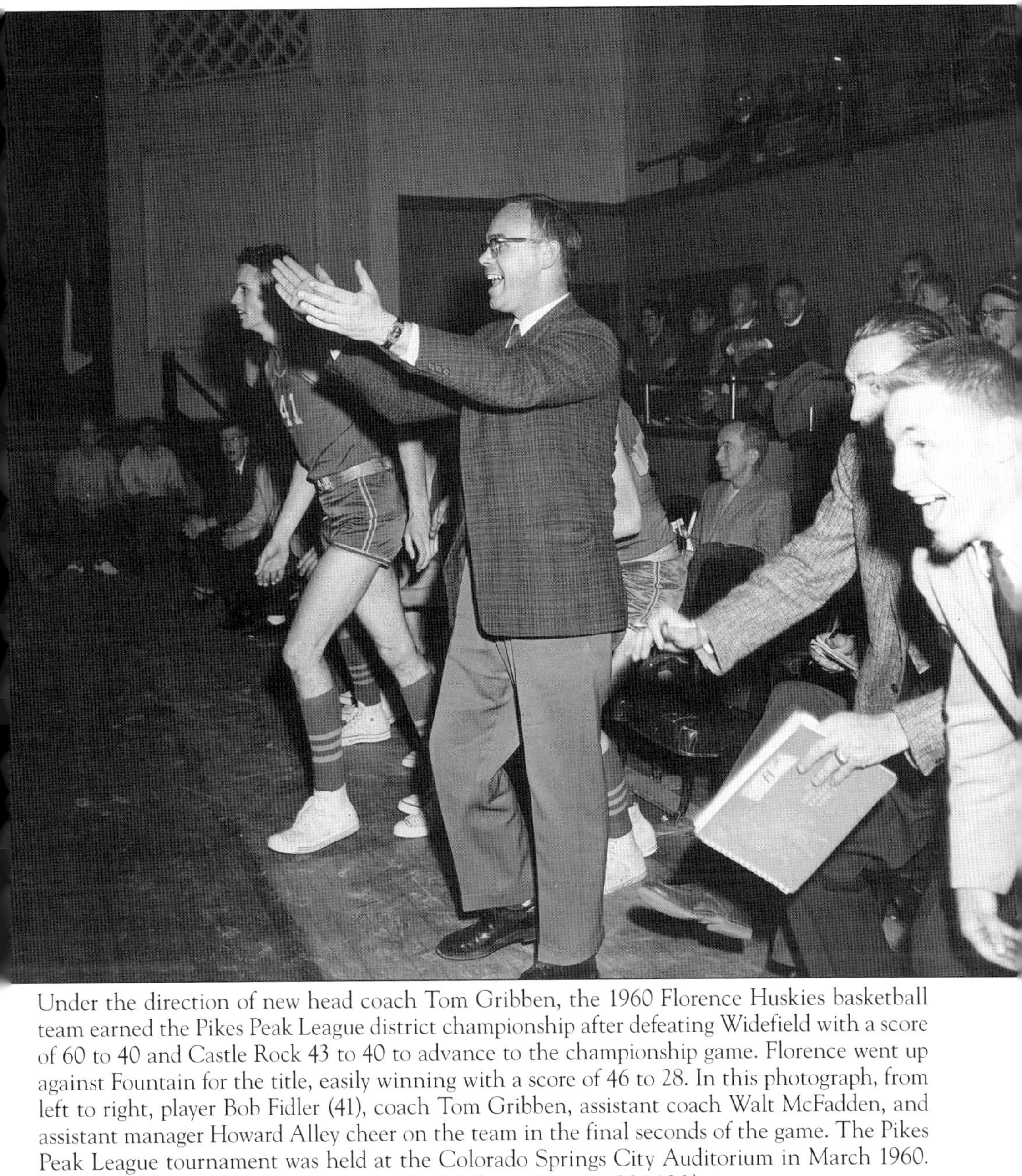

Under the direction of new head coach Tom Gribben, the 1960 Florence Huskies basketball team earned the Pikes Peak League district championship after defeating Widefield with a score of 60 to 40 and Castle Rock 43 to 40 to advance to the championship game. Florence went up against Fountain for the title, easily winning with a score of 46 to 28. In this photograph, from left to right, player Bob Fidler (41), coach Tom Gribben, assistant coach Walt McFadden, and assistant manager Howard Alley cheer on the team in the final seconds of the game. The Pikes Peak League tournament was held at the Colorado Springs City Auditorium in March 1960. (Courtesy of Special Collections, Pikes Peak Library District, 004-136.)

Index of Family Names

About the Florence Pioneer Museum and Research Center

The Florence Pioneer Day Association was founded in 1927 with the mission of honoring the area founders and settlers with an annual celebration. The idea of a museum was brought to the association in 1964 by Charles "Chopper" Price. The association formed a committee to research and develop the concept, appointing Chopper as committee chairman with members Eda Calhoun, Phillistia Huiatt, Darrell Lindsey, and Ty Scutti.

The first order of business for the committee was to locate a home for the new museum. They identified the Branden-Griffith Block, constructed in 1894 on the corner of South Pikes Peak Avenue and Front Street, as an ideal location. It was a three-story yellow sandstone commercial building, unique to Florence. The building had been vacant since the Eagles organization relocated several years earlier. Through a very aggressive fundraising campaign, the building was purchased from the Eagles for $1,500.

Knowing that a successful museum project would be driven by community spirit and volunteerism, the committee, with additional volunteers and donations, immediately took on the task of creating a museum. On September 12, 1964, the day of the annual Pioneer Day celebration, the Florence Pioneer Museum opened its doors to its first official visitor.

From 2015 to the present, significant growth has occurred within the museum, including expansion into adjacent properties, becoming a year-round operation, and changing its mission and name to the Florence Pioneer Museum and Research Center. The current leadership runs monthly programs relating to historic events and maintains expansive files on all families and organizations involved with the making of Florence. Under the guidance of president Gayle MacKinnon, the board of directors includes vice president Paul Villagrana, secretary Marty Lamm, treasurer Dale Johns, and members Dana Angel, Berton Lamm, Terry Nelson, Skip Older, Gloria Stenzel, and the late Gene MacKinnon.

Through years of dedicated, 100-percent volunteerism, relying on donations alone—along with the ever important "community involvement"—the museum has expanded and evolved into one of the most popular sites in Fremont County for locals and visitors alike.

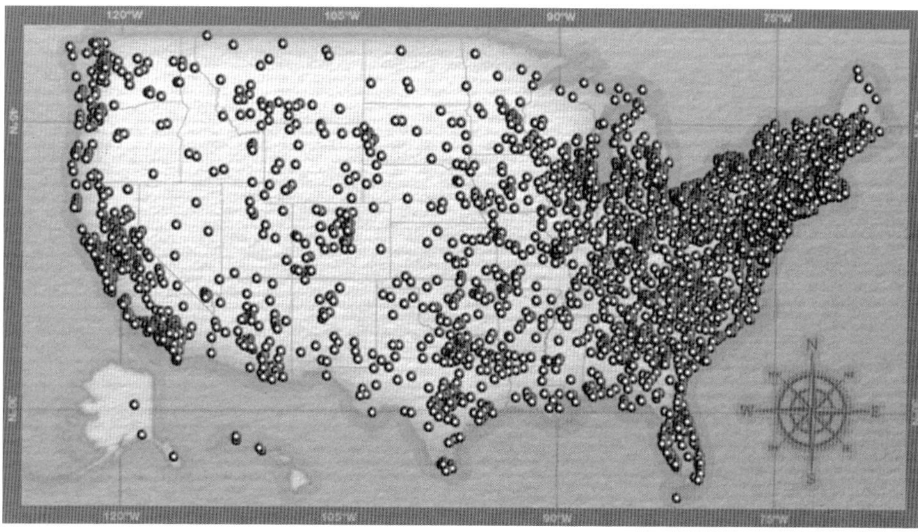